Icebergs,
Zombies,
and the
Ultra Thin

Icebergs, Zombies, and the Ultra Thin

Architecture and Capitalism in the Twenty-First Century

Matthew Soules

PRINCETON ARCHITECTURAL PRESS · NEW YORK

Published by
Princeton Architectural Press
202 Warren Street
Hudson, New York 12534
www.papress.com

Printed and bound in Singapore
24 23 22 21 4 3 2 1 First edition

ISBN 978-1-61689-946-2

Editor: Sara Stemen
Designer: Paula Baver
Cover design: Paul Wagner

Library of Congress Cataloging-in-Publication Data
Names: Soules, Matthew, author.
Title: Icebergs, zombies, and the ultra thin : architecture and capitalism
    in the twenty-first century / Matthew Soules.
Description: First edition. | New York : Princeton Architectural Press,
    [2021] | Includes index. | Summary: "An exploration of how finance
    capitalism converts architecture to financial assets and alters the fabric
    of our global urban landscapes"—Provided by publisher.
Identifiers: LCCN 2020036598 (print) | LCCN 2020036599 (ebook) |
    ISBN 9781616899462 (hardcover) | ISBN 9781648960291 (ebook)
Subjects: LCSH: Architecture and society—History—21st century. |
    Financialization. | Architecture—Economic aspects.
Classification: LCC NA2543.S6 S6423 2021 (print) | LCC NA2543.S6
    (ebook) | DDC 720.1/03—dc23
LC record available at https://lccn.loc.gov/2020036598
LC ebook record available at https://lccn.loc.gov/2020036599

Contents

Preface

A residential floor plan painted on the back of a model as part of a marketing strategy, at 55th Housing Fair, Nantong, China.

The impetus for this book arose from the 2007–8 global financial crisis. The crisis underscored, among other things, the importance finance had come to play in global capitalism and placed the financial system under tremendous scrutiny. Alongside popular and political discourse, a large amount of work in fields ranging from economics to sociology addressed what is termed "finance capitalism" and the process of "financialization." While much of this attention focused on the seemingly immaterial workings of things like Wall Street and "too big to fail" banks, some of it was attuned to the material dimensions of the crisis. After all, the crisis had subprime mortgages and housing at its core. Foreclosed homes in Florida, ghost estates in Ireland, and empty towers in China all entered the popular imagination, if they were not already the stuff of firsthand experience.

The financial crisis catalyzed widespread discussion and actions centered on the financialization of housing and cities that continue to the present. These range from debates on affordability to the implementation of taxes on empty homes. The United Nations established a special rapporteur, who in 2017 issued a report on "structural changes in housing and financial markets and global investment whereby housing is treated as a commodity, a means of accumulating wealth and often as security for financial instruments that are traded and sold on global markets."[1]

But while politicians, economists, popular media, and the general population are at least topically attuned to the financialization of the built environment, the discipline of architecture is largely mute. The degree to which the asset function of architecture has increased has not been met with a corresponding conceptual or operational framework on the part of architects. Current design discourse appears mostly outmatched by the agility and scale of capital that now drives the processes of architecture and urbanization across much of the globe. This is a pressing shortcoming for those interested in buildings and cities as well as anyone concerned with contemporary economic issues. This book aims to address this blind spot.

I commenced work on this topic with a grant from Canada's Social Sciences and Humanities Research Council that I received in 2012.[2] The grant funded investigations of locations where the built environment experienced some of the most pronounced changes—often in the form of massive amounts of speculative construction followed by dramatic oversupply and the associated social, political, and economic challenges—leading up to and following 2007–8. Between 2013 and 2015, I conducted on-the-ground documentation and analysis throughout Ireland and Spain, and in Florida and the Southwest in the United States. This initial work provided the seed from which the broader concerns of this book emerged.

The Intellectual Context

The importance of finance is the defining characteristic of contemporary capitalism. Indeed, the ascent of finance capitalism is arguably the most important sociocultural transformation of the past four decades, and buildings play a uniquely significant role in this ascent. To fully understand architecture in the twenty-first century, it is imperative to understand its role within finance capitalism. And to fully understand how finance capitalism operates, it is vital to situate architecture within its workings.

Part of the challenge of addressing the relationship between finance and architecture is the isolation between disciplines interested in the financial dimension of buildings and those interested in design. While everyone accepts that buildings need to be both financed and designed, and there have been numerous efforts to make connections between finance and design, those involved in each domain usually view the other with distrust and maintain that money does not really affect design in any truly meaningful way (and vice versa). Academia embodies this schism. Those interested in the financial aspect of architecture and urbanism tend to work within the broad category of "real estate." Architecture schools typically do not employ real estate experts, and if they do, their numbers are small and they often operate at the margin. And business schools, where real estate expertise is typically located, almost never have design knowledge represented on the faculty. Simply put, the two worlds are estranged. This long-standing isolation becomes all the more problematic as architecture increasingly functions as a medium of finance.

Many writers have examined the relationship between architecture and capitalism. The Italian architectural historian Manfredo Tafuri made exceptional and influential contributions, including his 1973 book *Architecture and Utopia: Design and Capitalist Development.* Tafuri's thesis that capitalism renders all aesthetic ideologies useless for social production was received as the pronouncement of the death of architecture when it was first articulated in 1969.[3] Among the contemporary Italian architect Pier Vittorio Aureli's numerous contributions, *The Project of Autonomy: Politics and Architecture within and against Capitalism,* from 2008, reevaluates Tafuri and the broader architectural discourse of 1960s and '70s Italy as a way to help locate the political possibility of architecture today. The American architect Peggy Deamer considers questions of architectural labor and, in 2014, edited a fantastic collection of texts, *Architecture and Capitalism: 1845 to the Present.* While these writers address issues that have profound contemporary relevance and have in various ways informed my position, none focus on finance capitalism. Instead, some of the more insightful work on the spatial and material character of financialization can be gleaned from writings on sociology and geography and those where political economy intersects with housing. The Marxist economic geographer David Harvey has been vital in conceptualizing urbanization as an agent of surplus capital absorption and in illuminating the characteristics of finance capitalism. Of his prodigious authorship, a good place to find the former is in *The Urbanization of Capital: Studies in the History and Theory of Capitalist Urbanization*, from 1985, and the latter, in his now-classic *The Limits to Capital*, from 1982. The geographer and sociologist Manuel B. Aalbers's work, including his 2016 book *The Financialization of Housing: A Political Economy Approach*, offers an in-depth analysis of the essential role housing plays in finance capitalism.

While architecture's blind spot toward finance capitalism continues to be substantial, the discipline did begin to shift its attention in the wake of the 2008 crisis by documenting the material detritus of the collapse. Ireland, Spain, and the United States each saw small groups of architects discretely conceptualizing their respective crisis landscapes. Isabel Concheiro's "Interrupted Spain," in the 2011 collection *After Crisis: Contemporary Architectural Conditions*, and Julia Schulz-Dornburg's 2012 book *Ruinas Modernas: Una topografía de lucro* both make important contributions in the case of Spain. Reinhold Martin, Leah Meisterlin, and Anna Kenoff's *The Buell Hypothesis: Rehousing the American Dream* contributes to understanding conditions in the United States. Christopher Marcinkoski's *The City That Never Was: Reconsidering the Speculative Nature of Contemporary Urbanization*, from 2015, is perhaps the apex of documentations of the ruinous landscapes of 2008's aftermath. And these efforts have continued with the likes of the Dutch architect Reinier de Graaf's 2018 Harvard GSD studio Phantom Urbanism, which cataloged empty urban projects throughout the world. Collectively, this work documents and describes some of the spatial and material consequences of finance capitalism but does not provide a sustained and specific examination of finance capitalism and architecture.

Since finance capitalism began its current ascent around 1980, there has been a small but important body of analysis focused on the nexus of finance and design. Carol Willis's 1995 book *Form Follows Finance: Skyscrapers and Skylines in New York and Chicago* is an important analysis of spatio-financial formation in the first half of the twentieth century in the United States. While Willis provides insight into the relationship between corporate finance and the skylines of New York and Chicago, she is concerned with a time period prior to finance's current ascendancy. London-based architect Jack Self's design and editorial work, on the other hand, is squarely embedded within contemporary conditions. Self's design projects, such as *The Ingot*, a gold-plated housing tower proposed for a site next to London Bridge, add financial algorithms to the architect's tool kit. He explores this notion of the architect as financier in response to the overwhelming presence of financial logic in contemporary architecture and urbanism. Douglas Spencer's 2016 book *The Architecture of Neoliberalism: How Contemporary Architecture Became an Instrument of Control and Compliance* is an outstanding exploration of the parallels between contemporary architecture and neoliberal ideology. Financialization operates in conjunction with neoliberalism, and while Spencer does not address finance capitalism, his work is nevertheless relevant.

The work of the American literary critic, philosopher, and political theorist Fredric Jameson and that of the American architectural historian Reinhold Martin is especially significant for any analysis of finance capitalism and architecture. Both Jameson and Martin explicitly explore finance and architecture in the post-1980 era, often vis-à-vis an interest in postmodernism.

Jameson argued that postmodernism is the cultural condition unique to what he variably called late capitalism, multinational capitalism, and finance capitalism. While his subjects often included such things as paintings, photographs, and novels, he considered architecture exceptionally useful for his analysis because it was "virtually unmediated" with economics.[4] In his 1992 *Postmodernism, or, the Cultural Logic of Late Capitalism*, he famously described the Westin Bonaventure Hotel in Los Angeles, designed by architect-developer John Portman, as a "full-blown postmodern building."[5] Casting it as a hermetic substitute for the city, wrapped in reflective glass, with a profoundly disorienting interior lobby, Jameson said of the building that it "can stand as the symbol and analogon of...the incapacity of our minds...to map the great multinational and decentered communicational network in which we find ourselves caught as individual subjects."[6]

Jameson and I share the conviction that architecture occupies an exceptional position in the logic of finance capitalism and that this position has resulted in architectural mutations. I am deeply indebted to his insights, and we share multiple overlaps, but we diverge on a few key points. Although Jameson at times tries to consider buildings as more than representations of capitalism, he nonetheless remains mostly constrained within this model. For him, architecture is primarily an aesthetic space of symbols, analogies, illustrations, and expressions. While I think architecture is always partly symbolic, this book is more concerned with how architecture serves not only as a symbol or analogy of finance capitalism, but also as a functional component integral to the workings of finance capitalism.

This difference relates to how we both conceive the relative autonomy of the discipline of architecture. Jameson positions himself in relation to debates concerning architectural autonomy: Is architecture, alongside literature and the visual arts, part of the sphere of culture and therefore autonomous from the ostensibly practical world, or is it wholly of the practical world? Jameson says he wants to inhabit an in-between position in which architecture is informed by capitalism while respecting "the specificity, the autonomy or semi-autonomy, of the aesthetic level and its intrinsic dynamics."[7] While he aims to understand architecture as a mediation between economics and aesthetics, he maintains this binary and spends more time on the side of aesthetics. In contrast, while I recognize that, like any discipline, architecture possesses internal logics and cultures that are unique to itself and that therefore those internalities can be said to be autonomous, I believe they have no meaningful autonomy from the workings of capitalism.

In the late 1990s, Jameson turned his attention more explicitly to finance capitalism in two important pieces of writing. While his 1997 essay "Culture and Finance Capital" addresses the cultural sphere broadly, his essay a year later, "The Brick and the Balloon: Architecture, Idealism and Land Speculation," is crucial for initiating a focused conversation about the formal and aesthetic characteristics of architecture that might be specific to finance capitalism. A central preoccupation in this work is the topic of abstraction and how it plays out in both the economic and the cultural spheres. He argues that the logic of finance capital has "radically new forms of abstraction" that can be observed in "cultural production."[8] He posits that two features of architecture illustrate this abstraction: "extreme isometric space" and "enclosed skin volumes."[9] The move toward this dematerialized abstraction is akin to shifting from the brick to the balloon.[10] While I concur that finance capitalism entails increased abstraction, and that this sometimes enlists isometry and particular types of building envelopes, I do not focus on abstraction because of what it often entails in relation to abstract versus representational or realist art and architecture. Also, there seems to be an emphasis on particular material conditions in Jameson's use of abstraction: glass walls,

Condominium towers, including Zaha Hadid Architects' One Thousand Museum
(second from left), 2020, in downtown Miami.

mirrored glass, and weightlessness. In this book, I prefer to augment
abstraction with *simple* and *complex*. These terms capture more of what
is operative in finance capitalist architecture than does a preoccupation
with abstraction alone. Finance capitalism involves a simultaneous move
toward heightened simplicity and complexity that can be found across
material and formal conditions; it is thus that *both* the brick and balloon
play a role in not the dematerialization but rather the rematerialization
of architecture.

Reinhold Martin is also concerned with postmodernity, abstraction, and architecture's relation to capitalism but seeks to more fully
develop Jameson's suggestions concerning abstraction and architecture's mediation between economics and culture, ultimately aiming to
move beyond them. He writes in 2011 that "we must read architecture
and urban form not only as tangible, material evidence of the abstraction of modern life but also as abstraction itself" and that finance capitalism both defines and is defined by architecture." He further states,

"In today's cities, the construction and circulation of cultural meaning through architecture and other aesthetic forms is a primary characteristic of political-economic processes, rather than a secondary effect."[12] It is thus that Martin is closer to my position than Jameson's in regard to the tighter connection between architecture and political economy.

While Martin and I both understand architecture as a political-economic process, we differ in what we emphasize when considering how architecture operates within that process. While he goes further than Jameson in dissolving the separation between culture and economics, Martin still adheres to understanding architecture's role as primarily aesthetic in a traditional sense—the construction and circulation of *cultural meaning*. This allows Martin to compare twenty-first-century developer architecture to nineteenth-century landscape painting because they both attempt to capture the sublime (the latter, the sublime of nature and the former, the sublime of finance capital).[13] He claims that the undulating forms of Frank Gehry's IAC Building in Manhattan's far West Side are where "the vicissitudes of multinational capitalism are converted into the gentle rippling of a summer breeze."[14] I don't necessarily think Martin is wrong in these assertions; the construction of cultural meaning is indeed a vital aspect of architecture functioning as finance capitalism. It is only that it is just one aspect of architecture's unique role, and Martin seems less interested in the rest.

In contrast to both Jameson and Martin, I argue that architecture and urbanism mutate in a manner that allows architecture to better function as a medium of finance capitalist investment in itself. This mutation occurs comprehensively, altering how buildings are designed to be used, managed, and operated. And make no mistake—these design changes are formal and aesthetic, but they arise equally from financial functionalism as well as an imperative to cultural meaning.

Scope and Methodology

While finance capitalism and financialization are global in scope, this book focuses primarily on Europe and North America. That the book does not more than cursorily address a larger geographic scope is clearly one of its limitations and is due to nothing more substantial than the constraints of time and resources. Europe and North America offer ample opportunities to explore the relationship between finance capitalism and architecture, partly because their economies tend to be highly financialized, yet future in-depth work focusing on additional territories within Africa, Asia, and South America is clearly necessary. Financialization is a highly uneven process, affecting different neighborhoods, cities, and countries in very different ways. Although the insights gleaned from the limited number of buildings and cities in this book have broad relevance, examining the local particularities of architecture and capitalism in a wider set of locations will undoubtedly change the conceptualization of architecture and capitalism everywhere.

Finance capitalism plays a role in all building types, but this book focuses on housing because this is where the characteristics of finance capitalism can be witnessed in sharpest relief, due to finance's exceptional integration into the real estate of housing. Some studies of finance and its relationship with architecture have focused on buildings, such as those that house corporations involved in finance, that present direct and obvious connections.[15] Others have emphasized avant-garde

Housing subdivision in metropolitan Phoenix, shown in 2015,
partially incomplete since the 2007–8 financial crisis.

architecture and exceptional buildings.[16] This book looks at both the exceptional and the everyday, since both work together in a spatio-financial system. While the corporate headquarters of finance may seem to present the best opportunities to analyze the architectural logics of finance, these are not the means through which finance primarily actualizes itself; housing is its primary medium and is therefore the focus of this book. Other building types or urban and landscape features, from destination museums to golf courses, operate in a real estate investment ecology in which housing is the dominant species. The financial function of housing can be traced in formal, aesthetic, programmatic, maintenance, and use practices—and all these categories are treated with equal significance in this book.

Periods of heightened significance for finance capitalism are often described as emphasizing the circulation of capital over the production of commodities. Where Karl Marx's general formula for capital is M-C-M (money-commodity-money), finance capitalism foregrounds the C-M aspect of the formula, as money "sets itself free" and profit accrues through financial deals, as Marx describes in the M-M (money-money) formulation.[17] Some authors emphasize the role of the developer when considering capitalism and building; in contrast, the developer is almost entirely absent from this book.[18] This is not because the developer ceases to be important but rather because developer financing practices, while changing over time, have been a constant feature of the production of buildings in capitalist economies. What is unique to architecture in the era of finance capitalism has little to do with the developer directly but rather with how architecture operates as a spatio-financial instrument that facilitates financial transactions that are relatively separate from the developer.

My methodology is primarily argumentation that draws on philosophy, political economy, political economy's extensions into the cultural sphere, economic theory and history, the popular press, and architectural discourse. And cast into this argumentation is a net of observations and analyses of selected built environments and buildings. The result is a body of architectural and urban criticism that articulates the function of buildings as spatio-financial constructs that are one of the main vehicles of financialization.

Organization

This book is organized into an introduction and eight chapters. The introduction provides context regarding both the characteristics of current capitalism and its conceptual history. It defines finance capitalism and the associated process of financialization and briefly demonstrates their significance by touching upon economic data. While the historiography of finance capitalism is extensive, the introduction focuses on a handful of figures—including Karl Marx, Rudolf Hilferding, Fredric Jameson, Giovanni Arrighi, and Costas Lapavitsas—who offer useful touchstones. These thinkers situate the ongoing issues of finance capitalism that provide the conceptual backdrop for the material in subsequent chapters. Further, as financialization has been contemporaneous with the rise of neoliberalism and globalization, the introduction addresses the relationship between all three while adopting the position that financialization is the most apt concept to describe the operations of twenty-first-century capitalism.

Following the introduction's broader contextualization, chapter 1 focuses on the relationship between finance capitalism and architecture in a general sense. I begin by identifying real estate as a critical component of finance capitalism and then discuss more narrowly housing as a category of real estate that is exceptionally significant, as the arena where finance capitalism's relationship with architecture can be witnessed in sharpest relief. The chapter introduces five characteristics of finance capitalist architecture and urbanism:

1. It is inherently unstable and creates spaces of crisis.
2. It increasingly functions as speculative wealth storage.
3. It is the means of uneven development and heightened inequality.
4. It has a simultaneous propensity for highly iconic and extremely standardized spaces.
5. It increases liquidity.

These five characteristics are explored in greater detail in the remaining chapters.

Chapter 2 develops the concept of crisis space as a key characteristic of finance capitalist urbanism. Crisis space is broken down into two categories: zombie urbanism and ghost urbanism. Zombie urbanism describes the phenomenon of significantly underoccupied secondary homes that function as investment properties. The chapter traces this condition in large and powerful global cities like London and Paris and also in smaller cities like Melbourne and Barcelona that tend to be perceived as desirable because of climate, culture, or natural setting. Ghost urbanism signifies a greater amount of vacancy than zombie urbanism and typically exists in overt crisis conditions. The discussion of ghost urbanism is organized around an in-depth examination of conditions in Ireland and Spain and a brief discussion of China.

Chapter 3 explores five architectural types that have arisen during finance capitalism's current ascent: iceberg homes, exurban investment mats, superpodiums, ultra-thin pencil towers, and financial icons. These five spatio-financial types can be found in different locations and in varying degrees. Therefore, this chapter jumps from location to location, visiting iceberg mansions in London, exurban investment mats in Mexico, the superpodium at Zorlu Center in Istanbul, ultra-thin towers in Manhattan, and financial icons in southern Spain and Miami. This tour conveys the international reach of an extensive spatio-financial ecology.

Billboard advertising model homes along Interstate 15 in Southern California.

Inequality has increased in the current era of finance capitalism, and chapter 4 examines the emergence of new categories of the very rich and the architecture that caters to them: the ultra-high net worth individual (UHNWI) and superprime properties. This chapter examines One Hyde Park in London as an example of superprime architecture and unpacks its main architectural traits to provide insights into the tendencies of architecture for the very rich. To further illuminate this phenomenon, I situate One Hyde Park in relation to the work and thinking of the architects Patrik Schumacher and Pier Vittorio Aureli.

Chapter 5 is devoted entirely to how simplifying the ownership, management, and design of buildings serves the purposes of finance capitalism. After addressing real estate investment trusts (REITs) as mediated forms of simplified investment and the legal invention of the condominium as a simplified form of ownership, I spend the bulk of the chapter focusing on the design of buildings. Their spatial simplification occurs through implementing specific strategies for handling security and maintenance as well as through diminishing opportunities for social interaction. In ultra-thin towers, these types of spatial simplification function in an extreme fashion. Chapter 5 then examines how seemingly complex attributes are used as paradoxical components of simplification. It considers finance capitalist architecture's proclivity for recreational leisure spaces, invented nature, and constructed views as simplified complexities tuned to the purposes of finance capitalism.

Chapter 6 considers Danish architect Bjarke Ingels's Vancouver House condominium tower and what its marketers call the world's first one-for-one home-gifting program to explore the role of philanthropy in architecture and urbanism in the era of finance capitalism. In doing so, I ask how spatial philanthropy works in concert with practices like using shell companies and intermediary agents to invest in real estate to propagate new forms of global urbanism, where luxury cities like Vancouver are ever more distant from the slums of the world.

Chapter 7 focuses on New York–based architect Rafael Viñoly's 432 Park Avenue condominium in Manhattan as a zenith of finance capitalist asset architecture. I argue that the building can be understood as a posthumanist totem serving the spiritual dimension of contemporary capitalism. The chapter spins a strategic yet promiscuous web connecting apparently disparate elements and ideas: the Dutch architect Rem Koolhaas's description of the Downtown Athletic Club in New York

City, the philosophical ideas of transhumanism, the Italian architect Aldo Rossi's ossuary structure at the San Cataldo Cemetery, and the discourse concerning the spiritual aspects of capitalism. Ultimately, I position 432 Park as a novel form of tomb for those seeking immortality through the means of finance capitalism.

Chapter 8, the final chapter, centers on condominium presales (the buying and selling of condo units before the building has been completed) and what this market implies for architecture. The phenomenon of presales is presented as the architectural version of the financial market for futures derivatives. This market foregrounds the importance that finance capitalism places on digital representations of architecture and resonates with markets for virtual real estate that can be found in virtual environments such as Second Life and Decentraland. By incorporating into the discussion the role of science fiction in architecture and the emergence of financial technology (FinTech) and a subset devoted to real estate (property technology, or PropTech), I reflect on what constitutes reality and fiction in architecture and beyond. I ultimately argue that a useful lens for understanding the current state of architecture is a revision of the genre of science fiction: from science fiction (sci-fi) to financial fiction (fi-fi). Finance capitalism emphasizes what Marx called fictitious capital—as distinct from real capital and money capital. As the "real" of real estate shifts toward the fictitious state of financial instruments like stocks and bonds, the always-fictional character of architecture accelerates. And as a material fiction premised upon the defining technologies of the current era—the technologies of finance—architecture is a preeminent manifestation of financial fiction, the defining fiction of the early twenty-first century.

Introduction

The shift from investments in production to speculation on the stock market, the globalization of finance, and...the new level of a frenzied engagement with real estate values, these are realities with consequences for social life...;and the effort to theorize those new developments is very far from being an academic matter.

FREDRIC JAMESON, 1998

ceberg homes in London, where a global investor class buries wealth architecturally, deep into the earth. Zombie urbanism, where subtle but persistent underoccupancy has become common in cities from Melbourne to Paris. Ultra-thin pencil towers in Manhattan, where astronomically priced units are purchased by numbered companies under a cloak of secrecy. Extreme scales of commodity repetition in housing archipelagoes on the periphery of Madrid. The predilection for new natures. Parametrically designed complex building forms serving as singular icons in more and more cities. Millions of purchased but unoccupied units in the ghost cities of China. Speculative housing estates constructed in Ireland only to be demolished before being inhabited. The emergence of a tomb-like neo-spiritualism. Housing affordability crises in cities around the world. The confounding opacity of mortgage-backed securities. The expanding role of real estate investment trusts in configuring the United States' built environment. The globalization of real estate brokerage firms. Over the last four decades, something fundamental seems to have changed in how architecture works.[1]

Capitalism and Its Ever-Changing Character

Capitalism constantly changes, shape-shifting from place to place, time to time, and subject to subject. Historians describe the transformation of dominant modes of capitalist accumulation: mercantile, agricultural, industrial, and consumer capitalism. Varying social relations can be foregrounded: state, welfare, laissez-faire, monopoly, or corporate capitalism. Or capitalism can be described in temporal stages: advanced, late, and postcapitalism. Specific avatars are routinely christened in relation to almost any phenomenon: cognitive capitalism, eco-capitalism, surveillance capitalism, spiritual capitalism. This fluid ubiquity captures the challenges of addressing capitalism while signaling its importance. But of the exhaustive nomenclature, the most appropriate term for capitalism in the twenty-first century is *finance capitalism*.

The terms *finance capitalism* and *financialization* occupy prominent positions in contemporary discourse, yet their definitions are nebulous and often vague. Finance capitalism is here understood in two senses. In the first, it is a type of capitalist behavior that facilitates the circulation and accumulation of capital through issuing and exchanging credit, securities, and their numerous avatars. Since credit plays an integral role in capitalism, finance capitalist behavior has been a necessary and always-present feature of capitalism since its very inception. Finance capitalism pursues profit through the exchange of financial instruments rather than through the production of commodities that are sold at markup. Examples of financial instruments include currency, bonds, stocks, and derivatives.

In the second sense, finance capitalism is a stage of capitalism in which the pursuit of profit through financial transactions is so ubiquitous that it is the defining character of an era. This book adopts the position that finance capitalism is *both* a constant, yet varying, feature of capitalism *and* a phase in its history.

Associated with these two senses of finance capitalism is the term *financialization*. Like the other widely deployed terms *globalization* and *neoliberalism*, financialization risks signifying everything and nothing. The sociologist Greta R. Krippner, who published a highly regarded empirical analysis of financialization in the US economy, defines financialization as "a pattern of accumulation in which profits accrue primarily through financial channels rather than through trade and commodity production. 'Financial' here refers to activities relating to the provision (or transfer) of liquid capital in expectation of future interest, dividends, or capital gains."[2] In this book, I utilize Krippner's definition but expand it to include a whole host of human behaviors and practices that are associated with the pattern of accumulation she identifies. In this model, everything from aspects of individuals' daily lives to large-scale industrial production can be financialized. For example, the widespread adoption of credit cards and the prominence of the stock market in media reporting are both parts of how everyday life has been financialized. This book takes the position that finance capitalist behavior has increased in such significance and to such a degree that it defines our era.

Shelter—Culture—Wealth

Architecture, as a mode of production and a part of the cultural superstructure, has necessarily always had a relationship with capital. Addressing architecture's manifold connections to capital has invariably been, therefore, a relevant concern of architectural criticism and theory. But the rise of finance capitalism in the years since 1980 is of exceptional and unprecedented significance for architecture. "Architecture and twenty-first-century capitalism" should really be viewed as "architecture and its relationship with finance capitalism."

The quanta of architecture and urbanism (land, buildings, and their subdivided elements) have served as investment assets and vehicles to store wealth since at least the time of Vitruvius, the first century BCE, when Roman properties were bought and sold in markets not entirely dissimilar to contemporary capitalist models. Karl Marx describes what he calls primitive accumulation: the transformation in Western Europe from feudalism into early capitalism through the appropriation of the means of production—which started with land.[3] Through such acts as enclosure and assembly, a small number of people took over the commons and transformed it into private property. Private land property—what came to be categorized as real estate—is thus the "primitive" location of capital accumulation, the original site of wealth storage.

While real estate has long played a vital role for wealth storage, the ascendancy of finance capitalism has continuously and dramatically accelerated the investment asset function of buildings. By emphasizing profit acquisition through speculative real estate investment, finance capitalism entails the most symbiotic and synthetic relationship architecture has ever had with capitalism.

Buildings simultaneously fulfill three elemental roles: providing shelter, manifesting culture, and embodying wealth. A building always provides protection from the elements. At the same time, by necessity, it embodies cultural ideas and practices. And because buildings require labor to design and construct and because they incorporate physical materials, they are always an embodiment of wealth. Individual buildings vary in their proportions of the shelter-culture-wealth triad, with some structures more determined by the pragmatics of shelter, others the performance of culture, and yet others the storage of wealth and production of profits. The same can be said about different historical moments and geographical locations: the relative proportion of shelter-culture-wealth in buildings shifts over time and place. The premise of this book is that in the current era of finance capitalism, since around 1980, the wealth function of buildings has significantly increased. And as the wealth function rises, it recalibrates its relationship with the shelter and culture roles of buildings. Within finance capitalism, the function of buildings as profit-generating investment assets rises to such significance that in many instances it overshadows the historically more prominent roles of shelter and culture.

Finance Capitalism's Current Ascendancy

The rise of finance capitalism since approximately 1980 has been extensively documented.[4] Since this ascendancy is integral to the workings of contemporary capital, there is no shortage of opportunities to measure its magnitude. But those aspects of the economy at the core of finance capitalism—such as stock and currency markets—and what is more broadly categorized as the finance industry are convenient.

From all vantages, the stock market has grown in scope and scale. In 1980, there were 14,000 companies listed on the world's stock exchanges compared to 43,000 now.[5] In today's dollars the total value of stocks traded globally in 1984 was $1.7 trillion and by 2018 had reached $68 trillion, after peaking at just under $100 trillion in 2015.[6] (All figures in this book are quoted in adjusted US dollars, unless otherwise noted.) This is an increase from 17 percent to 98 percent of world GDP.[7] In 2015, the value of stocks was more than 160 percent of world GDP. Even more explosive growth can be found in the market for derivatives, which are contracts that derive their value from an underlying entity such as a stock or mortgage.[8]

The highly speculative character of currency markets is especially indicative of finance capitalism's rise. In the 1970s the daily volume of foreign exchange transactions was between $10 and 20 billion, but by 2000 a typical day had a volume of about $2 trillion—150 times greater than the value of all goods and services traded worldwide each day.[9] Roughly 80 percent of foreign exchange transactions in 1975 involved the trading of an actual product or service, while the remaining transactions were speculative, but by 2000 that ratio had dramatically shifted, with speculative transactions at 98 percent.[10] By 2019, the foreign exchange market had an average daily transaction volume of $6.6 trillion, making it by far the largest financial market in the world.[11]

As the scope and scale of financial markets have mushroomed, so have the financial sector's profits. In the United States, annual corporate profits in finance are higher than in any other industry. In 1982, about 14 percent of corporate profit in the United States was earned through financial corporations; two decades later it had risen to roughly 40 percent.[12] But the profits of financial corporations capture only a portion of the degree to which the US economy has financialized. Krippner demonstrated how nonfinancial corporations increasingly derive significant portions of their profit from financial transactions.[13] Examples of this include car manufacturers offering automotive financing products to dealerships and individuals, and large-scale housing developers making profit from financing the homes they sell.

The growth of financial markets and their associated profits has occurred in parallel with a change in finance's sociocultural position. In Western countries, marketing for financial products such as mutual funds, credit cards, and mortgages saturates the media. Ordinary people—even teenagers and children—are encouraged to become financially literate. By the 2000s, Wall Street had begun to draw a large percentage of elite US college graduates.[14] And the advent of online trading has made it easier for people to become active in trading financial assets. In 1980, 13 percent of people in the United States directly or indirectly owned stock.[15] According to polling by Gallup, that number reached a high of 63 percent in 2004 and in 2019 was at 55 percent.[16] When people do not directly own stock, they often indirectly own it through such things as pension funds. As more people own stock, use credit cards, and watch movies like *The Wolf of Wall Street*, everyday life is transformed. As Randy Martin, professor of art and policy at New York University, wrote in *Financialization of Daily Life*:

Finance, the management of money's ebbs and flows, is not simply in the service of accessible wealth, but presents itself as a merger of business and life cycles, as a means for the acquisition of self. The financialization of daily life is a proposal for how to get ahead, but also a medium for the expansive movements of body and soul."

It is in this manner that the stock market comes to be treated as an elemental barometer for not just the economy at large but also the vicissitudes of human existence in its entirety.

Marx and the Fictions of Finance

Without labeling it as such, Karl Marx pioneered the critique of finance capitalism in *The Process of Capitalist Production,* volume 3 of *Capital: A Critique of Political Economy.* Here, Marx discusses the essential role of credit in capitalism and demonstrates its basis for the function of banks and the stock market, writing that credit is a "necessary formation…on which the whole of capitalist production depends."[18] With extensive narration of the function of "bills of exchange" that exist between creditor and debtor and the intermediary role of entities such as banks, he establishes financial instruments and institutions as constant features of capitalism. For Marx, the joint-stock company (a business whose stock can be bought or sold by shareholders) is an extension of the credit system. A company can raise money by borrowing it (credit) or by issuing stock (equity). Both require the intermediation of financial institutions and instruments and can be thought of on a continuum.

Marx labels a critical aspect of the credit and joint-stock system as "fictitious capital." He understands fictitious capital as distinct from "real-capital" (capital in the form of the physical means of production) and "money-capital" (actual funds in the form of paper money, gold, or some other currency). The fictitious character of capital within the credit and the joint-stock system derives from its ability to increase or decrease through transactions and associated accounting practices alone and in a manner that appears to Marx to be relatively disconnected from real conditions of production:

> With the development of interest-bearing capital and the credit system,
> all capital seems to be duplicated, and at some points triplicated, by the
> various ways in which the same capital, or even the same claim, appears

in various hands in different guises. The greater part of this "money capital" is purely fictitious.[19]

Marx elsewhere quotes a Yorkshire banker, W. Leatham, in regard to bills of exchange specifically:

> It is impossible to decide what part arises out of real *bona fide* transactions, such as actual bargain and sale, or what part is fictitious and mere accommodation paper, that is, where one bill of exchange is drawn to take up another running, in order to raise a fictitious capital, by creating so much currency.[20]

Thus "fictitious capital has its characteristic movement." For Marx, most banking capital is fictitious, taking the form of bills of exchange and stocks.[21]

The problems of fictitious capital are numerous, according to Marx. *Capital*, volume 3, recounts various economic crises in nineteenth-century England, providing Marx with evidence for some of finance's most egregious characteristics. "The credit system appears as the main lever of overproduction and excessive speculation," he argues, due to the separation it creates between owners of capital and managers of production. Its ascendancy engenders novel dimensions in the class struggle of capitalism, reproducing "a new financial aristocracy, a new kind of parasite in the guise of company promoters, speculators and merely nominal directors."[22]

Hilferding and Lenin on Finance Capitalism

Since "fictitious capital" appears only in volume 3 of *Capital*, which was completed by Friedrich Engels after Marx's death, the term cannot be said to occupy a central position in Marx's body of work. Its importance grew among early twentieth-century Marxists who extended his preliminary work on finance. Some of the more prominent figures to grapple with finance capitalism in the early part of the century include Russian revolutionary and Soviet head of state Vladimir Lenin and the Austrianborn economist Rudolf Hilferding.

Hilferding's 1910 book *Finance Capital: A Study of the Latest Phase of Capitalist Development* attempts to extend Marx's initial work concerning credit and the joint-stock company. The emergence of close structural and personal links between industrial and bank capital that

Hilferding witnessed in parts of Europe defined finance capitalism for him.[23] Because, in Hilferding's view, Marx did not grasp the full significance of the joint-stock company, Marx "does not yet conceive dividends as a distinct economic category and hence fails to analyse promoter's profit." Hilferding argues that a shareholder in joint-stock companies does not rely on profits from those companies, but rather becomes a type of money capitalist who profits from a form of interest unique to shareholder securities. He calls this gain promoter's profit and recognizes it as an entirely new type of profit, writing that "promoter's profit is neither a swindle, nor some kind of indemnity or wage. It is an economic category *sui generis.*" This new category of profit accelerates a schism between production and finance, as "the share of interest in the total profit increases to some extent at the expense of entrepreneurial profit. In other words, the share of rentier grows at the expense of productive capitalists."[24]

Promoter's profit incentivizes the creation of joint-stock companies and thus enlarges the stock market, which Hilferding identifies as having a "true sphere of activity…as a market for titles to interest, or fictitious capital." Because many functions of a stock exchange overlap with those of other entities—for example, one can buy shares in a joint-stock company from both a bank and a stock exchange—Hilferding argues that the distinctive "specific activity of the stock exchange is really *speculation.*" Thus finance capitalism is inextricable from fictitious capital that allows for unique profits in a speculative structure. Hilferding recognizes that speculation is unproductive, yet nevertheless necessary to the function of capitalism.[25]

Lenin's *Imperialism: The Highest Stage of Capitalism* was published in 1916 and is largely derivative of Hilferding. However, its significant contribution was to articulate the imperialist dimension of finance capitalism. According to Lenin, the world is divided into a small number of "usurer states" and a much larger number of "debtor states" through the credit system that finance capital extends across the planet.[26] Finance capital had become global by his era and had rewritten the modes of production and superstructure everywhere.

Finance Capitalism as a Phase of History

Finance capitalism can be understood as integral to the cyclical nature of capitalist economies. The Italian economist and sociologist Giovanni

Arrighi envisioned two cycling stages of capitalist accumulation, prying Marx's general formula of capital, M-C-M (money-commodity-money), into a separate first M-C stage that is then followed by a C-M stage. Arrighi writes, "The central aspect of this pattern is the alternation of epochs of material expansion (MC phases of capital accumulation) with phases of financial rebirth and expansion (CM phases)."[27] During the first phase, there is an increasing "mass" of commodities, and in the second phase, "an increasing mass of money capital 'sets itself free' from commodity form, and accumulation proceeds through financial deals (as in Marx's abridged formula MM)."[28] Arrighi's *The Long Twentieth Century: Money, Power, and the Origins of Our Times* makes the case that there have been four great "hegemons" of capitalism, each defined by their capital city: Genoa (1340–1630), Amsterdam (1560–1780), London (1740–1930), and New York (1870–present). Each hegemonic period encapsulates one "systemic cycle of accumulation"; Arrighi calls the second, financial phase the autumnal phase, marking the decline of that particular hegemon.

Building upon Arrighi, Fredric Jameson describes capitalism's development as an "epidemic of epidemics" distributed across time and space in which a repeating cycle "replicates itself and reproduces a series of three moments."[29] The first moment is defined by the accumulation of money through trade. The second arises when this accumulation becomes capital that is invested in agriculture and manufacture. As this inevitably results in increasingly saturated markets that constrain production and consumption, the third moment—speculation—emerges:

> Speculation—the withdrawal of profits from the home industries, the increasingly feverish search, not so much for new markets (those are also saturated) as for the new kind of profits available in financial transactions themselves and as such—is the way in which capitalism now reacts to and compensates for the closing of its productive moment. Capital itself becomes free-floating.[30]

The Greek politician and economist Costas Lapavitsas, in his 2013 *Profiting without Producing: How Finance Exploits Us All*, argues that capitalism has had two "waves of financial ascendancy," the first spanning the final quarter of the nineteenth century and lasting until roughly the interwar years (the period that informed Hilferding) and the second starting in the late 1970s and continuing to the present.[31] In his explicit focus on financialization, distinct from Marx, Lapavitsas understands the financial system as "neither a minor adjunct, nor a parasitical excrescence of the capitalist economy, but an integral part of sustaining its accumulation." Lapavitsas describes an asymmetry in the current period of ascendancy between the sphere of production and "the ballooning sphere of circulation" in which financialization entails an entirely new form of profit. This is not promoter's profit, as identified by Hilferding, but rather what he calls financial expropriation, in which profit originates in the money revenue of workers.[32] He uses pooled mortgages as an example of financial expropriation, arguing that the future revenue of workers is the source of profit for these traded assets. Recognizing that Marx's and Hilferding's theories have limited application to contemporary finance capital, Lapavitsas is cautious about fictitious capital. He recognizes its utility as a conceptual category in analyzing finance capitalism but emphasizes that financial profits are enormous and real and that the notion of fiction should not distract any analysis. Furthermore, he believes that loanable capital, not fictitious capital, is at the root of financialization.[33]

Authors such as Marx, Hilferding, Lenin, Arrighi, Jameson, and Lapavitsas work in different contexts, offer different positions on finance capitalism, and have varying applicability to contemporary conditions. Nevertheless, the essential contours of finance capitalism are common to them. They all recognize that finance capitalism is a constant, yet varying, feature of capitalism that entails unique forms of profit that arise from the exchange of financial instruments unto themselves, the heightened role of speculation, and a separation of ownership and production. At the same time, the more recent writers—Arrighi, Jameson, and Lapavitsas—recognize that something significant and unique has occurred since roughly 1980. As Jameson observed in 1998, "I think everyone will agree that finance capital, along with globalization, is one of the distinctive features of late capitalism, or in other words of the distinctive state of things today."[34]

Neoliberalism, Globalization, Financialization

The post-1980 financialized economy is interrelated with two contemporaneous phenomena: neoliberalism and globalization. The relationship is so intimate that it is hard to disengage them from one another. The three concepts compete to serve as the most appropriate organizing concept for post-1980 capitalism.[35]

While the definition of neoliberalism is diffuse, in current discourse it tends to signify economic policies—such as privatization, deregulation, and decreased government spending—that expand the role of the private sector. Many neoliberal policies and practices played a key role in the ascent of finance capitalism. One of the most important occurred in 1971, with Richard Nixon's New Economic Policy, which suspended the gold standard. This effectively ended the Bretton Woods system that had established rules for commercial and financial relations among the United States, Canada, Western European countries, Australia, and Japan since 1944. What began in the 1970s gained momentum in the 1980s with the policies of Margaret Thatcher in the United Kingdom, Ronald Reagan in the United States, and Deng Xiaoping in China. In the early 1980s, the first major financial deregulation laws were passed in the United States; they were key to neoliberal restructuring and enabled current financialization to commence. Deregulation reached a high point with the 1999 Financial Services Modernization Act, which repealed the Glass-Steagall Act of 1933. It allowed commercial and investment banks to affiliate and enabled ever-larger financial conglomerates. These legal changes permitted financial institutions to grow rapidly and appropriate a much greater share of profit in the economy than they had previously.[36]

The processes of globalization date back centuries; Hilferding and Lenin described the extent to which finance capitalism operated at a worldwide scale by the late nineteenth and early twentieth centuries. This long-standing process of globalization has nevertheless accelerated in recent decades and coincides with post-1980 financialization. As the International Monetary Fund (IMF) reported in 2007, "Technological innovations and faster information flows, aided by a sharp increase in total savings being channeled into financial instruments across borders, have fostered the dramatic globalization of capital flows."[37] Cross-border capital flow was less than $1 trillion in 1990, rose to more than $12 trillion in 2007 (just before the 2008 crash), and was at $4 trillion in 2015.[38] The globalization of financial transactions is now so integral to the economies of the world that it is hard to conceive of globalization without finance and vice versa. While the rise of finance capitalism has coincided with globalization, financialization captures the specific transformation of capitalism since 1980 more directly than globalization. As Lapavitsas writes, "The deeper character of capitalism during the last three or more decades can be more easily captured by focusing on financialization rather than globalization."[39]

Architecture as Finance Capitalism

Finance capitalism has an especially pronounced effect on architecture. This is not merely because it is the dominant contemporary economic mode that, by necessity, impacts all sociocultural conditions, but rather because real estate is one of the primary mediums through which finance capitalism operates. By arguing that contemporary architecture is a primary operative medium of finance capitalism, the idea that architecture is the outcome or product of any economic structure is eschewed. Architecture is not the result of finance capitalism but rather *is* finance capitalism. As architectural historian Reinhold Martin wrote:

> Architecture…does not (or does not only) represent or "mirror"
> late capitalism as its cultural equivalent. It *belongs* to late capitalism.
> Asserting this might seem like attributing or conceding to architecture
> a near absolute immanence. But seen from another direction, it also
> extends the dialectical model that both [David] Harvey and [Fredric]
> Jameson deploy, perhaps to a point of no return, a point at which what
> is culture and what is capital cannot be distinguished in any useful way.[40]

Just as architecture has helped produce finance capitalism, finance capitalism has helped produce architecture. Any binary between capital and culture resonates with that of fiction and reality. Marx's term *fictitious capital* describes a distinction between capital directly bound up with production and a specific form of capital within the comparatively abstract layers of credit and speculative markets. Fictitious capital denotes a tension between ostensibly material, real conditions and immaterial, fictional conditions. A Marxist analysis of any process of financialization has to grapple with whether that process is also a fictionalization. Finance capitalism does indeed entail a shift toward greater importance for Marx's fictitious capital. As architecture in the twenty-first century *is* finance capitalism, it is perhaps best described as a financial fiction. Architecture is finance and finance is a fictional dimension of capitalism.

But the profits arising through finance capitalist transactions are very real, and financial fictions are not immaterial. The architecture described in this book is just as physical as any. So architecture becoming financial fiction is not only its virtualization or dematerialization, but rather its rematerialization. As architecture becomes financial fiction, its material conditions transform and adjust. Exploring architecture as finance capitalism reveals what the British political theorist Timothy Mitchell notes as "the distinction between virtual and real, model and reality, [that] is found at every point," helping to "engineer the modern sense of the real, or the material, as that from which we are cut off."[41]

CHAPTER ONE

FINANCE CAPITALISM AND ARCHITECTURE

In the free market, architecture=real estate.

REM KOOLHAAS, 2003

W hile architecture and capitalism have always been related, the ascent of finance capitalism since 1980 has uniquely implicated architecture because built space is a preferred operating medium of finance. As architecture has become finance and finance has become architecture, key aspects of both have changed. These changes involve how buildings are conceptualized, used, and managed and at the same time how they are designed, entailing everything from their proportions to their programmatic composition. The result can be experienced in the landscapes and cities that many of the world's citizens inhabit.

The FIRE Economy

As Fredric Jameson recognized in the late 1990s, "One of the privileged forms of speculation today is that of land and city space."[1] Indeed, some observers argue that real estate is now the single biggest component of certain economies. The American economist Michael Hudson wrote that the "'postindustrial' economy turns out to be mainly about real estate," adding that, in Western economies, increases in property values are "the driving force in today's financialized mode of 'wealth creation.'"[2] Financial tactics and logics are increasingly interconnected with real estate. The fact that real estate investment is primarily debt financed conveys one important aspect of the tight symbiosis between the finance and real estate sectors.

To capture this symbiosis, the term *FIRE economy* emerged in the 1980s; it has come into more common economic parlance since. An acronym for *finance, insurance, and real estate*, it indicates the economic ecology connecting landowners, banks, insurers, mortgage brokers, investment brokerages, real estate developers, real estate agencies, and hedge funds. Not only are the finance and real estate industries tightly interdependent, but so is the insurance industry to them, since insurance corporations are among real estate's largest investors. For example, in 2018, the largest investor in global real estate was Prudential, a multinational insurance corporation headquartered in London, with a reported $64 billion in real estate assets.[3] The monthly periodical *Institutional Investor* reported in 2018 that insurance corporations account for 21 percent of institutions with at least $1 billion invested in real estate.[4] A large portion of the FIRE sector's revenue comes from fluctuating asset prices and interest on loans—making it an embodiment of finance capitalism.

As finance and insurance became increasingly integrated with real estate during the 1990s, the way that real estate had functioned for centuries fundamentally changed. It transformed from what had historically been a local endeavor into an asset class traded in various forms in global financial markets.[5] While this recent financialization of real estate is widely recognized as unprecedented in scope and scale, it is important to note that just as finance capitalism is a constant feature of capitalism itself, so is real estate. Vladimir Lenin wrote in 1916 that "speculation in land situated in the suburbs of rapidly growing towns is a particularly profitable operation for finance capital."[6] Giovanni Arrighi described the earlier two of his four hegemons, the Renaissance Italian city-states and Enlightenment Amsterdam:

> The profits that were being made in long-distance trade and
> high finance…could not be reinvested in these activities without
> jeopardizing their profitability. Then as now, a significant portion
> of this surplus capital tended to flow into speculation and into
> conspicuous consumption; and then as now, investment in real estate
> within the capitalist cities themselves were [*sic*] the most important
> means of combining speculation with conspicuous consumption.[7]

The role that real estate plays in finance capitalism is as integral and therefore as long-standing as finance capitalism is to capitalism at large.

One of the keys to understanding the important role that real estate plays in finance capitalism is the relationship between rent and fictitious capital. In Marxist economic geographer David Harvey's analysis, when land is traded, it becomes a special type of commodity. It does not have any value in the Marxist sense, as it is not a product of labor, yet it can secure for the owner a stream of rent. Harvey states that the rent revenue on land is in principle no different from the revenue acquired through investments in such things as government debt and corporate securities. He writes, "The land becomes a form of fictitious capital, and the land market functions simply as a particular branch—albeit with some special characteristics—of the circulation of interest-bearing capital."[8] Therefore real estate finds its function as a vehicle of finance capitalism in the structural condition of capitalism and land rent.

The Central Role of Housing

While real estate takes many forms—including raw land and a variety of building types—housing plays an especially important role in the current era of finance capitalism. And while housing, like all real estate, is a long-standing site of finance capital, it has assumed heightened importance in contemporary capitalism. Costas Lapavitsas identifies three tendencies of accumulation that have given financialization its current character, one of which is that "individuals and households have come increasingly to rely on the formal financial system to facilitate access to vital goods and services, including housing, education, health and transport. The savings of households and individuals have also been increasingly mobilized by the formal financial system."[9] This unique distinction of current financialization is critical for real estate and housing, since housing is the primary way that individuals and households are financialized. The geographer and sociologist Manuel B. Aalbers demonstrates what he calls "the specificities of housing as a central aspect of financialization" in his 2016 book *The Financialization of Housing*. He writes:

> Housing-based wealth, that is housing valued at current market prices minus mortgage debt, has risen to historically unprecedented heights, implying that real estate has become more important as store-of-value for households in the age of financialization.[10]

Aalbers identifies five mechanisms through which housing is financialized: the securitization of mortgage loans; the rise of subprime and predatory lending; rising mortgage debt for households; the entry of private equity firms, hedge funds, and publicly listed real estate firms in rental markets; and the reliance of housing providers on bonds and complicated financial derivatives.[11]

It is hard to overstate the importance of housing to current capitalism. Market-based financing of housing has grown dramatically since the deregulation of financial systems.[12] The result is that, for instance, in 2010 in the United States, Britain, and Australia, 70 percent of all bank loans were real estate mortgages.[13] In the United States, the total value of mortgages for one- to four-family residences climbed from around $900 billion in 1980 to almost $11 trillion by the end of 2019.[14] Household debt, of which mortgages are typically the largest component, has risen significantly in the era of finance capitalism. In the United Kingdom, it has risen from 30 percent of GDP in 1980 to 87 percent in 2018, and over the same period from about 46 percent to 100 percent in Canada, 50 percent to 76 percent in the United States, and 38 percent to 120 percent in Australia.[15]

While financialization entails vast markets, complex transactional chains, and powerful intermediaries, it is important to remember that housing serves as the physical construct through which people become most heavily engaged with financing. In many economies, houses are the most widely owned asset, the biggest asset of the majority of households, and the asset that is simplest to borrow against.[16] This engagement with finance typically occurs through a decades-long relationship with a bank. At the same time, the IMF observes that the rise and fall of housing prices are becoming more synchronized across the planet.[17] This is because housing is no longer only a physical construct that is bought, sold, and financed locally but also a global asset class.

The Giant Pool of Money

The drivers of the financialization of housing and real estate are numerous and complex, but the growing magnitude of global capital is a critical basic backdrop of it. This large mass of capital has been referred to as the "giant pool of money" and the "wall of money."[18] There are a variety of methods to measure the total amount of global capital. One can consider global assets under management—the aggregate amount of capital savings in various forms of management funds, such as pension funds, mutual funds, or insurance funds. Different institutions offer varying statistics for assets under management, but all agree that growth in recent decades has been staggering. For example, PwC (formerly PricewaterhouseCoopers) issued a report in 2017 titled *Asset & Wealth Management Revolution: Embracing Exponential Change*, which states that global assets under management more than doubled from $37 trillion in 2002 to $85 trillion in 2016.[19]

Where is all this money coming from? A major source is "emerging market economies," generally defined in mainstream economic discourse as markets—currently including those of Brazil, China, and India—transitioning from less developed to advanced. In essence, the productivity of global economic systems and their dramatic role in these emerging territories have resulted in a historically unprecedented amount of capital. Other factors such as loose monetary policy and the accumulation of profits by transnational corporations also play an important role in feeding the giant pool of money.[20] The relevance of this for architecture lies in how and where the growing surplus of capital is absorbed.

There exists a heightened imperative for capital investment to be made in asset categories that offer profitable returns coupled with reasonable risk. While this imperative may be understood as a basic premise of capitalism, with what David Harvey calls the "perpetual need to find profitable terrains for capital-surplus production and absorption shap[ing] the politics of capitalism," it can be argued that the drive to newly profitable terrains is amplified in the context of the giant pool of money.[21] For most of modern history, the majority of investment capital went into relatively safe and stable locations such as treasuries and municipal bonds.[22] But as capital grew, those instruments became less attractive, while the search for new terrains resulted in more and more capital being absorbed by real estate. As Harvey describes, the processes of contemporary urbanization are "driven by the need to find outlets for overaccumulating capital."[23] Indeed, Harvey notes, "Urbanization has played a particularly active role, alongside such phenomena as military expenditures, in absorbing the surplus capital that capitalists perpetually produce in their search for profits."[24] The financialization of real estate and housing improves their capacity to perform this absorption function.

Aerial image, taken in 2015, of the incomplete Ascaya development in metropolitan Las Vegas.

The Emergence of Asset Architecture and Urbanism

Real estate, and especially housing, is a primary medium through which finance capitalism actualizes itself, and it is because of this that architecture can be described as a primary medium of financialization. As most real estate incorporates architecture, architecture exists at the center of finance capital, not just in a peripheral domain merely affected or influenced by it. Instead, it is one of the main agents of financialization and better understood as financialization itself. Through mortgages, mortgage-backed securities, home equity loans, and other financial constructs, the buildings that are necessarily connected with these financial instruments are a major component of the current era of financialization.

But at the same time, these buildings are physically present in the everyday lives of the people who inhabit them. And because these buildings are both designed and used to suit the logics of finance capitalism, they imprint the logics of finance onto how humans move through space, what is in their field of vision, and how they interact with others both inside the buildings and in the public spaces between them. It is in this way that architecture serves as an overarching means of financialization for the human condition. The building is literally the object that ties more and more people into the seemingly immaterial flows of finance capital at the very same time that it configures financialized ways of moving, seeing, and behaving.

As finance capitalism has ascended and pulled architecture toward the center of finance, how has architecture changed? What are the

For years, laborers have continually raked the rocky ground of Ascaya, keeping this massive earthwork in an odd state of sublime purity.

characteristics of its financialization? The shift entails changes to almost every aspect of built space. This includes physical attributes such as siting, scale, program, organization, form, aesthetics, and materiality, as well as how buildings are conceptualized, managed, maintained, and used. The architecture of finance capital has five broad characteristics:

1. It is inherently unstable and creates spaces of crisis.
2. It increasingly functions as speculative wealth storage.
3. It is the means of uneven development and heightened inequality.
4. It has a simultaneous propensity for highly iconic and extremely standardized spaces.
5. It increases liquidity.

Architectural changes in form and function that are unique to the contemporary era of finance capital can all be understood in relation to these five financial functions.

Spaces of Crisis

While the cyclical disposition of capitalism is constant, financialization, observers argue, increases the tendency for crisis, with some describing it as being in an almost perpetual state of crisis.[25] As architecture and urbanism increasingly absorb surplus capital, they begin to behave more like stocks, complete with their instability. Such things as rapid development, the oversupply of built space, mass vacancies, and volatile fluctuations between growth and decay mark the resulting urbanism and present unique socio-spatial challenges and opportunities. Zombie and ghost urbanism, characterized by a subtle but persistent underoccupancy in the former and by extreme vacancy in the latter, are now worldwide phenomena. Housing costs are increasingly detached from local economies, prompting crises of affordability. Overt crises that have architecture at their core — like the savings and loan crisis in the mid-1980s and the subprime mortgage crisis in the mid-2000s — have become more common. Financialized architecture and urbanism create an unstable landscape marked by the detritus and absurdities of simultaneous expansion and collapse.

The inherent instability and the unforgiving vicissitudes of economic booms and busts result in spaces of crisis that are themselves characteristic of finance capitalist architecture and urbanism. These include land cleared and prepared for development that sits in fallow decay for more than a decade and neighborhoods that are eerily underpopulated. These conditions — historically associated with failures and crisis — are typical of spaces of crisis that finance capitalism propagates.

Finance capitalist crisis space often juxtaposes the semiotics of success and failure in unusual ways. An example can be found at Ascaya, a "luxury" single-family-home subdivision in suburban Las Vegas. With 313 lots carved into a mountainside, the project stalled with the 2008 housing collapse in the United States. More than twelve years later, the site remains largely unoccupied, with just a few multimillion-dollar homes sitting on what is essentially a massive earthwork. Here, a few wealthy homesteaders occupy a kind of financial wasteland — a new nature. The scale of speculative development in the era of finance capitalism, in combination with the propensity for swings between growth and collapse, results in surreal territories like Ascaya.

Speculative Wealth Storage

Financialization elevates architecture as a site for both wealth storage and speculative capital gains. Unlike safe-deposit boxes (as condominiums are sometimes referred to by the media) or savings accounts, buildings have prices that can fluctuate significantly and therefore offer the opportunity for spectacular gains. Manuel B. Aalbers recognizes that housing has become more important as a store of value for households during financialization.[26] And Giovanni Arrighi notes that investing in urban architecture is the most important means of combining speculation with conspicuous consumption.[27] Architecture is transformed as the sheer amount of money entering real estate distorts the form and scale of buildings, which mutate as they get thinner and taller, extend deeper, and repeat ever more relentlessly across ever-larger scales.

An example of speculative wealth storage is Pentominium in Dubai. The project has one 6,000-square-foot (550-square-meter) unit per floor—an entire tower of penthouses! (The name Pentominium is a portmanteau of *penthouse* and *condominium*.) At 122 stories and more than 1,600 feet (500 meters) tall, the structure would have been the tallest residential building in the world upon completion. Construction commenced in 2009 but stalled in 2011, when the tower had risen only twenty-two floors. The partly finished tower sits abandoned to this day. During construction, the developers boasted in promotional marketing, "The Pentominium has one of the deepest excavations done in the world—an exercise necessary for this awe-inspiring proposition."[28] The carcass of this ambitious scheme of future wealth storage sits among neighboring towers, long ago complete.

Inequality

As the French economist Thomas Piketty has shown, the post-1980 era of finance capital has coincided with growing inequality in most advanced capitalist economies. The growing number of very wealthy individuals and the amount of money they control has resulted in a proliferation of architecture uniquely tailored to them. Take, for example, the emergence in the twenty-first century of "gigamansions" in Los Angeles. While the wealthy have always built large and conspicuous houses, the number and extremity of these structures is new. *Gigamansion* tends to signify a home that is at least 20,000 square feet (1,850 square meters), sells for $50 million or more, and has an array of ostentatious amenities such as champagne rooms and bowling alleys. In contrast, a few hours' drive from the gigamansions of Los Angeles, subdivisions blanket the Inland Empire with the single-family homes that are the physical constructs through which lower- and middle-class families obtain mortgages.

Iconic Standardization

Certain architecture projects emphasize standardization in order to better function as tradable assets, while others aim to attract investors by being what Arindam Dutta, an MIT associate professor in architectural history, labels "financial icons."[29] Standardized and iconic buildings sometimes work in concert. A specific financial icon, such as a signature museum, can seed an urban territory with investor desire. This then increases the surrounding, and often highly standardized, buildings' ability to function as spatio-financial instruments for wealth storage and speculation.

In other instances, the standardized and the iconic coexist within the same building. Herzog & de Meuron's 56 Leonard Street in Lower Manhattan is a fifty-seven-story tower with 145 condominium units that have sold for prices ranging from $3.5 to $50 million. As a site for

McClean Design, Opus (Hillcrest II), Beverly Hills, California, 2016. A 20,500-square-foot (1,900-square-meter) gigamansion with seven bedrooms, eleven bathrooms, and two swimming pools. A 170-bottle Cristal champagne vault, a gold Lamborghini, and a gold Rolls-Royce were included in its purchase price.

ABOVE A marketing "teaser" poster for Herzog & de Meuron's 56 Leonard Street, New York City, 2017, with an accumulation of text such as "global landmark" and "sculpture in the sky" conveying an icon of standardized elements.

UPPER RIGHT A model and box, part of the marketing campaign for 56 Leonard Street.

RIGHT 56 Leonard Street.

speculative investment (one German investor bought three units), it is a slender column of standardized condominium units, yet its unique form also renders it a financial icon. The form departs from a typical tower extrusion through its increasingly uneven projections and recesses as it rises—what has been called pixelated—earning it the nickname "Jenga Tower." It achieves an iconic status through the nonstandard shuffling of standardized quantities of luxury investment.

Liquidity

The process of financialization presents challenges that arise from the internal logics that have historically differentiated finance and architecture. The synthesis of these different internal logics results in particular socio-spatial outcomes. The most important of these challenges for architecture's financialization is liquidity—the degree to which an asset can be readily exchanged for cash (cash being the ultimate liquid asset). Those investment assets that function as the optimum instruments of finance capitalism require a relatively high degree of liquidity to facilitate the requisite scale of buying, selling, and investing. Financial instruments such as stocks are designed to provide this degree of liquidity—allowing investors to easily own incremental portions of diverse corporations in a market context that facilitates simple and efficient transactions. A non-financial entity, in contrast, typically has a much lower degree of liquidity. Introductory lessons on the concept of liquidity often use real estate as the quintessential example of an illiquid asset. It is difficult to exchange quickly and easily because land, buildings, and units are immovable, are comparatively large and expensive, require ongoing maintenance, tend to be highly idiosyncratic, and are situated within complex and nuanced sociopolitical contexts. Because of all these factors, buildings are bought and sold in a time-consuming process.

Financialization aims to increase the liquidity of buildings and land in a number of ways. These include embracing new financial instruments that serve as liquid intermediaries for property ownership, increasing market size through the invention of the condominium and global expansion, and changing the social performance, physical form, and aesthetics of buildings themselves.

Real estate investment trusts (REITs) and mortgage-backed securities (MBS) are examples of relatively new financial instruments that have gained in popularity since the 1980s. REITs, which were legalized in the

United States in 1960, allow investors to buy and sell shares in a company that owns or finances real estate on well-established stock markets. MBS, which first appeared in their contemporary form in the United States in the late 1960s, enable investors to trade securitized shares of mortgage debt. Transactions in the shares of REITs and MBS are far more streamlined and efficient than direct purchases of real estate, thereby offering more liquid forms of real estate investment. REITs have proven to be popular worldwide. In 2009, the Financial Times Stock Exchange created the EPRA Nareit Global Real Estate Index, which tracks the performance of listed real estate companies and REITs; by 2019, it had a market capitalization of $1.8 trillion.[30] MBS have a far larger market and played a major role in the 2007–8 global financial crisis.

Directly owning real estate is expensive in comparison to other asset classes and is also highly locally specific, hence the saying, "All real estate is local." High cost and local specificity constrain the size of any given market, but finance capitalism's emphasis on real estate has been abetted by multiple factors that have increased market size and the ease of real estate transactions. Two primary ones are the invention of the condominium and the globalization of the real estate market. Legalized in North America in the 1960s but not gaining popularity until the 1990s, condominiums have provided a low-cost way to enter the real estate market with streamlined transactions. In parallel, the increase in individuals and entities purchasing real estate in far-flung locations has expanded the market. This has been facilitated by the emergence of global real estate brokerage firms such as Colliers International, currently the world's largest residential real estate brokerage firm by volume of sales. Founded in 1976, the company now employs more than 15,000 people in 485 offices spread among 63 countries.[31] Colliers competes with other global real estate brokerages such as New York–based Newmark Knight Frank and London-based Savills. The recent large-scale global expansion of these firms mirrors the exponential growth of real estate values in the early to mid-2000s.

At the same time that buildings have acquired heightened liquidity through new financial instruments and practices, their physical form and function also have changed, transforming buildings into optimized, more liquid, spatio-financial instruments that facilitate the accumulation of profit within the complex milieu of laws, regulations, and practices that constitute finance capitalism. These changes occur in four primary ways:

1. Simplifying space
2. Maximizing the number of assets
3. Facilitating remote ownership
4. Adding compensatory complexity

Simplifying architecture has myriad social and spatial consequences. Common tactics include diminishing sociality and abstracting locality—that is, diminishing the possibility of social interaction within and among buildings while incorporating standardized spaces that are relatively isolated from unique local characteristics. Maximizing the number of assets translates into repeating standardized housing units in large numbers, thus building taller towers and more extensive arrays of single-family homes. Facilitating remote ownership centers on adjusting the siting, massing, and organization of buildings so as to reduce maintenance and security demands, thus making architectural assets easier to own from afar. Paradoxically, as heightened liquidity is achieved through the first three techniques, the unique characteristics of each building are diminished to such a degree that their very viability as real estate assets is threatened. Overly simplified and standardized, they risk becoming undesirable purchases. In other words, the "real" of real estate is diminished to a degree that threatens its desirable attributes for investment. To resolve this inherent tension in the drive for liquidity, architectural conditions that *seem* complex compensate for what has been lost. This compensatory complexity, a simplified version of conditions that only appears complex, primarily serves to maintain the investment asset function.

The Aquarius residential complex in Vancouver, designed by the Vancouver architect James Cheng and completed in 1999, is an early example of all four tactics being used to increase liquidity. The project incorporates 480 condominium units in four towers, with a podium that houses retail at its base along with a modest amount of office space. An elevated courtyard sits on top of the podium, providing a private recreational domain complete with a fish-stocked lagoon and gardens. The project achieves spatial simplification through a variety of tactics, including the repetition of simple and standardized units. The podium raises these units off the ground, disentangling them from the messy complexities of public street life. Maximum asset provision is ensured through the sheer number of units. The condominium provides the legal apparatus

James KM Cheng Architects, Aquarius, Vancouver, 1999.
Condominium towers sitting atop a retail podium.

The fish-stocked lagoon and lush gardens in the new ground plane
on top of the podium at Aquarius.

that helps separate ownership from occupancy. The typology of the relatively slender tower placed atop a podium minimizes security and maintenance by controlling access to units through centralized lobby entrances and reducing contact with areas such as the roof that are prone to failure. These operations of architectural simplification are compensated for by the reproduction of a naturalistic ground plane on the roof of the podium; this artificial and controlled nature becomes the seemingly unique and complex site for the liquid commodities of the investment-oriented condominium units that rise above it.

While architecture optimizes its asset function, it simultaneously becomes a spatial territory in which users directly engage the logics of finance capital. It is not merely that architecture is changed by finance capital but also that it becomes the medium in which humans directly inhabit financialization in their everyday lives. In financial ruins like Ascaya, investment icons like 56 Leonard Street, and standardized condominium units like those at Aquarius, the scale of investment capital, its inherent inequalities and propensity for failure, and the spatial sameness cloaked in invented "natures" all function as the rematerializations through which finance capital builds itself.

CHAPTER TWO

ZOMBIES AND GHOSTS, GROWTH AND DECAY

I n the years since Occupy Wall Street emerged, it has begun to seem that the most meaningful aspect of the movement was the name itself—"Occupy." It has become clear that the very notion of occupancy is a fulcrum of contemporary capitalism. What else can one make of the normalization of the owned but empty housing units in so many buildings in cities around the world? As housing is increasingly treated as an investment asset, its basic function of providing bodily shelter is beginning to appear outmoded. A sober assessment of current global real estate trends cannot avoid the conclusion that vacancy is a preferred investment class. While vacancy rates are always shifting over time and changing from context to context, in the United States, for example, the vacancy rate, including seasonal use-related vacancies, increased by 44 percent between 2000 and 2010—growing from 10.4 million to 15 million units.[1] Economist Michael Hudson's 2010 declaration that the "'postindustrial' economy turns out to be mainly about real estate" might reasonably be updated to pronounce that today's economy turns out to be mainly about *unoccupied* real estate.[2]

A by-product of finance capitalism's emphasis on asset value over use value is the underuse of architectural space. High residential vacancies in parts of cities that are widely perceived as desirable (because of some combination of climate, culture, and setting) as well as abandoned or largely empty developments are prominent attributes of twenty-first-century urbanism. As these two conditions convey, not all underoccupancy is the same. A neighborhood's high proportion of owned but empty residential units generates an in-between state of vitality—zombie urbanism—whereas a more dramatic proportion of vacant or unfinished units in the context of a perceived crisis amounts to a distinct phenomenon—ghost urbanism. The divergence between use and asset values problematizes an array of widely held beliefs about buildings. Historically, underuse exists on one end of the spectrum, where it is closely associated with blight, decay, and ruins. On the opposite end is the vibrant utility of new growth. But twenty-first-century urbanism abounds with newly created ruins. Zombie and ghost urbanism problematize the opposition between the success of new utility and the failure of ruinous decay. And in the process, they recalibrate theoretical and emotional conceptions of architecture.

Zombie Urbanism

Zombie urbanism occurs when an area has large numbers of owned but empty housing units, resulting in a de facto density that is significantly below designed capacity. These areas mix present populations with absent populations, exhibiting an eerily low level of vitality in relation to their scale. They are not dead, but they are also not quite alive.

No urban area has full residential occupancy at any given time, because there is never a perfect alignment between housing supply and demand. In addition, there is a steady rate of turnover as people move in and out, buy and sell units, and spend time away from primary residences—all of which contribute to a certain number of empty units at any moment. What is considered an optimal level of vacancy depends on local conditions that change over time. According to the US Census, the vacancy rate in rental housing in the entire United States fluctuated between 7.6 and 10.6 percent from 1995 to 2018.[3] Over the same period, the vacancy rate of homeowner housing moved between 1.5 and 2.6 percent.[4] The equilibrium vacancy rate (EVR) is that which poses no upward or downward pressure on housing costs. As an example, Seattle has an EVR between 4.97 and 5.25 percent.[5] Zombie urbanism occurs in specific locations when vacancy rates are significantly higher than these ranges.

Owned but empty units in zombie urbanism tend to serve three functions: as wealth storage, as speculative assets, and as secondary residences. These functions can operate discretely but more often work in combination. For instance, the purchase of a secondary home for recreational use is often at least partly informed by speculation. While a typical investor will rent out a unit for ongoing revenue, very wealthy investors increasingly let units sit empty. These individuals' substantial capital propels their interest in diversifying wealth storage and also facilitates their lifestyle of global mobility, in which they perceive multiple residential properties as desirable. The growth of this wealthy population and the amount of capital it controls are having a significant effect on numerous locations around the world.

Secondary homes fall into either recreational or urban categories; some regions and cities have long been the site of these properties, from

Rogers Stirk Harbour + Partners, One Hyde Park, London, 2011. Dark units at the famously expensive building adjacent to London's Hyde Park.

rural dachas outside Moscow to urban pieds-à-terre in London. While they have served as manifestations of wealth and privilege for centuries, recreational properties became more common during the Industrial Revolution, as the upper class and growing middle class sought relief from the challenges of modern urban life. By the early twentieth century, large areas of London—the so-called cocktail belt and stockbroker's belt—contained country and weekend homes.[6] The French term *pied-à-terre* (foot to the ground) was first used in the nineteenth century to describe short-term or secondary lodging. Since then, the term has come to denote a secondary urban home, typically an apartment.

Finance capitalism has increased the prevalence of secondary housing. In Manhattan, for example, Midtown is a center of underoccupied housing. When the *New York Times* analyzed data from the Census Bureau's 2012 American Community Survey, they found that on the eight blocks from East Fifty-Ninth Street to East Sixty-Third Street between Park Avenue and Fifth Avenue, 628 of 1,261 homes were vacant the majority of the time.[7] While Midtown is an epicenter of pieds-à-terre, the phenomenon can be found across much of Manhattan and beyond. The 2017 New York City Housing and Vacancy Survey has shown 75,000 vacant pieds-à-terre in New York City compared with 55,000 in 2014.[8] Of course, there are other forms of vacancy. The US Census Bureau's 2017 American Community Survey counted 122,000 vacant housing units in Manhattan—almost 14 percent of all units. This compared to about 25,000 vacant units, under 5 percent, in the Bronx.[9] There are many reasons for vacancy, ranging from units awaiting demolition to those that are empty while awaiting sale, but the single biggest census category is those "held for occasional, seasonal, or recreational use."[10]

Underuse in Paris appears to be even more widespread. A 2017 report by the Paris Urbanism Agency shows that 26 percent of homes were empty in the 1st, 2nd, 3rd and 4th arrondissements.[11] While seldom-used second homes have long been features of central Paris, they have experienced a significant uptick between 2008 and 2013, according to the same report. Ian Brossat, Paris Housing Commissioner, was quoted as saying, "It's a really worrying issue, it's not normal to have 200,000 empty or semi-occupied homes. It represents twice the housing available in a big arrondissement like the 18th."[12]

London also has substantial zombie urbanism. "Some of the richest people in the world are buying property here as an investment," the *New*

York Times quoted Paul Dimoldenberg, a Westminster Council politician, as saying. "They may live here for a fortnight in the summer, but for the rest of the year they're contributing nothing to the local economy. The specter of new buildings where there are no lights on is a real problem."[13] Savills World Research reports that during 2011–12, 59 percent of sales of existing residences in prime areas of central London, such as Chelsea and Kensington, were purchased by overseas buyers.[14] A significant number of these properties were not primary residences and were not occupied for much of the year.

While finance capitalism increases the number of owned but empty units in major global centers of power like New York, Paris, and London, it affects a large roster of cities throughout the world. The latest Canadian census indicates nearly 100,000 vacant or underoccupied housing units in Toronto.[15] In certain parts of central Vancouver, up to 25 percent of condominiums sit largely empty.[16] In Miami, hard numbers are difficult to obtain, but real estate data suggests the perfect combination of factors for high second-home vacancy. In 2007, more than a third of all houses and almost 60 percent of condominiums in Miami-Dade County were secondary residences.[17] In 2015, 31 percent of condominium purchases in the county were made by buyers who lived at least fifty miles away.[18] It is also difficult to obtain accurate numbers for Panama City, but it is widely believed that a large portion of that city's residential towers are empty. Reports indicate that a system of using buildings for money laundering works alongside legitimate real estate investment in the city.[19] In Melbourne, the Australian NGO Prosper analyzed domestic water usage in 2014 to determine the number of vacant units and found just over 100,000 empty or hardly used homes.[20] The municipal government in Barcelona identified more than 100,000 units with zero or very little water consumption in 2016, indicating they were likely vacant or underoccupied.[21] Beirut's city center appears full of sparsely occupied condominium towers. Central Beirut experienced a surge in luxury condominium construction between 2007 and 2011 that was aimed toward expatriates and foreigners within the Persian Gulf region.[22] Many of these units were sold and are now rarely inhabited.

These locations are all perceived as both desirable places to live and good places to bank wealth in real estate. This is in no small part because there is good reason to believe that real estate values will rise over the long term. Vancouver offers the transparency and stability of Canadian law and governance, alongside exceptional natural beauty. Beirut is perceived as a liberal oasis in West Asia and has been fast growing since the end of Lebanon's long civil war. Melbourne is seen as a safe city with an excellent climate, located in relative proximity to Southeast Asia's population centers. While the particularities of desirability change from place to place, these cities are invariably considered good locations for investment and are thus magnets for real estate investment capital.

In response to the challenges posed by zombie urbanism, many jurisdictions are exploring tools to reduce its incidence. Paris introduced a 20 percent tax on second homes in 2015 and increased it to 60 percent in 2017. As a result, second-home owners pay 50 percent higher property tax than owners of primary residences.[23] Vancouver enacted its Empty Homes Tax in 2016, which charges an annual 1 percent tax on the assessed property value of units that are unoccupied for more than 180 days per year. Melbourne enacted its Vacant Residential Property Tax in 2017, which applies to sixteen areas of the city and imposes a 1 percent annual tax on properties that are unoccupied for six or more months of the year, regardless of whether they are continuous. Washington, DC, and Oakland, California, have their own versions of vacancy taxes. In 2020, Hong Kong, Toronto, and Los Angeles were among cities debating whether to implement vacancy taxes.

It has long been accepted that recreational properties sit empty for much of the year. A modest cabin on the edge of a lake, a few hours' drive from the city, is expected to be vacant most of the time. However, as the number, location, and extravagance of secondary homes have shifted, accepted norms are being challenged. In some locations, recreational properties have increased exponentially to the point of forming entirely new types of urban environments. For example, Spain's Mediterranean coast from Valencia to Málaga merges the globalized tourist economy with finance capitalism's predilection for real estate investment by providing a vast linear city of secondary vacation homes for Northern Europeans. This collection of megaprojects transforms recreational properties into a distinct urbanism of epic proportions.

Zombie urbanism is now a defining attribute of the contemporary city, yet dominant modes of designing, managing, governing, and conceptualizing the city rely on assumptions of certain levels of occupancy. Basic decisions regarding provisions of services and scaling of amenities are based on historic notions of occupancy for their integration and deployment. Zombie urbanism upends these assumptions and problematizes myriad aspects of urbanism. New York State Senator Liz Krueger recalls, "I met with a developer who is building one of those billionaire buildings on Fifty-Seventh Street, and he told me, 'Don't worry, you won't need any more services, because the buyers won't be sending their kids to school here, there won't be traffic.'"[24] As ongoing vacancy is normalized, should cities rethink zoning requirements, infrastructure, and public services? Given the long-standing correlation between the number of housing units and population density, the separation of the two presents a challenge to the operation and management of cities. When population drops 10 percent in an area, it can be the make-or-break difference for local stores and services. In this way, zombie urbanism can translate into vacancies not only in residential space but in locations that are more visible, such as commercial storefronts.

The vacancies of zombie urbanism are not the result of an overt system failure, deficiency, or calamity, as in the postindustrial Ruhr Valley or in post-Katrina New Orleans, but rather a vacancy of success. This vacancy emerges not from oversupply or low demand, or in relation to a declining job market, but instead tends to exist within the context of both strong demand and economic growth. Buildings sell out, developers make profits, governments collect fees, and property values often continue to escalate, yet things remain not quite alive.

Ghost Urbanism

While zombie urbanism is defined by a state of reduced occupancy that operates in its own form of success, ghost urbanism is distinguished by two primary differences: higher vacancy and the perception of failure. Ghost urbanism's radical departure from intended levels of occupancy renders a space experientially dead and leads to an overt perception of failure—most commonly a noticeable and persistent amount of unsold or incomplete housing units that may be in a state of decay.

As increased capital flows into real estate, exaggerating periods of expansion and subsequent contraction, a disposition toward overbuilding results in mass vacancies. This resonates with the Austrian-born economist Joseph Schumpeter's "creative destruction."[25] As David Harvey states, "Under capitalism there is…a perpetual struggle in which capital builds a physical landscape appropriate to its own condition at a particular moment in time, only to have to destroy it, usually in the course of a crisis, at a subsequent point in time."[26] Ghost urbanism, which occurs when something has ostensibly not gone according to plan, is always a form of crisis, and its spaces of crisis can be found throughout the world.

While there is no shortage of ghost conditions, exceptional insights can be found in the boom and bust that pivoted around 2007 to 2008 in Ireland and Spain. In many respects, these countries experienced the most radical relative transformation during the global economic crisis, a crisis that centered on the financialization of housing. The ghost conditions that emerged in these countries persist today and offer poignant portraits of the ruthless vicissitudes of built territory operating primarily as an investment asset.

Ghost Urbanism in Ireland

The Irish property boom, commencing in approximately 1995 and lasting until roughly 2007, radically altered the nation's landscape. During this period, more than 750,000 units of housing were constructed, amounting to approximately 40 percent of the total housing stock in Ireland at the time.[27] As the boom gained momentum between 2001 and 2007, an average of 70,000 units of housing were constructed each year, with more than 90,000 in 2006 alone.[28] In a country with a population of nearly 4.6 million, this translates into 18 units per 1,000 people per year, giving Ireland, along with Spain, the highest rate of construction in the European Union and nearly triple the rate of the next-highest nation, France.[29] This construction blanketed the entire island in everything from urban perimeter blocks to peripheral megaprojects, exurban commuter estates, and a proliferation of one-off rural houses. And the boom was not constrained to housing. Millions of square feet of shopping malls were constructed, resulting in the second-highest per capita area of shopping malls in Europe.[30] Nearly 13 million square feet (1.2 million square meters) of office space was constructed between 2000 and 2007.[31] Between 2004 and 2008, more than 18,000 new hotel rooms were built.[32] At the zenith of the property boom in 2006, the construction sector in the Republic of Ireland accounted for €37 billion ($47 billion), or nearly 25 percent of GNP.[33]

Irish scholars have compiled no shortage of statistics that convey the magnitude of the property boom: Between 1995 and 2006, Irish house prices rose by more than 300 percent nationally, and by more than 400 percent in Dublin. Raw land prices increased in the same period by approximately 1,200 percent, jumping from about €5,000 ($6,368) to almost €60,000 ($76,416) per hectare (2.5 acres).[34] The value of commercial real estate grew by between 250 percent.[35] This data conveys the enormity of a real estate expansion that involved large numbers participating in the market. Many Irish people described owning second, third, fourth, and fifth investment homes in addition to their primary residence. Banks were said to cold-call customers and encourage them to acquire more property and more mortgages.

One way to account for the degree to which speculation fueled home purchases in Ireland is to look at the distribution of two dominant

Battery Court, an Irish ghost estate in the town of Longford, County Longford, shown in 2013.

mortgage types: primary dwelling home (PDH) mortgages and buy-to-let (BTL) mortgages, which are used by investors. In most cases, BTL properties are purchased as a source of both ongoing rental income and capital gains to be realized from price escalation—speculation in the proper sense.[36] Of Ireland's outstanding mortgages in 2011, approximately 16 percent were BTL.[37] This is a significant portion of the total stock produced during the boom and conveys the degree to which built space functioned as a site of speculation. But the BTL statistics capture only one aspect of built space's asset function, as new primary home purchasers, many aiming to build capital to leverage future purchases, entered the market. The prominent Irish economist John FitzGerald noted a disposition on the part of home purchasers that emerged during the 1990s and continued into the 2000s. According to FitzGerald, Irish families had formerly been more likely to buy a property that they intended to live in for their entire lives, whereas during the boom a new norm came into being in which individuals and families approached home purchases as investments to jump between as equity was created through rising property value.[38]

Faster than investment had swelled during the boom, in 2008 the contagious perception that the supply of Irish real estate was radically decoupled from real demand resulted in an almost overnight freezing

of the market. Mortgage markets collapsed, property purchases halted, and prices plummeted. By 2012, prices for existing homes had dropped by 34 percent, existing apartments by 49 percent, and new apartments by 54 percent.[39] Mortgage holders frequently found themselves in negative equity and developers buried in debt. Builders packed up, leaving a landscape of partially completed projects. It became painfully clear that Ireland had built far too much. In 2011, 294,000 units of housing sat empty, with many situated in what the Irish came to call ghost estates, housing projects that sometimes have finished construction but are mostly or entirely empty, and other times only partly built, with one or two occupied dwellings sitting amid a bleak context of homes frozen in various states of construction, as if a catastrophe had forced the builders to flee.[40]

While ghost estates capture much of the popular imagination because of their intimate connection with the struggles of individuals and families, there has existed a related world of zombie hotels, phantom golf courses, and large amounts of vacant retail and office space. Sometimes a finished hotel sits empty as a target for vandals; other times, only 30 percent of its rooms are finished, which are offered at rock-bottom rates. Mixed-use developments lumber along with empty ground-floor retail, and the carcasses of half-finished shopping malls hulk on the horizon. Golf courses without patrons have been converted to agricultural fields for the production of silage or the roaming of horses. Postcrisis Ireland was strewn with these high-vacancy failures that together constitute a twenty-first-century ghost landscape.

The housing constructed during Ireland's property boom occupies the full spectrum of typologies, from detached homes to apartments in high-density mixed-use developments. Of the housing produced in 2003, approximately 32 percent were detached homes, 34 percent semi-detached duplexes, 12 percent row houses (what in Ireland is called terraced housing), and 22 percent apartments.[41] The prototypical housing development constructed during the boom is a distinct development parcel, called an estate, usually with one access point feeding an arrayed combination of single-family detached homes, semidetached duplexes, and three- to six-unit row houses. Almost every Irish city, town, and hamlet witnessed amoeba-like growth at its periphery in addition to estates popping up seemingly out of nowhere within agricultural fields; in the period between 1997 and 2007, around 40 percent of total house completions took place in rural settlements of fewer than 1,500 people.[42]

Asset urbanism needs to be understood in relation to both global and local parameters. Ireland's economy started to grow around 1995, as multinational corporations were drawn to low taxes and wages alongside a highly educated, English-speaking workforce. Ireland's EU membership offered tariff-free access to the single European market. As the Celtic Tiger took off, the country reversed emigration to strong immigration for the first time in decades. In parallel to this globally configured local milieu of real demand, the liberalization of international credit markets

Complete but unoccupied homes shown in 2013 at a ghost estate in Drumshanbo, County Leitrim, Ireland.

helped lubricate a flow of lending capital from German and French banks to Irish banks in the early 2000s, which fueled the height of the building and buying boom. Irish banks responded to the heated demand for mortgages with increasingly lax lending requirements in the form of longer mortgage terms and diminishing down-payment requirements, ultimately landing on the infamous zero-down mortgage with a forty-year term. The ease of acquiring mortgages combined with government policies designed to encourage construction and home ownership to create a perfect storm of speculative construction and property purchasing.

Ghost conditions have shifted in the years following the crisis. The first four years after 2008 were devoted to sorting out the financial and physical debris while the real estate and construction industries largely stalled. In 2010, the Irish government started surveying "unfinished housing developments" and began a multiyear effort, through various programs and initiatives, to "resolve" these developments. Its first survey counted approximately 3,000 ghost estates with 180,000 units. Over the subsequent seven years, that number dropped to 420 estates with a total of just under 25,000 units.[43] Empty units were eventually occupied, and construction resumed on partially finished projects. A small number were simply demolished without ever being inhabited (given the sensitivity of the topic, it is difficult to determine from the government just how many). Irish media reported in 2013 that a plan authored by the Minister of Housing and Planning identified roughly forty estates as candidates for destruction.[44] While there has undoubtedly been a major reduction in ghost estates in Ireland since 2010, the official statistics seem improbably low, and they likely undercount physical conditions on the ground. This is because the government removes developments from its list of unfinished projects once they have been

designated as resolved. Because of the specific definitions of resolution, it is possible that the government is undercounting. For example, resolution does not require the estate to have an electrical connection but rather only a supply of potable water.[45]

While the situation of ghost urbanism in Ireland has dramatically improved, it has taken a long time. For years after 2008, the Irish landscape was pockmarked with various combinations of fenced-off and cleared land waiting for development, roads and infrastructure that went nowhere and fed nothing, arrays of concrete foundation slabs

An uncanny territory of roads enclosed in "temporary" walls as seen in 2013 at the Castlepark ghost estate in Mallow, County Cork, Ireland.

The Waterways ghost estate in the process of being demolished
in 2013 in Keshcarrigan, County Leitrim, Ireland.

sitting empty, buildings with no roofs, shells of homes without their
siding or glazing, and row upon row of perfectly completed dwellings
awaiting a population that did not yet exist, with the stains of weather
and biotic growth conveying their slow descent into ruins. Even now,
almost fifteen years after the global financial crisis started, it is easy to
find its ruins.

Ghost Urbanism in Spain

While Ireland and Spain built about the same amount of housing per
capita during the boom, Spain witnessed a much larger amount of absolute building activity. Roughly four million homes were built in Spain
between 2001 and 2008, at an average rate of 565,000 per year, which
is more than double that of the previous decade.[46] In 2006, there were
865,000 housing starts, more than in Germany, France, and the UK combined.[47] A huge amount of infrastructure was also constructed. The highway system was extended by roughly 8,000 miles (13,000 kilometers)
between 1993 and 2011.[48] Spain now has the third-largest high-capacity
highway system in the world, surpassed only by the United States and
China.[49] Five new international airports were built, and thirteen existing

airports received new terminals. At the market's height, construction accounted for approximately 11 percent of Spain's GDP.[50] All of this activity occurred within a context of dramatically rising property values: between 1996 and 2007, raw land values increased by 260 percent.[51] During the same period, the national average price for housing grew by 200 percent.[52]

In tandem with its intensified construction and price escalation, Spanish real estate became increasingly financialized. Between 1996 and 2007, the average length of a home mortgage grew from eighteen to twenty-eight years.[53] As the Spanish economist José García-Montalvo reported in 2006, "Today we are talking about forty-year loans....The majority of the mortgages are for 100 percent of the purchase price plus 10 percent for additional costs."[54] Within this milieu of easy credit, mortgage debt mushroomed, and by the height of the boom the value of Spanish mortgages reached 100 percent of GDP.[55] And Spanish financial institutions, like those in the United States, securitized mortgage debts and thereby directly connected indebted Spanish households to global financial markets. It is reported that between 2000 and 2006, the gross value of securitized assets in Spain rose from €8 billion ($10 billion) to €100 billion ($127 billion).[56]

An indicator of speculative investment and the heightened role of the investment asset function is the prevalence of secondary-home ownership. By the height of the boom, a remarkable number of Spanish households owned two or more homes. The Madrid-based economists Isidro López and Emmanuel Rodríguez reported that 35 percent of Spanish households owned multiple residential properties by 2007.[57] A stream of Britons, Germans, and other Northern Europeans purchased units in Spanish developments that in many instances explicitly catered to them, greatly exacerbating the magnitude of construction in Spain. In the municipalities of Santa Pola, Guardamar del Segura, and Torrevieja on the southern coast of Alicante, almost 80 percent of all homes were secondary vacation properties and 47 percent of the population were "registered foreign holiday home residents" in 2010.[58] While numerous factors influenced this influx, speculative investment was undoubtedly significant. As the Spanish sociologist Aitana Alguacil Denche stated, "The fundamentally speculative character of foreign investment can be appreciated from its high concentration in certain geographic areas....Foreign housing investment tended to be concentrated in island communities

The two-thirds-incomplete Residencial Francisco Hernando, shown in 2014,
in Seseña, Toledo, Castile-La Mancha, Spain.

(Canary and Balearic Islands) and the eastern Spanish coast (Andalusia, Murcia, and the Valencian Community), which are the areas that registered the highest increases in prices during the upswing of the cycle."[59]

Spanish avatars of neoliberalism facilitated Spain's investment and development frenzy. In 1998, the Spanish government passed the Land Act, which effectively reclassified the entire country as a single territory open to development. In the words of the government, "The present Law aims to facilitate the increase in land supply, meaning that all land which has not yet been incorporated into the urban process, in which there are no reasons for preservation, can be considered capable of being urbanized."[60] This law, which coincided closely with the beginning of the property boom, is emblematic of the type of market liberalization that characterizes neoliberalism and facilitates finance capitalism.

In 1994, the Valencian Community signed into effect the Regulatory Law of Urban Activity (LRAU), which created a new actor in land development—the *agente urbanizador*, or developer agent. In subsequent years, other regional governments passed laws modeled on Valencia's, with the effect that the agente urbanizador became a key propagator of development across Spain. The role and powers of the agente are considerable. Granted powers of expropriation, the agente is an individual or private corporation able to develop land regardless of the desires of private landowners. In other words, the agentes can develop land for market purposes against the will of landowners, with the only requirement being that they must compensate them for the expropriated land. In practice, this compensation is derived from the value created through "urbanization" (the process in which an area is subdivided into lots, road and utility infrastructure installed, and buildings constructed). It is important to note that almost any private business was able to act as an agente urbanizador.[61] As the Spanish architect Isabel Concheiro described, "The creation of this figure was to end the retention of land by owners who refused to participate in urban development [and] to speed up the urbanization process."[62] It should also be noted that the original Valencian law emerged from the left side of the political spectrum, as its central hypothesis was that by increasing the supply of urbanized land, the price of housing would fall.[63] However, prices did not fall. Fernando Gaja i Díaz, a chief critic of the law and a professor at the University of Valencia, states, "The LRAU has contributed to the increased production of urbanized land without reducing the land prices that have accompanied the spiraling, inflationary real estate market, meanwhile [it has aided] the concentration of property in the hands of large urbanizing businesses."[64]

One of the profound by-products of Spain's (as Ireland's) investment-driven building frenzy was a dramatic overproduction of built material. By 2010, Spain had more than one million unsold homes on the market, and by 2012 that number was reported to be closer to two million.[65] Large numbers of megadevelopments on Madrid's periphery, each with thousands of units, were largely vacant. Spain's so-called ghost airports sat empty for years; while the Murcia Airport was completed in 2012, it did not open for flights until 2019.[66] Similarly, the Ciudad Real

Leisure-oriented investment developments shown in 2013 along the Mediterranean coast north of Valencia, Spain.

Arcosur, the incomplete urban ensanche in Zaragoza, Aragon, Spain, shown in 2014.

Central Airport, made infamous by the international media and said to have been constructed for more than €1 billion ($1.2 billion), sat empty and decaying between 2012 and 2019.

A vast amount of land in Spain underwent urbanization during the boom, only to sit empty and in various states of decay. It is difficult to accurately account for the total area of empty urbanized land, but some estimates are as high as 290,000 hectares (716,606 acres), a surface area that is more than three-and-a-half times larger than that of New York City's five boroughs.[67] It is reported that this stock of empty urbanized land has a built potential capable of meeting demand until almost 2040.[68] And then there are the partly constructed buildings that litter the landscape. Taken collectively, these states of incompletion and vacancy constitute the ghost urbanism of postcrisis Spain.

The built environment produced during the property boom, along with the aftermath states of incompletion and vacancy, present morphological patterns that constitute archetypes of Spanish ghost urbanism. Three dominant archetypes are postmetropolitan islands, foreign investment enclaves, and urban *ensanches*.

Postmetropolitan islands are megadevelopments that are discrete and geographically separate from existing urban fabric — isolated satellites

Empty urbanized land in Majadahonda, Madrid, Spain, shown in 2014.

orbiting an urban center at a distance.[69] Their tendency to amass an over-whelming amount of housing without including meaningful amounts of complementary programs renders them postmetropolitan. Such projects can be found around many of Spain's large and midsize cities, forming what can be described as investment archipelagoes. The most infamous example is Residencial Francisco Hernando (named after its developer) in Seseña, approximately nineteen miles (thirty kilometers) from Madrid. The design organizes 13,500 units in a series of mid-rise housing blocks that emphasize repetition and efficiency in the extreme. All aspects of the development maximize the quantity of units at minimum construction expense, resulting in an almost inhuman space of speculation. One inves-tor's experience with this project during the boom, as recounted in the Spanish newspaper *El Mundo* in 2007, was typical:

> My family bought various units in Residencial Francisco Hernando at
> a very good price with the intention of getting a high return. And that is
> how it has been. We have seen the rise of the end of the real estate cycle,
> and we have decided to get rid of them. I have gotten rid of three units
> that cost me 120,000 euros for 180,000 [161,000 dollars for 242,000].[70]

Just over 5,000 units were completed before the market collapsed. It was reported in Spain's national press that 2,000 were unsold and vacant in 2009.[71] For years after the collapse, the development was referred to as a wasteland, with thousands of residents occupying a partially complete and entirely isolated territory. The completed buildings sit within a much larger context of barren building sites enclosed with fencing—a persistent crisis space some twelve years after Spain's housing bubble burst.

The construction of new housing that attracts a disproportionate amount of foreign purchasers occurs primarily along Spain's Mediterranean coast in what can be called foreign investment enclaves. Building for this market segment was a significant factor in creating what is in effect a linear city that stretches along the Mediterranean. These developments are often organized around golf courses or beaches in an alluring combination of a sunny climate and speculation. In a manner that echoes the isolation of the postmetropolitan islands, "these new developments are increasingly more segregated from the existing urban fabric and homogeneous in terms of nationalities from rich European Union countries," says the Spanish urban planner and activist Ramón Fernández Durán.[72]

At the time that foreign investment enclaves proliferated, so did urban ensanches. Almost all major and midsize cities in Spain experienced hyperexpansion at their peripheries, in twenty-first-century versions of Spain's traditional ensanches (city extensions). In most instances, these massive territories of rapid development sat in various degrees of partial completion and emptiness for at least five years. Isabel Concheiro noted that Madrid's "southeastern landscape is currently a 'stand-by' landscape, defined by land works and the construction of new roads and infrastructure," awaiting the development halted by the market's collapse.[73]

Smaller cities experienced similarly massive development programs. Zaragoza, a city in northeast Spain with a population of 700,000, has a single urban ensanche called Arcosur that was planned to house 70,000 new residents. In 2014, only 2,100 units had been completed, resulting in a surreal social condition in which a small number of residents inhabit an immense but largely empty tabula rasa of urbanization. In 2020, this condition remains completely unchanged, again providing an example of the persistence of landscapes of crisis in Spain.

More than ten years since the financial crisis, Spain's ghost urbanism continues. Considerable amounts of empty urbanized land still exist. Partially constructed projects can be found throughout the country. The longevity of this ruinous landscape signifies the new intensity of building booms and busts in the context of neoliberal investment practices that are now global.

Ghost Urbanism in China

Ghost urbanism is not limited to Ireland and Spain. The phenomenon can be found in countries throughout the world, from Angola to Brazil, but the scale of ghost urbanism in China appears exceptional. In 2018, the Dutch architect Reinier de Graaf, a partner at the Office for Metropolitan Architecture, and students at Harvard studied worldwide ghost urbanism. They located and examined fifty developments in twenty-two countries, each one square kilometer or more in area, with reported vacancy rates above 50 percent that persisted for a minimum period of one year.[74] China's growth over recent decades has been accompanied by large increases in real estate prices. In thirty-five major cities, average real housing prices are reported to have increased roughly 380 percent over ten years.[75] China's property boom is likely the largest in history, and the country's unprecedented urbanization includes enormous examples of ghost urbanism.

The most infamous instances are China's so-called ghost cities: underoccupied or incomplete new towns at the periphery of second- and third-tier cities. Christopher Marcinkoski of the University of Pennsylvania writes that examples "abound," including Chenggong, near Kunming; expansions of Bayan Nur and Erenhot, Inner Mongolia; the periphery of Changsha, Hunan; and an unnamed satellite city northeast of Xinyang, Henan.[76] The Kangbashi District on the edge of the city of Ordos in Inner Mongolia is frequently covered by the Western media—and inspired the term *ghost city* in 2010.[77] Inaugurated in 2006, the district was planned to house one million people upon eventual build-out, but by 2014, the official population was 30,000 residents, and 70 percent of finished buildings were empty.[78] Reliable statistics are difficult to acquire, but photographs from 2020 provide clear evidence of a largely empty urban environment. The local government redrew the boundary of Kangbashi to exclude an area with a large number of unfinished residential buildings, and in 2016 it reported the population had

Kangbashi District, Ordos, Inner Mongolia, China, shown in 2012.

reached 153,000—but with an original population aimed at one million, the report still suggests significant underoccupancy.[79]

In 1980, less than 20 percent of China's population lived in urban areas; by 2020, more than 60 percent does.[80] The staggering amount of new building all but necessitated significant gaps between supply and demand and led to high vacancy at certain points in time. However, it appears that the practices of finance capitalism have exacerbated this inevitability and amplified its proportions. China's newly rich and its burgeoning middle class seek to invest newfound wealth but have relatively limited options. Regulations make it comparatively challenging for Chinese citizens to own foreign stocks and bonds, and Chinese banks offer low returns on investment compared to their Western counterparts. At the same time, China has no property tax. The result is that real estate is a very popular investment. As Marcinkoski writes, "Investment in housing has been understood to be…the most stable available investment.…It is not uncommon for middle-class Chinese families to own two or three apartments as investment vehicles."[81] According to the Survey and Research Center for China Household Finance, in the first quarter of 2018, 41 percent of all home purchases were of a second home and a shocking 31 percent of a third home.[82] In 2011, the state-owned *China Daily* reported that the Beijing Municipal Government banned Beijing families who own two or more apartments and non–Beijing residents who own one or more from purchasing more property in the capital city.[83] In subsequent years, other jurisdictions have enacted similar regulations. Xinhua News Agency, China's official press agency, reported in 2017 that Hangzhou prohibited single adults from purchasing second homes.[84] It is unclear whether these types of policies will have much effect. The 2017 China Housing Finance Survey concluded that roughly 21 percent of housing units sat empty in urban areas of China.[85] Underscoring the challenge, Chinese President Xi Jinping stated in his address to the Nineteenth Party Congress in 2017, "Houses are built to be inhabited, not for speculation."[86]

The Simultaneity of Growth and Decay

Zombie neighborhoods and ghost cities present a newly dynamic terrain for architecture. It is a topography shaped by ever-shifting investment flows, where states of radical growth are simultaneously collapsing into states of decay and waste.

Much twenty-first-century architectural discourse has orbited around one or the other of two dominant paradigms of urbanism: the rapidly growing city-region, represented by locations such as China's Pearl River Delta, or, conversely, the shrinking city, represented by the likes of Detroit. These two paradigms are ontologically premised upon temporal and spatial isolation—growth happens at a certain time and place, and decay happens in a separate time and place. While this may have been the case over much of history, the particularities of finance capitalism are propelling novel manifestations of this dyad in which characteristics of growth and shrinkage are increasingly found together, in spatial and temporal proximity.

Why are growth and decay collapsing upon each other? One major reason is the giant pool of money and its flow through architecture.

A complete but largely unoccupied Kilamba New City, Luanda, Angola, shown in 2012.

The sheer volume of capital now in architecture results in more extreme peaks and valleys in the expansion/contraction cycle. Increased capital tends to produce a greater volume of architecture during expansion and therefore a larger oversupply when the market shifts. This enlarged volume is more at risk of disrepair and decay, and it is harder for it to be absorbed once the market eventually rises. Therefore, empty and sometimes ruined buildings persist so far into a downturn and recovery that some remain throughout the next expansion period, constituting an overlay of growth and decay.

Growth/decay simultaneity also appears to originate from the rising frequency of the expansion and contraction period in real estate markets. Nobel laureate Robert Shiller of the widely referenced Case-Shiller Home Price Indices, which track home prices in the United States, remarked in an interview, "There's been a rise in speculative culture all over the world. I think the volatility of real estate may be going up in a long secular path. I don't believe home prices will go up [over the long run], but they might be more vulnerable to bubbles."[87] If the new contours of real estate cycles are defined by a larger amplitude between boom and bust, and the frequency of these intervals increases, the resulting social and spatial challenges of rapid production and price escalation followed by oversupply and vacancy might become defining attributes of financialized architecture and urbanism.

Traditional concepts of real estate posit the primacy of "market fundamentals" as the determining factors of growth and decline. These fundamentals foreground the basic relationship between supply and demand as being driven by employment, population, and wages. Common wisdom is that an increase in these three will drive rising demand for housing and vice versa. The magnitude and fluidity of capital in real estate increasingly decouple expansion and contraction from these fundamentals. It is no longer a given that rising prices are connected to a local job market, nor is it always the case that increased demand is related to a growing population.

The 2007–8 bust offers many remarkable examples of the instant ruins that the dynamics of finance capitalism engender. In Ireland, scenes juxtaposing inhabited buildings and the various manifestations of vacant, partly constructed structures and territories were stark: families living alone among a sea of half-built, empty homes; patrons of rooftop bars overlooking abandoned construction sites; and drivers moving through uncanny landscapes defined by construction hoarding or security fencing that had become permanent. It became common for teenagers to believe that growing up among decaying relics of half-built housing was normal. These unfinished adjacencies are a defining characteristic of asset urbanism. The degree to which plant life and rural activities overtook many abandoned building sites is striking. Many projects were halted after only utilities were installed, resulting in field landscapes with entire below-grade electricity, water, and sewage infrastructure in place, with conduits, pipes, and manholes emerging from vegetation the only clues of intended development. These electric fields have been informally appropriated by recreational and agricultural users, complete with roaming horses and children playing ball. While many unfinished structures sit totally empty, there is a parallel set of instances: one or two tenants occupying a structural carcass, a fully operational retail bank tucked under the scaffolding of an incomplete concrete tower, a working supermarket with raw apartment shells above. This carcass occupancy conveys the situational agility and resilience of those inhabiting the crisis spaces of finance capitalism.

Life, Death, and Finance Capitalism

In the years following the 2007–8 crash, the figure of the zombie occupied a prominent position in fiction, television, and film. Some sought to make connections between this pop-culture phenomenon and more general attributes of political economy. Chris Harman's *Zombie Capitalism: Global Crisis and the Relevance of Marx* appeared in 2009, and David McNally's *Monsters of the Market: Zombies, Vampires and Global Capitalism* was published in 2011. Romance literature professor David Castillo and literary critic William Egginton wrote in the *New York Times* in 2014, "Today's zombie hordes may best express our anxieties about capitalism's apparently inevitable byproducts: the legions of mindless, soulless consumers who sustain its endless production, and the masses of 'human debris' who are left to survive the ravages of its poisoned waste."[88] Juan Carlos Fresnadillo's film *28 Weeks Later* was released at the height of the global property boom in 2007 and envisioned a radical vacancy that would soon become actualized in some parts of the world. Near the film's opening, the camera pans over a London without pedestrians and cars; the city has been depopulated by a zombie-producing virus. Also released in 2007, Francis Lawrence's *I Am Legend* shows

TOP The strange juxtaposition, as seen in 2013, of a long-lasting unfinished adjacency in Ireland.

ABOVE Below-grade infrastructure rearing its head in 2013 at a large, abandoned development site in Mallow, County Cork, Ireland.

RIGHT Shown in 2013, a Bank of Ireland branch operating at the base of a stalled housing project in Dublin.

Will Smith's character living alone in an emptied Manhattan, except for the zombies that come out once the sun has set. In Marc Forster's *World War Z* (2013), the highest-grossing zombie film of all time, a global battle between the living and the undead is won once humans discover that they can effectively camouflage themselves by temporarily infecting themselves with lethal viruses, rendering them unattractive for the zombie reanimation. In other words, individual humans must begin the active process of dying in a manner that zombies perceive in order for them to be protected against becoming zombies.

This solution resonates with the paradox of zombie urbanism as well as ghost urbanism and the associated simultaneity of growth and decay. These nonliving states of architecture and the city rely on the belief that full life is the current condition or the future likelihood. While zombie urbanism is a necessary outcome of the current inclinations of finance capitalism, it is predicated on the viability of its host's livelihood. London is a magnet of international investment capital in real estate precisely because it is considered a safe and stable investment over the long run. Investors believe it will live forever. Vulture capitalists scoop up Irish ghost estates because they believe they will eventually return to life—ushering in a simultaneity of growth and decay. A further irony is how some of these undead city-states rank on global livability indexes: Melbourne and Vancouver are stars. Within the logics of finance capitalism, to be highly livable is also to be the perfect host for exactly the types of spatio-financial conditions that enervate urban life as it has been known.

CHAPTER THREE

THE FORMS OF FINANCE

The financialization of architecture occurs through the formal conditions of buildings, including their siting, massing, proportions, and dimensions. This formalism serves the absorption of surplus capital while simultaneously increasing opportunities for speculative investment and the liquidity that such investment necessitates. It is possible to trace the financialization of architecture across many instances where intensified conditions allow widespread characteristics to be seen in sharp relief. This chapter identifies five specific spatio-financial types: iceberg homes, exurban investment mats, super-podiums, ultra-thin pencil towers, and financial icons. These types collectively function in a financial ecology. Some serve primarily as providers of investment liquidity, while others more solely as absorptive sites of wealth storage, but collectively they work in concert for different movements and moments of capital in the built environment.

Iceberg Homes

London and New York attract a disproportionate amount of global investment in real estate.[1] In 2011, for instance, overseas investors spent £5.2 billion ($8.5 billion) on London housing—an amount greater than

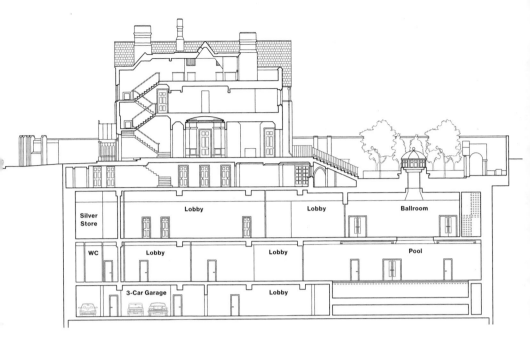

A proposed basement extension from 2012 in the Royal Borough of Kensington and Chelsea, London.

the UK government's investment in the Affordable Housing Programme for the entire country.[2] The giant pool of money's influx into London resulted in a unique spatio-financial type that locals call iceberg homes.

Many of the most desirable areas for the wealthy in London—such as Chelsea, Mayfair, Knightsbridge, and Westminster—consist primarily of Victorian mansions and townhomes that are modestly sized in relation to the contemporary standards of the very rich. These neighborhoods are governed by zoning regulations that strictly limit above-grade additions. Starting around 2005, the superwealthy began to exploit the absence of laws concerning building activity below grade, inventing a new way to store wealth. Ademir Volic, one of the architects involved in designing some of the more extravagant iceberg homes, was quoted as saying, "We analyzed the planning laws and realized they covered everything about the surface of the ground, but nothing beneath it. There was nothing whatsoever that could stop us from drilling all the way down to the south pole."[3] In these neighborhoods, it became common for existing mansions to be augmented by two or three stories of underground space that extends beyond the footprint of the original aboveground structure.

Subterranean pool in a basement extension completed in 2017 on Lonsdale Road in the Royal Borough of Kensington and Chelsea, London.

Pool in a basement extension completed in 2018 on Winnington Road in Hampstead Garden Suburb, Greater London.

In Kensington and Chelsea alone, there were 393 basement extension planning applications in 2014 compared to 180 in 2010.[4] A study conducted at Newcastle University examined the approved development plans for basement extensions to existing homes across seven London boroughs between 2008 and 2017. During this period, 785 "large basements" (defined as two stories in depth or one story extending far beyond the footprint of the existing house) and 110 "mega basements" (at least three stories in depth or two stories extending far beyond the existing footprint) were approved.[5]

Roger Burrows, who spent time mapping London's iceberg mansions, called the phenomenon "luxified troglodytism."[6] As the icebergs reach varying depths and extents under the earth, lighting becomes critical. Some homes have an array of skylights extending across the garden lawn to bring light to rooms below. But as natural light cannot make it everywhere, artificial lighting takes on greater significance; photographs of underground spaces reveal a wealth of cove and accent illumination. Programmatically, these subterranean zones are very particular. The pre-existing above-grade structure remains the primary location for every-day activities of cooking, eating, sleeping, and living. The below-grade spaces typically function as an extended territory of leisure, entertainment, and luxury-goods storage and display. The large and megabasements analyzed by Newcastle University include roughly 1,000 gyms, 375 pools, 450 cinemas, and 380 wine cellars. The pools and movie spaces function as devices of escape, enveloping the senses to transcend the immediate. The aesthetic range within these leisure territories appears broad, from contemporary minimalism to colorful traditional Turkish tiling. The lighting, themed interior decorating, pools, and cinemas create parallel worlds entirely separate from above-ground conditions.

Near the beginning of the BBC documentary *Millionaire Basement Wars*, the owner of an iceberg mansion with a waterfall-fed subterranean pool adorned with Buddhist statues remarks that visitors often say the space is "better than the Four Seasons."[7] Jon Hunt, the billionaire founder of British real estate agency Foxtons, caused a minor media sensation when he proposed an extension roughly 80 feet (24 meters) beneath grade and with a total floor area of over 50,000 square feet (4,600 square meters).[8] His proposal included a car "museum" and a Ferris wheel alongside the more standard tennis court and swimming pool.[9] The hotel reference and Ferris wheel are not coincidental; they make explicit the operations of these underworlds of capital absorption, which function as private hotels and personal Disneylands.

Iceberg homes have proven contentious in London. Westminster City Councillor Robert Davis said in 2016, when the council enacted new rules aimed at curbing icebergs, "We are sticking up for local residents, many of whom have found the explosion of basement development in recent years hellish."[10] In some cases, exuberant excavations led to the gradual sinking of land and nearby buildings. In a sensational case

Recreational room in a basement extension completed in 2019 in Hampstead Garden Suburb, Greater London.

Screening room in a basement extension completed in 2015 on Egerton Crescent in the Royal Borough of Kensington and Chelsea, London.

reported in the London press, an excavation for a managing director at Goldman Sachs purportedly resulted in a neighbor being trapped in her house." In 2015, the city of Westminster and the borough of Kensington and Chelsea adopted a policy that limited the footprint of basement extensions to 50 percent of the exterior area of the lot and banned them under listed heritage buildings.[12] Westminster also introduced a basement tax and established a "subterranean squad" of council officers dedicated to policing basement extensions.[13] The restrictions appear to have reduced the amount of subterranean construction. The real estate market analysis firm Glenigan compiled data that showed applications for basements declined by 27 percent in Kensington and Chelsea and 22 percent in Westminster in 2016.[14]

The emergence of iceberg homes demonstrates the agility of capital in finding new territories for spatial absorption. These wealth caves, removed from weather and other humans, manifest a kind of fantasy reality. There the body can be perfected through fitness or altered through the sensual pleasures of bathing and intoxication, and anything can be heard or watched through audiovisual systems. These private theme parks of wealth are sensual pleasure machines, but by hiding underground, like inverted mini-towers, any sense of metropolitanism has been replaced by the lone isolation of capital absorption.

Exurban Investment Mats

The exurban investment mat is a financial typology that houses middle- or lower-income inhabitants at the periphery of existing urban fabric. Its primary mandate is to maximize the number of discrete spatial investment assets in the form of the home. It is akin to a mass stock offering. To provide a large number of inexpensive assets, the exurban mat minimizes expenses for both developer and owner/investor by reducing three things: land cost, construction cost, and parcel of ownership. These strategies allow housing units to enter the market with relative speed and to be sold at relatively low prices. It is in the exurban periphery where cheap land is found, which is why exurban mats fuel urban sprawl. Construction costs are reduced through the economies of scale achieved through building large numbers of standardized and repeated units. The parcel of ownership is minimized by increasing the density of a given development so that each unit of ownership bears less land cost and by minimizing the actual size of the house.

An exurban investment mat, as seen in 2014, flowing over the landscape like lava on the Mediterranean Coast in Alicante, Spain.

The architectural forms of exurban commodity housing vary from culture to culture. In Spain, the peripheries of larger cities have witnessed an immense increase in mid-rise courtyard housing. These projects are sometimes lumped into new satellites of investment in postmetropolitan islands such as Residencial Francisco Hernando in exurban Madrid. While some vertical exurban commodity housing exists, housing that appears detached defines the type. Exurban investment mats are therefore best understood as simple, discrete housing units that are repeated and arrayed across a large horizontal expanse. At its apotheosis, the space between homes is compressed to such a degree that they begin to function as one continuous mat.

The speculative logic of exurban investment mats becomes especially apparent during real estate booms. Leading up to 2008, Spain, Ireland, and parts of the United States, for example, saw large extensions of these mats. In Ireland, the replication of an essentially standardized housing estate model dramatically expanded small and medium towns across the country. Before-and-after satellite photography reveals many centuries-old hamlets that more than doubled their footprint in the relatively short period of the boom. This is so dramatic that it is perhaps its own expansionary model: town doubling. In the United States, locations such as exurban Phoenix, Las Vegas, Southern California's Inland Empire, and large areas of Florida all demonstrate big increases in mat-like single-family housing. This is the spatial reality of the policies of finance capitalism, which George W. Bush promoted in 2004 when he declared, "We're creating…an ownership society in this country, where more Americans than ever will be able to open up their door where they live and say, welcome to my house, welcome to my piece of property."[15]

One of the most intense and perfected forms of the exurban investment mat is found in Mexico. In 1991, in a legal shift similar to the

Discrete subdivisions of exurban investment mats popping up across the desert near Las Vegas in 2015.

An exurban investment mat, photographed in 2010, at the edge of Ensenada, Baja California, Mexico.

Backyards within an exurban investment mat in Durango, Durango, Mexico, photographed in 2010.

enactment of Spain's 1998 Land Law, Mexico allowed *ejidos*, a traditional form of communal land that was largely agricultural and on the periphery of cities, to be privatized.[16] Approximately ten years later, under President Vicente Fox, Mexico embarked on a public-private venture to provide affordable housing for millions of the country's poor. By 2012, more than fifteen million housing units had been constructed and $100 billion spent in the largest residential construction boom in Latin American history.[17] Thousands of housing developments were built across the country, often on far-flung former agricultural or compromised land. Approximately one-sixth of Mexico's population moved to one of these new developments.

These housing mats were a primary means of financialization in Mexico. The government lender INFONAVIT provided millions of mortgages to people with little income or savings. In the 1970s, INFONAVIT built around 25,000 social housing units per year; by 2012, it was giving out more than 500,000 mortgages per year.[18] The World Bank and the Inter-American Development Bank invested heavily in the government's effort—and encouraged the introduction of mortgage-backed securities.[19] A significant portion of Mexico's population became first-time homeowners, pulled into a financial orbit

An aerial image taken in 2006 of the relentless repetition of the San Buenaventura
housing complex in Ixtapaluca, near Mexico City.

with mortgages that were often tied to an inflation index and payments directly deducted from paychecks. The purchases of this privately built social housing were financed with mortgages that were securitized. By 2006, Mexican mortgage-backed securities reached a value of $6 billion, making Mexico the largest market of its type in Latin America.[20] Private developers built the housing, fueled by global investors hoping to generate large capital profits. In 2002, the Chicago-based fund Equity International invested $32 million into a small construction company in Sinaloa called Homex. Ten years later, the company went public on the New York Stock Exchange with a valuation of $100 million and soared to $3 billion as global investors, including Wall Street investment banks and US pension funds, poured capital into the company.[21]

In San Buenaventura in Ixtapaluca, on the edge of Mexico City, exurban investment mats comprise 20,000 identical housing units.[22] These units are within two-story duplex structures with party wall conditions that form 300-foot (90-meter) row-housing blocks. The blocks are repeated over a large expanse with no other programs or amenities such as parks, schools, or retail spaces. Each unit has a small front yard, with an entry door visible to the street. The individual duplexes project forward in plan to give the visual impression that each is freestanding. While all the units, duplexes, and blocks are constructed identically, the buildings sometimes have varied color schemes to give the minimum semblance of variation.

An inhumane scale of repetition maximizes mortgageable units across a horizontal expanse of inexpensive land in Ixtapaluca. The financial logic of the mat is made possible and also concealed by appealing to the desire for a single-family home. While expansive and unrelenting, these tracts have been conceived with formal characteristics that generate the semiotic impression of the single-family home with yard. There is a visual lineage stretching back to the post–World War II Levittown housing developments in the United States, but this similarity is barely maintained, as the open space between discrete structures in that model has been compressed to only a visual effect in San Buenaventura. In describing this and similar developments across Mexico, the Mexican architect Tatiana Bilbao writes, "Living here becomes a nightmare. You can paint them in bright, lively colors, but the situation beneath is just as bleak and horrible."[23]

Superpodiums

For as long as there have been towers, there have been variants that sit atop podiums. But podium towers have taken on a newfound prominence in the era of finance capitalism. An important origin of the finance-capitalist superpodium can be traced to Vancouver in 1990, when Cambridge Gardens, a condominium with two towers sitting atop a podium of New York–style row houses, was completed. Architect James Cheng has said of his project, "In those days in Vancouver, you either had a tower or houses, and nobody ever combined the two….[Cambridge Gardens] sold out in two hours, which was unheard of in Vancouver at the time."[24] The podium and tower formula went on to become the basic building block of new Vancouver. It can now be found in many cities around the world, especially those with a combination of rapid new growth and heightened international real estate investment, such as Dubai, Miami, and Toronto. What is sometimes claimed to be the largest master-planned urban community in the world, Dubai Marina, deploys residential podium towers as its basic urban type.

Podium towers are defined by a low-rise base from which one or more towers rise. There are many iterations, but the podium often contains ground-oriented housing or ancillary programs such as retail, shared amenities, and parking. The popularity of podiums is due to a broad array of city-making ideas, chief of which is "livability." From this ideological vantage, podiums seemingly mitigate the perceived shortcomings of high-density housing. When they include townhomes, as in Vancouver, they are advocated for their ability to provide Jane Jacobs–style eyes on the street. They sometimes include neighborhood amenities such as day care centers and art galleries. In other instances, they are more overtly marketed as private enclaves separated from the messy unpredictability of the public domain. In many respects, the podium tower is a perfect neoliberal avatar, a postpolitical middle ground between the diminutive premodern scale of the town house and the large scale of mass-housing towers.

Subject to the intensity of finance capitalism, the podium sometimes contorts into the extreme, becoming a superpodium. Compared to earlier forms of podiums, the superpodium tends to exhibit some combination of being extra-expansive, formally exuberant, or programmatically baroque. Vancouver's Aquarius condominium project is an early example

ABOVE Arquitectonica, Icon Brickell
Residences + W Hotel, Miami, 2008.
Icon Brickell's pool and leisurescape-
topped superpodium.

LEFT Emre Arolat Architecture, Zorlu
Center, Istanbul, 2014. Superpodium
roof plan.

OPPOSITE Residential towers floating
above the green roof of Zorlu Center's
superpodium.

of such a superpodium. The privately accessible podium roof incorporates an artificial and elevated ecology of various plants and species, including a large, fish-stocked pond where local herons and eagles feed. It is a romantic enclave of apparent sustainability that functions as an experiential and optical amenity for the units towering above it.

This basic model has since taken on more grandiose dimensions and ambitions. Icon Brickell, located in downtown Miami and designed by Arquitectonica, has three towers rising from a podium, with an immense pool and leisurescape raised far above the ground plane (one of the three podium-top pools is 210 feet [64 meters] long). In Istanbul, Zorlu Center incorporates a large shopping mall under an undulating green roof, from which more than five hundred units of housing rise in four generic towers. In all these instances, the podiums have enlarged and absorbed ambitious formal and programmatic roles, providing isolated worlds of purported specificity upon which generic large-scale, investor-driven housing assumes a semblance of uniqueness.

Superpodiums heighten the liquidity of housing by raising residential towers off the ground and placing them on new and isolated

"ground." This elevated ground plane assumes the programmatic and formal language of contemporary desire: romantic nature in the form of ponds, ferns, rocks, and fish at Aquarius. Permanent vacation in the form of sunbathing decks, swimming pools, and poolside bars at Icon Brickell. A folded greenscape at Zorlu Center, synthesizing the appearance of both sustainability and art. A continuum of leisure, nature, shopping, and sculptural formalism offers an almost infinitely extended site for investor housing. The podium roofscapes provide interchangeable "sites" that are disconnected from the ground, which allows commodity housing units to hover separately above in a global pool of investment assets. This delamination between the specificity of the podium and the tower's standardized units allows those units to become more interchangeable and readily exchanged, thereby increasing their liquidity.

Ultra-Thin Pencil Towers

While capital absorption responded to strict bylaws in London by extending below grade, in New York speculative wealth storage reached skyward. The architecture critic Paul Goldberger wrote in 2014 that Manhattan's new crop of residential towers are

> much taller, much thinner, and much, much more expensive than
> their predecessors. And almost every one of them seems built
> to be taller, thinner, and pricier than the one that came before.
> Few people are inclined to mourn the end of the age of the luxury
> apartment building as a boxy slab. But what is replacing it, which
> you might call the latest way of housing the rich, is an entirely
> new kind of tower, pencil-thin and super-tall.[25]

The easily tradable units of these condominium spindles combine the wealth-storage function of the London iceberg home with the asset-number maximization of the exurban investment mat, but with a liquidity that exceeds what the superpodium provides; while the podium effectively abstracts the units by providing a buffer from the ground, the pencil tower accelerates this function by being ultra-thin.

Structural engineers generally define a tower as slender—what is sometimes called a pencil tower—if it has a width-to-height ratio of 1:10 or higher.[26] The World Trade Center towers, by comparison, had a 1:7 ratio. It is important to note that pencil towers are an exclusively

SHoP Architects, 111 West 57th Street, New York City,
under construction, rendering.

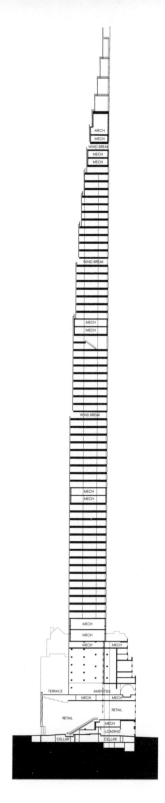

SHoP Architects,
111 West 57th Street,
section drawing.

residential housing phenomenon—their small floor plates are not suitable for most types of office work. The form is intimately related to elevated real estate prices in the era of finance capitalism. Pencil towers started to emerge in Hong Kong in the 1980s in concert with that city's dramatic housing cost ascent; Hong Kong still has the highest number of slender towers in the world. Highcliff, completed in 2003, with a ratio of 1:20, is the world's slenderest residential building. But the ultra-thin towers that have emerged in twenty-first-century Manhattan are unique in being both very slender and very tall—taller than their Hong Kong counterparts. The current iteration of pencil towers in Manhattan had precrisis roots. For example, One Madison, which began construction in 2006, has a slenderness ratio of 1:12 but a relatively modest 621-foot (189-meter) height. As of 2020, there are ten new supertall (more than 900 feet [275 meters]) and ultra-thin residential towers in Manhattan, with at least two additional ones proposed; they have been designed by architects including David Childs, Robert A. M. Stern, and Jean Nouvel.

These towers are magnets for capital. As of 2020, the most expensive home purchase in the history of the United States is a condominium unit in a building with a slenderness ratio of 1:18. In 2019, Ken Griffin, the founder of Citadel, the giant hedge fund and financial services company based in Chicago, paid $238 million for the penthouse at 220 Central Park South. Frequently, the ownership of Manhattan's pencil towers is shrouded in secrecy, concealed through numbered companies and complicated networks of intermediaries. And units often sit largely empty, revealing their true function as speculative wealth storage assets among the portfolio holdings of the global elite.

A building's slender proportion is not coincidental to this financial function, as it allows individual units of investment to become highly abstract and simplified. The ultra-thin proportion allows fewer units (often just one) per floor, essentially placing a unit alone in the sky and disentangling it from messy interactions with the public and neighbors. The very proportions help achieve a frictionless spatial commodity that can be owned from afar and exchanged relatively easily.

The epicenter of these towers is midtown Manhattan, where they command preeminent views over Central Park. The first of this new phalanx was One57, designed by Christian de Portzamparc and finished in 2014. With 92 condominium units on top of a 210-room hotel, 1:8 slenderness ratio, and a height just over 1,000 feet (305 meters), it was the tallest residential building in the Western Hemisphere upon completion. One of its two penthouses sold for more than $90 million to a hedge fund manager who, according to the *Wall Street Journal*, did not plan to live there but to hold it as an investment.[27] In 2015, Rafael Viñoly's 432 Park Avenue surpassed One57's height to become the tallest residential building in the world and the tallest building in New York City by roof height. With just 104 units, it is 1,396 feet (426 meters) tall, with a 1:15 slenderness ratio. Its top residence sold for $95 million. Towers currently in construction will surpass 432 Park by various measures. Scheduled for completion in 2020, Central Park Tower, designed by Adrian Smith + Gordon Gill Architecture, will reach a height of 1,550 feet (472 meters) with a 1:12 slenderness ratio. SHoP Architects' 111 West 57th Street's 1,428-foot (435-meter) roof will not overtake Central Park Tower's, but its 1:23 slenderness ratio will surpass Highcliff's to make it the slenderest residential tower in the world. It will be the world's second-tallest residential building and will have only fifty-eight individual condominium units. Smaller units will occupy entire floors, while larger ones will span multiple floors. By offering a vertical column of housing units that are freestanding on all four sides, 111 West 57th Street will achieve some of the spatial attributes of a single-family home, but far from the unpredictability of the public ground plane.

While Manhattan is a center of this asset-based architectural arms race, it is not the only location in which pencil towers are being built. Collins House in Melbourne has a slenderness ratio of 1:16 and a roof height of 669 feet (204 meters). The ÏCE Condos, completed in 2015 in Toronto, have a slenderness ratio of just over 1:10; Marina 101, 2018 in Dubai, a ratio of greater than 1:11; and The Point, 2010 in Panama City, a ratio of 1:9.

Financial Icons

Cultural and institutional facilities with unique and highly differentiated forms, materiality, and scale have assumed a heightened financial role in the era of finance capitalism. More than ever, this architecture seems attuned to attracting investment. This function is famously enshrined as the Bilbao Effect, by which Frank Gehry's undulating, titanium-clad Guggenheim Museum in Bilbao, Spain, and the global media attention it received generated new investment in and attracted millions of tourists to the city, thereby increasing its employment, wages, and real estate values.

In the years following its 1997 opening, many cities and neighborhoods wanted to experience their own Bilbao Effect. The architectural historian and theorist Arindam Dutta writes of spectacular architecture during the burst of financial speculation from the mid-1990s to 2008:

> This iconicism relied on two major funding doctrines: the use of sovereign or federal moneys to privilege particular "primary" cities within each nation-state as privileged attractors of global investment; and for "secondary" cities, given the directed retreat of public money for infrastructure support, to use the "cultural" heft from these icons to raise real estate values (and revenue).[28]

These financial icons, as Dutta calls them, are increasingly used to seed a given territory with investment desire, facilitating investment in housing units in neighboring areas.

Financial icons have many manifestations, from large, federally funded institutions to privately funded museums. François Mitterrand's Grands Projets in Paris used public funds to erect structures intended to attract foreign capital to France. As Dutta writes,

> The Projets were in fact emblems of the ideological defeat of the Mitterrand Socialists at the hands of large-scale capital flight. The new monuments were explicitly commissioned to foreign architects to convey an impression of being receptive to foreign investment and capital.[29]

The Projets sought to attract capital to the nation. But many financial icons operate at a more direct scale of real estate investment. The *Routledge Companion to Real Estate Development* notes of flagship projects and urban transformation:

> A real estate project with positive external effects will…lead to a rise in land values of the surrounding plots, since their use prospects for retail or residential purposes are improved and the demand is increased, while negative external effects will lead to a decline. Owners of land that happens to be in the vicinity of a project generating added social value enjoy windfall profits without investments. Hence, landowners are one of the driving forces behind "growth machine" coalitions identified in studies of local power distributions.[30]

Toyo Ito & Associates, Torrevieja Relaxation Park, Alicante, Spain, 2006. The unfinished and decaying financial icon, as shown in 2014, sits adjacent to an exurban investment mat.

Many of the competitions that sparked so much excitement and innovation in Spanish architecture in the early twenty-first century worked in concert with the speculative property boom in that country. Towns, small cities, and developments all competed with each other to attract real estate investment. The Japanese architect Toyo Ito, for example, designed an iconic pavilion for the Torrevieja Relaxation Park, directly adjacent to large tracts of exurban investment mat–type housing. The project offered a constructed starchitect attraction to an area otherwise devoid of significant features. With the collapse of the boom, the project stalled; more than a decade later, it is still an unfinished shell.

The Pérez Art Museum Miami (PAMM), designed by Swiss architects Herzog & de Meuron and opened in 2013, anchors a new district of condominium towers in downtown Miami. The building was funded with a $100 million general obligation bond supported by Miami-Dade County voters and $120 million from private donors. These included Jorge M. Pérez, who offered the largest amount, thus securing naming rights. Pérez is the cofounder of the Related Group real estate development company and, as of 2018, 316th on the Forbes list of the world's richest people, with a net worth of $2.6 billion. His role in PAMM is typical of real estate moguls' involvement in art museums throughout the Western world. His surplus capital is significantly derived from developing, selling, and renting housing throughout South Florida. This surplus gets absorbed in tax-deducted philanthropic donations like his to PAMM, which further seed an area for future profits. Zaha Hadid's condominium tower across the street from PAMM is indicative of the power of the museum in generating future potential. Marketed as One Thousand Museum, with a height of just over 700 feet (213 meters), making it the fifth-tallest building in Miami, the project's eighty-four condo units are explicitly advertised for their proximity to PAMM.

While the particular form of any given financial icon is not that significant, what is critical is its pronounced difference from the architecture of its context. Given the homogenized and standardized form of most commodity housing, it is expected that financial icons would be disproportionately formally complex. Morphogenic, ecologically inspired, parametrically derived forms occupy a privileged position. As Douglas Spencer so convincingly argues in *The Architecture of Neoliberalism*, it is no coincidence that this type of form making is explicitly aligned with the political logics of contemporary capitalism. These complex spaces of "smooth" flows that purport to be nonhierarchical and flexible compared to their neighbors are the ceremonial training grounds for the postpolitical subjects of finance capitalism.

Accelerations and Mutations

To provide increased opportunities for investment, to create more places to store wealth, to give everyone a mortgage, and to heighten liquidity, the architectural formalism of finance is often characterized by extremes. Horizontal expanses of similar single-family homes can be found in Levittown and countless similar developments. Iconic buildings have a long history; the wealthy have always built expensive monuments. But finance capitalism accelerates these practices in relation to the giant pool of money. Thus, buildings extend deeper into the earth, arrays of horizontal sameness become more expansive, towers taller and thinner, and icons ever more radically distinct. It is no small shift that the tallest buildings in many cities in the world are no longer offices—a change that has happened during the ascent of finance capitalism. This change symbolically announces the shift from an emphasis on wealth accumulation through production to wealth accumulation through financial speculation. The extremism in scale and proportion is an important change in itself, but it invokes architectural and technological mutations along other fronts to make that change viable. Icons find novel ways to bend, contort, and shine. Changes to elevator cabling and structural systems allow pencil towers to stand. Excavation strategies alongside dynamic LED lighting make underground wealth vaults possible. The function of buildings as finance necessitates a comprehensive transformation of almost all things architectural.

CHAPTER FOUR

UHNWIS AND THE SUPERPRIME

There are only two markets, ultraluxury and subsidized housing.

RAFAEL VIÑOLY, 2013

If we can find a bunch of billionaires around the world to move here, that would be a godsend. Because that's where the revenue comes to take care of everybody else.

MICHAEL BLOOMBERG, 2013

H ousing, and architecture along with it, is at the center of the twenty-first century's growing inequality. Architecture has always been a primary means to manifest and display wealth, and as more money flows into the built environment in this era of heightened economic extremes, it is under increased demand to fulfill this role. Projects aimed at social progress have largely been subsumed by the logics of investment-driven real estate. The very rich are growing in number and wealth, and as architecture becomes synonymous with marketing and real estate, it becomes increasingly aligned with these most powerful market actors. The result is that architecture appears significantly different than it did during the relative economic equality of the 1960s.

Increasing Inequality

A useful frame in which to consider the correlation between inequality and finance capitalism is the Organisation for Economic Cooperation and Development (OECD). The thirty-seven OECD member nations include those commonly accepted as possessing the world's most advanced capitalist economies, which for the most part exhibit pronounced attributes of finance capitalism.[1] Their rising state of financial inequality can be seen in their Gini coefficient, a widely accepted yardstick of inequality, which grew on average from 0.29 to 0.32 between 1985 and 2018.[2] Inequality has risen over the past twenty-five years in every OECD country except Turkey, Chile, and Mexico.[3]

The French economist Thomas Piketty argues that whenever the rate of return on capital is larger than the rate of economic growth over a significant period of time, wealth inequality increases.[4] Piketty believes that the concentration of wealth is a fundamental quality of capitalism itself and that it was only under a unique set of conditions that the wealth gap decreased between 1930 and 1975. Yet it is a compelling correlation that the current ascent of finance capitalism started around the same time as the current growth in wealth inequality.

Piketty's core position is that capitalism is structurally predisposed to favor returns on investment over wages from labor. Finance capitalism as it has risen since 1980 emphasizes investing as the preferred form of capitalist activity, accelerating the rate of return on capital and therefore generating heightened inequality. The concentration of wealth in a small minority animates many of the dynamics that have come to be associated with today's finance capitalism. Indeed, the very idea that the return on capital will be dependably higher than the return on labor is a proclamation of the significance of investing over production.

The Rise of the UHNWI

As inequality has increased, so has the sheer number of wealthy individuals. The finance industry refers to exceptionally wealthy people as high net worth individuals (HNWIs). The most prevalent definition for an HNWI is an individual with financial assets in excess of $1 million, excluding the value of a primary residence—essentially, a person who has more than a million dollars available for investment. Since HNWIs represent a lucrative client base for banks and investment managers, significant effort goes into analyzing them. Since 1996, the French multinational corporation now known as Capgemini, in collaboration with various financial institutions, has produced the annual *World Wealth Report*, which describes the investment needs of HNWIs. According to the 2001 report, there were 6 million HNWIs worldwide in 1998, owning a total of $22 trillion in financial assets.[5] By 2007, that number had grown to 9.5 million HNWIs with $40 trillion in assets, and by 2017 it had mushroomed to 18.1 million individuals collectively holding more than $70 trillion.[6] In seventeen years, both the number of HNWIs and their collective wealth tripled. At the same time that the number of HNWIs has exploded, their geographic distribution has shifted. In 1998 the Asia-Pacific region had 22 percent of the world's HNWIs.[7] By 2011 the number rose to 31 percent, equal to that of North America and just a touch above Europe.[8] In 2017 there were 4.8 million HNWIs in Europe, 5.7 million in North America, and 6.2 million in Asia-Pacific.[9]

The unprecedented scale and geographic scope of superwealth led to the creation of new subcategories in banking parlance. *Very high net worth individual* (VHNWI) is used to describe those with between $5 and $30 million in assets, whereas *ultra-high net worth individual* (UHNWI) defines those with more than $30 million in assets. In 2017, standard HNWIs accounted for 88.3 percent of total wealthy individuals, while 10.6 percent were VHNWIs and 1.1 percent were UHNWIs.[10] UHNWIs held 34 percent of all HNWI assets, amounting to more than $31 trillion in 2017[11]—doubling in just five years.[12] In fact, the number of UHNWIs grew by 12.9 percent and their wealth grew by 16.3 percent in just one year, between 2016 and 2017.[13] The 255,000 UHNWIs represent the wealthiest of the top 1 percent and possess a radically disproportionate amount of capital. Current forecasts point to a continued high growth rate for both HNWIs and UHNWIs; Wealth-X, a company specializing in data and analysis of the very wealthy, projects that the UHNWI population and its assets will grow by 41 percent between 2017 and 2022.[14]

The history of architecture is intimately related to concentrations of wealth; the fact that the very wealthy have a prominent impact on the built environment is nothing new. However, a number of factors have conspired to realign the spatio-financial ecosystem. Most of these are straightforward, yet in combination engender Doppler-like mutations. First is the simple fact that the sheer population size of both HNWIs and UHNWIs is unprecedented. It is this that enables wealth managers to refer to the HNWI as "the millionaire next door." Second is the relatively widespread geographic distribution of these individuals. Third is the interconnectivity of global financial practices and the communication and transportation systems that enable them. It is easy to forget how radical and recent a development it is for relatively large numbers of wealthy individuals to purchase real estate in globally far-flung locations en masse. These three basic conditions precipitate what might be called urban impact multiplication, in which the serial purchase of real estate in select cities multiplies, or greatly expands, the urban and architectural footprint of the superwealthy.

This also occurs because the very wealthy locate proportionally more of their wealth in real estate than do average investors. The average investor has historically tended to locate the majority of investments in stocks and bonds, whereas UHNWI investment portfolios are reported to allocate an average of 24 percent to real estate, the majority of which is in the form of direct ownership of residential real estate.[15] This investment is in addition to homeownership for personal use; the global average UHNWI owns 2.4 homes for personal use. Asian and Russian UHNWIs have an average of 3 personal-use homes each.[16] These investment behaviors allow the London-based global real estate brokerage Savills to state:

> Global real estate is mostly residential and held by occupiers. But in the world of traded investable property, private owners are becoming more important than institutional and corporate ones....Accounting for just 0.003% of the world's population, the real estate holdings of... UHNWIs...total over US$5 trillion, or around 3% of all the world's real estate value....Privately wealthy individuals are becoming an increasingly important force in the world of real estate.[17]

UHNWI Investment Tools

HNWI and UHNWI investment in real estate is facilitated by global real estate brokerages, which provide the means to invest around the world in a standardized platform. Real estate brokerages started to globalize in the mid-1970s; around the same time, new global brokerages that focus on luxury residential real estate also emerged. The two most prominent are offshoots of the Sotheby's and Christie's auction houses, with the former now having 990 offices in more than 72 countries with 22,500 sales associates, and the latter 1,200 offices in 45 countries with 32,000 agents.[18] These single-source brands enable purchasing continuity and fluidity across significantly different legal and economic contexts in a manner that is not entirely different from how multinational retail brands operate. In the words of Sotheby's promotional material, it has "the tools to

Rogers Stirk Harbour + Partners, One Hyde Park, London, 2011.

market each and every property with the same level of care and personalization in order to pair buyers and sellers around the world."[19]

The practice of positioning cities in relation to each other at a global scale appears to have assisted the investment practices of UHNWIs. The 2000s saw the emergence of a host of rankings that in various ways shaped conceptions of cities. While comparisons of the significance and power of cities at the global scale are long-standing hallmarks of modernity, the notion of a global city gained heightened prominence in the 1990s as expressed in sociologist Saskia Sassen's 1991 book *The Global City:*

New York, London, Tokyo. Rankings subsequently emerged that have helped shape a global competition among urban areas. The Globalization and World Cities Research Network was established in 1998 and has since issued a biannual categorization of more than three hundred cities into alpha, beta, and gamma tiers based on their level of economic connectedness. Rankings have grown in diversity since the 2000s and have expanded beyond direct measurements of power and influence. Newer rankings focused on livability appear to have the most impact on global real estate investment. The Economist Intelligence Unit's Global

Liveability Index was started in 2002 and now competes with numerous others. Initially intended to assist multinational corporations in determining hardship pay for far-flung employees, these indexes have served to propagate livability as a basic attribute of global urbanization. But they also can be used as global investment indexes, helping to ensure that both the world's alpha cities, such as London and New York, and the most livable, such as Melbourne and Vancouver, attract a disproportionate amount of global real estate investment. According to Christie's International Real Estate, in 2012, luxury residential purchases made by nonlocal buyers amounted to 60 percent of sales in London, 45 percent in Miami, 40 percent in San Francisco, 38 percent in Paris, and 30 percent in New York and Los Angeles.[20]

The Emergence of Superprime

Around the time that "ultra-high net worth individual" entered the lexicon of finance and banking, "superprime" property gained popularity in real estate parlance. The demographic segment of the extremely wealthy needed its correlative in real estate. The superprime designation depends entirely on price, and this determination is largely about promotion and marketing. A superprime building always has units that are expensive—sometimes a $1 million unit qualifies and other times a $10 million unit. There is now a whole subindustry within real estate specializing in superprime, and buildings are now explicitly marketed as such—the term itself signifies a structure's status. Frequently celebrity architects design these buildings. Richard Rogers's One Hyde Park in London, Rafael Viñoly's 432 Park Avenue in Manhattan, Herzog & de Meuron's Beirut Terraces in Lebanon—all superprime.

A prerequisite for the high cost that defines superprime is the perception of scarcity. At its most fundamental, this is a scarcity of location. First, the city is considered in relation to other cities: Is it a highly livable city, an alpha global city? Second is neighborhood, next site, and finally the specific location within a building. A penthouse with a view of London's Hyde Park is superprime by location alone. Given a prime location, the architecture could be anything. But of course, it is not anything—it is specific, at least in certain ways.

When it comes to what occupies a specific residential site, whether it is an entire lot or a three-dimensional volume in the sky, the prevailing conceptual and formal logic is that of differentiation: the design is meant to heighten the perception of scarcity. There is only one London and only one Hyde Park, yet how can this site be even more prime? The essential role of design in the context of superprime is to add hyperbole—to make it more super, finer, to add excellence and amplify luxury. Symptomatic of housing's complete submission to the demands of real estate, the spatial qualities of superprime residences are almost entirely a metrical matter. As Reinier de Graaf wrote, "Through the general deployment of the term 'real estate,' the definition of the architect is replaced by that of the economist."[21] Cost itself is the primary metric, in a sort of self-fulfilling loop in which cost both arises from a unit's inherent superprime qualities and produces the very perception of those superprime qualities. Closely related to cost is size: How many square feet? How many bedrooms? How many bathrooms? Add to this the age of the structure (either really new or a specific vintage upon which scarcity has been ascribed) and one has the entire metrical array of significance—the determining factors of superprime.

The view is perhaps the next most significant design attribute beyond overt metrics. While much of UHNWI housing is scarcely inhabited, posing an ontological challenge to the assumed purpose of these structures, the view plays a strategic role at the nexus of metrics and location. This is because the view is fundamentally premised upon an in situ human experience. While these structures may not be regularly inhabited, their viability as investment assets and places to store wealth is premised on the potential for pleasurable inhabitation. The view—a sort of mute entity, like a mirror, that becomes activated only in the presence of the owner—is extremely powerful in promising this possibility.

Beyond metrics and views, architectural design qualities both matter and do not. Physical design attributes are mainly about achieving exceptionalism in two ways: material finishes and details and formal/aesthetic differentiation. Architecture as a signifier of luxury tends to focus on certain attributes. An extreme focus on the building's exterior results in all manner of uncommon formal and aesthetic qualities whose sole purpose is to appear distinct and original. The best results of this emphasis on novelty above all else offer exceptional beauty and surprise. Distinction and originality also produce no shortage of vapid banality, a sort of global zoo of freaks and oddities all shouting, "Invest in me!" And it is not just top-heavy forms and proliferating cantilevers that achieve exoticism—sometimes minimal simplicity alone does it.

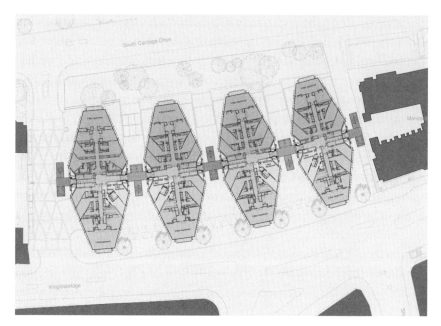

Rogers Stirk Harbour + Partners, One Hyde Park, level five (typical) floor plan.

A totally silent aesthetic can often provide the singularly unique structure on the block. Architecture as asset differentiator is entirely agnostic and supremely promiscuous when it comes to architectural qualities like color, shape, and style.

One Hyde Park, an Example of Superprime

Designed by London-based Rogers Stirk Harbour + Partners and completed in 2011, One Hyde Park, in the London district of Knightsbridge, is about as superprime as it gets. Since superprime is a marketing and cultural construct, popular media offer a good barometer of a building's superprime status. One Hyde Park is not short on hyperbole; newspapers frequently label the project as London's, Europe's, or even the world's most "elite" and "exclusive" building. A penthouse in the building was refinanced for £160 million ($213 million) in 2018—reportedly making it Britain's most expensive home ever sold.[22]

Situated directly on Hyde Park, the largest of London's Royal Parks, and in one of London's most expensive neighborhoods, One Hyde Park occupies the scarcest of locations. At the same time, it offers all the requisite metrical qualities of superprime. The eighty-six units, including four penthouses, have sold for enormous sums of money. A larger unit in the building occupies roughly 9,500 square feet (883 square meters) and includes five bedrooms, eight bathrooms, two kitchens, a breakfast room, a dining room, a media room, a study, a large principal reception room, and a second reception room. There are separate entrances to the units for residents and staff—and the building is serviced by the adjacent Mandarin Oriental hotel. In terms of its location, price, size, and standardized room types, the project has all the ingredients of superprime.

The formal logic of One Hyde Park's design works to amplify the perception of scarcity and to achieve the necessary qualities of the superprime. The building comprises four separate blocks, what the architects call pavilions, that are identical except in height: one is thirteen floors, two are eleven floors, and the shortest is nine floors. They are connected with glass circulation cores. The overall effect is four almost identical minitowers. At 700,000 square feet (65,000 square meters), One Hyde Park is a large building—for any residential structure, but exceptionally so for a superprime building. By comparison, SHoP's 111 West 57th Street project in New York City is 315,000 square feet (29,250 square meters). So, what it is often touted as the world's most exclusive residential address is also one of its largest. This registers one of the conundrums

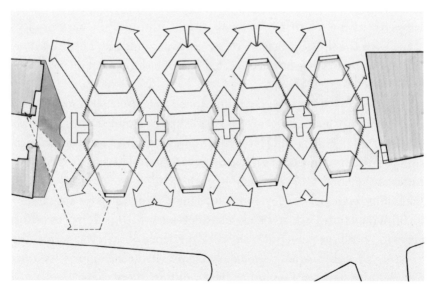

Rogers Stirk Harbour + Partners, One Hyde Park. A plan diagram created by the architects communicates the importance of views and aspect in generating the building's form.

of the UHNWI condition of finance capitalism: how to satisfy the demands of the increasing legions of the very wealthy while maintaining the sense of exclusivity and the perception of scarcity in the context of dense luxury. By breaking the building mass into discrete pavilions, One Hyde Park's architects divided one potentially massive block into a lighter-seeming series of smaller structures.

Much of One Hyde Park's formal logic is devoted to optimizing views. In comparison to a single rectangular mass, the arrayed pavilions increase its envelope-to-area ratio, thereby increasing exposure to views. The pavilions' plan shape is akin to a lozenge made of two mirrored trapezoids. The long faces of each pavilion are substantially angled rather than perpendicular to the street, allowing views of Hyde Park on the north and Kensington to the south from every single point of the perimeter. The walls of rooms deeper within the lozenge, nearer the center of the pavilions, are angled to the building facade so as to orient them toward the view. To reap the benefits of this view-optimizing geometry, the entire skin is floor-to-ceiling glass. And to further emphasize the view of the park and the cityscape beyond, the long faces of the pavilions are wrapped with vertical fins that visually shield inhabitants from neighboring units and adjacent pavilions. Each apartment's main living space occupies the narrow outer edge of the trapezoid, in what the architects call the promontory.[23] This placement provides panoramic views, thrusting the principal space of each unit into the park or cityscape with the illusion that no other unit surrounds it. The built density of this luxury has been concealed through the careful management of the view.

The long walls of each pavilion expose a concrete structural frame that is roughly a square grid. The grid supports and frames the glass units within. There is an elemental simplicity to this aestheticized version of structural purity. As the architects write, "The narrow promontories at the north and south end of each pavilion are intended to form the leading edges of the development. This gives it a slender appearance on both the Hyde Park and Knightsbridge sides."[24] This thin proportion generates both the perception and the experience of scarcity: despite the building's 700,000-square-foot mass, despite its dense luxury, its units feel secluded and few in number. The building's very shape accelerates its superprimeness. In its own way, One Hyde Park manifests finance capitalism's predilection for the ultra thin.

Two Opposing Positions on Architecture and Capitalism

It is useful to contextualize One Hyde Park in relation to the work of Patrik Schumacher and Pier Vittorio Aureli. Schumacher and Aureli are two of the highest-profile architects who combine active design work with writing explicitly focused on capitalism. Their positions are thus uniquely useful to situate the design qualities of superprime architecture particularly and finance capitalist architecture more generally. Schumacher is the principal of London-based Zaha Hadid Architects (ZHA), and Aureli teaches at the Architectural Association School of Architecture in London and is a partner at the Brussels-based architecture practice Dogma. Schumacher leads design work at ZHA and occasionally teaches, while Aureli engages architecture primarily through design propositions, teaching, research, exhibitions, and publications.

Patrik Schumacher and Zaha Hadid Architects

In 2013, Schumacher said he was "trying to imagine a radical free-market urbanism."[25] He has delivered talks titled "In Defense of Capitalism."[26] Schumacher is preoccupied with the notion that style aligns with "socio-economic epochs." From his perspective, the Renaissance is aligned with early capitalism, the Baroque with mercantilism, and so on. Within this schema, modernism assumes its common conceptual positioning as simultaneously aligned with Fordism, with its emphasis on efficient and standardized mass production, and international socialism.

Schumacher uses the term *parametricism* to identify the style of architecture that has emerged in the twenty-first century by those practicing parametric design. Parametric design utilizes algorithmic thinking to identify rules, or parameters, that determine the relationship between design input criteria and design output, and among design elements. Parametric design, and the complexity associated with Schumacher's brand of it, is rhetorically associated with post-Fordist organizational principles and their ostensibly progressive potentials.[27] Schumacher argues, "Parametricism is the only plausible contemporary candidate to become the global epochal style for the twenty-first century."[28] Schumacher does not use the term *finance capitalism*, preferring *post-Fordism* to describe contemporary capitalism. But *finance capitalism* is a more accurate description of current conditions and captures post-Fordist managerial practices under its umbrella of associated

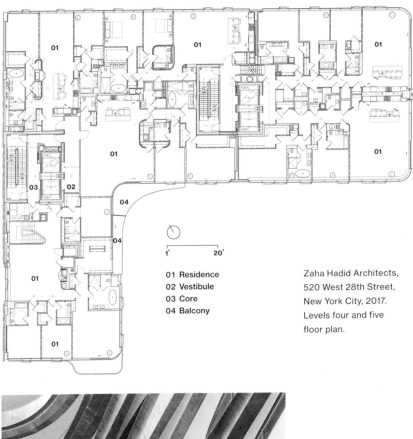

01 Residence
02 Vestibule
03 Core
04 Balcony

Zaha Hadid Architects,
520 West 28th Street,
New York City, 2017.
Levels four and five
floor plan.

Zaha Hadid Architects,
520 West 28th Street.
Chevron shapes on the
building's exterior skin.

Zaha Hadid Architects, 520 West 28th Street. The kitchen island—a location for sculptural differentiation inside the unit.

phenomena. From Schumacher's position, the formalism of parametric complexity is the spatial correlative of contemporary capitalism's logics. As the architectural historian and theoretician Douglas Spencer writes, "The order-words of this architecture—'self-organization,' 'emergence,' 'continuous variation,' 'material organization'—are circulated until they metabolize into a new doxa."[29]

While Schumacher and ZHA are best known for their cultural and civic structures, the practice is increasingly involved in luxury housing projects. One Thousand Museum in Miami, completed in 2019, and 520 West 28th Street in New York City, completed in 2018, are examples of this expansion. 520 West 28th is directly adjacent to the High Line, an elevated park in Manhattan's Chelsea neighborhood; it incorporates thirty-nine condominium units in a basic L shape that is extruded eleven floors. Units range from 1,500 square feet (140 square meters), with two bedrooms and three bathrooms, to an 11,000-square-foot (1,000-square-meter) penthouse with six bedrooms and six bathrooms. With condos selling for more than $3,000 per square foot during presales in 2017 and 2018, this building is superprime in terms of location and the metrics of size and price.

Unlike One Hyde Park, the design of which is primarily focused on views and thin proportions, 520 West 28th embodies a version of the epochal style of the twenty-first century that Schumacher advocates. In describing the project, ZHA emphasizes the "powerful urban dynamic between the streets of New York and the High Line" and the neighborhood's "multiple layers of civic space," which it seeks to "echo" and "convey" by "applying new ideas and concepts to create the latest evolution of the site's rich history."[30] These new ideas and concepts presumably involve the parametricism that Schumacher espouses. However, the L-shaped massing of the building and the interior layout of each unit is entirely standard. The only interior organizational element that differentiates this building from other housing projects of its size is the absence of hallways. Instead of a typical single elevator core with hallways that deliver people to their units, there are two separate cores that are strategically placed to offer the perception of private elevator lobbies for each unit. Seemingly parametric curved geometries can be found in the shared spaces of the building, such as the entrance lobby and swimming pool, but are otherwise confined to the building's exterior skin. In the unit interiors of projects like this, the kitchen island is one of the few places that offers the opportunity for sculptural differentiation. 520 West 28th is no exception in this regard; its kitchen islands present the style of parametricism.

Derived from the architects' impression of the site, the building's layering provides the opportunity for parametric "emergence." The floors in one bar of the L are offset by half a level from the floors in the other bar. This split becomes the opportunity for the building's main architectural operation: the resolution of the split levels on the skin of the building through the chevron form. As Zaha Hadid said, "The chevron comes from this idea of split levels. But because we don't stagger them, they become one single line."[31] The result is a skin that has a swooping metamorphosis in which one offset side fuses into the other around a zipper-like nexus. Since it is largely relegated to the skin, parametricism here seeks solely to differentiate the building from its context and provide scarcity in terms of exterior appearance. In contrast to One Hyde Park, which operates mainly as a place from which to experience a view, 520 West 28th relinquishes the interior in favor of a building as a sculptural object of desire, to be perceived from the outside.

Pier Vittorio Aureli and Dogma

While Patrik Schumacher marks one pole in contemporary architecture's association with capitalism, Pier Vittorio Aureli offers a strongly contrasting position. Far from celebrating the parametric style as an embodiment of the current political economy, Aureli foregrounds the *use* of architectural space in general and housing in particular. His particular notion of use is influenced by the Mendicant order of the Franciscans; he writes, "A fundamental tenet of their rule was the refusal to own things as a way of refusing their potential economic value and thus the possibility of exploitation of others."[32] As an example of architecture "against property," Aureli cites Swiss architect and Bauhaus director Hannes Meyer's 1924 Co-op Zimmer, in which the domestic space is reduced to a single room containing "only the essentials":

> Co-op Zimmer reveals what could be seen as an architecture of use
> against the architecture of property. While the latter must always
> be a reflection of the owner, Meyer's room is radically generic and
> anonymous. Precisely for this reason, it promises its inhabitant the
> possibility of a life liberated from the burden of household property.[33]

This focus on use positions a potential architecture disposed against the basis of capital: ownership.

For Aureli, this is an architecture intensely concerned with the interior as the primary site of a building's use. The lived space of housing is thus central to his project, "an approach intended to counter the present situation in which living space seems to be one of the most rigid societal realms, with very little typological flexibility."[34] Aureli's method of challenging the rigidity of living space is for architecture to become somewhat destructive and thereby to create a domestic tabula rasa. Architecture becomes its most elemental and facilitates the unfolding of a life of use within its boundaries. According to Aureli, architecture should

> become destructive in a symbolic sense, by ridding itself of illusions:
> for example, a wall has to be a wall and not an analogy for anything
> else. In performing this act of destruction, the architecture of housing
> can clearly state both its function as containment and its potential to
> formulate new and unforeseen forms of life.[35]

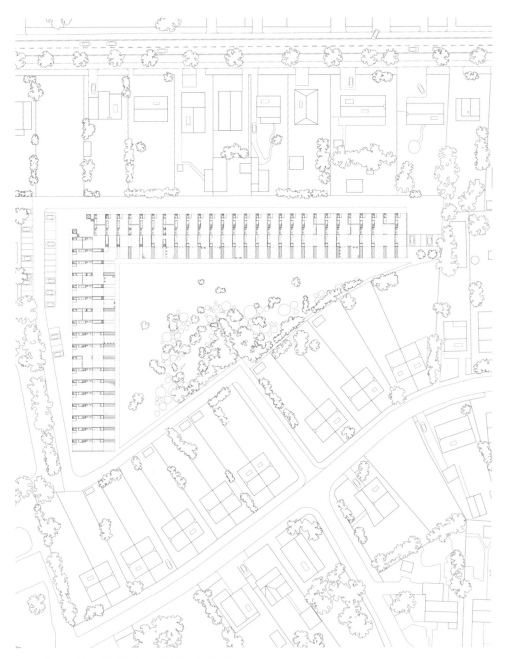

Dogma, Frame(s), Westerlo, Belgium, 2011, site plan.

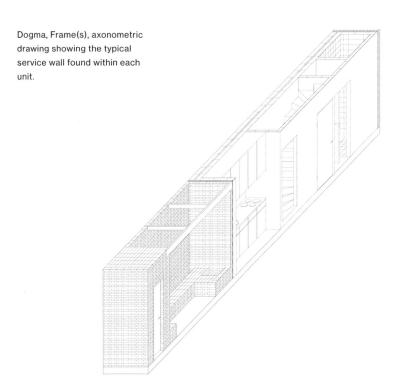

Dogma, Frame(s), axonometric drawing showing the typical service wall found within each unit.

Aureli's architecture is exceedingly reduced. Its basic increment at the urban scale is various formations of the rectangular bar: sometimes low-rise, other times high-rise, sometimes straight, and other times turned to form an L. These bars are generally composed with an unyielding, visible grid that is both organizational and aesthetic. Enacting its mandate of repetition and achieving a sublime austerity are the discrete elements of his simple architecture: flat floor slabs, vertical columns, and walls. A wall is nothing more than a wall—in an overwhelmingly elemental schema.

For an invited competition for forty-four units of social housing in Westerlo, Belgium, Dogma proposed Frame(s), a pair of two-story linear bar buildings pushed to the edge of an existing meadow and thereby making space for a shared garden. Each of the forty-four units has an identical volume, what Dogma calls a single tunnel-space, which is framed by a service wall. This service wall is a thickened band that incorporates a cooking area, stairs, bathrooms, and closet. It allows the rest of the unit to be clear and open—a background against which life can unfold in an undetermined manner. The narrow and deep rectangular dimensions of each unit in combination with fully glazed end walls reduce the envelope-to-area ratio (to lower construction costs) while extending the living space into the exterior. The exterior elevations communicate the interior plan condition—a simple rhythm of service wall and tunnel space for living. Each unit is essentially an open space where the primary role of architecture is to provide a container for life.

One Hyde Park and the Empty Interior

Aureli and Schumacher occupy opposing poles, with elemental form aligned with use at one end and complex parametric form aligned with ownership and speculation at the other. Dogma's Frame(s) project foregrounds the simplicity of architecture in service of the occupied interior, while ZHA's 520 West 28th Street finds its primary architectural purpose as a sculptural object to be perceived from the exterior—a reduced frame for social housing versus a zippy superprime skin.

Where does One Hyde Park sit in relation to these two versions of architecture? Its superprime status aligns it more closely with 520 West 28th. But, more significantly for architecture, both One Hyde Park and 520 West 28th are against use in the Aurelian sense. They both possess a modus operandi that is outside of themselves and therefore outside of actual domestic utility. One Hyde Park's architecture is primarily geared toward viewing, while 520 West 28th is primarily concerned with being viewed. Both are organized around vision and relatively incorporeal.

But the Rogers Stirk Harbour building is aesthetically closer to Aureli's than the Hadid/Schumacher project; both, for example, have a visible frame of containment. Both exterior elevations are to some degree a by-product of specific priorities—use and view. Both have touches of warm materials that accompany their operational logics: bricks and wood aligned with tabula rasa containment on one hand and patinated copper privacy screens aligned with optical positioning on the other. While Frame(s) is more austere than One Hyde Park, their proximity in appearance compared to the complex skin of 520 West 28th conveys how style and aesthetics operate in the era of finance capitalism. As Aureli has written:

> If we see how the political economy has worked over the past
> decades, we discover the significance of housing as a question of
> representation….This phenomenon has been a major contributor to

Dogma, Frame(s), rendering from inside a typical unit.

the financialisation of households: in other words, our economy of debt is also driven by the image of housing. The radical stylistic wealth of architecture in recent decades is also a by-product of this condition. Ironically, the more standardised the building industry becomes, the more architecture takes on the role of offering a "personalised" image.[36]

Superprime can thus be characterized by two versions of relinquishing the interior: one is the stylistically omnivorous elevation of differentiation; the other is the building operating as a view machine. Any emphasis on bodily use is antithetical to the investor-oriented architecture of the superprime.

Prefinance Wealth:
Kanchanjunga and the Waldorf Astoria

View and exterior novelty are the entire architectural design operations for superprime—leaving a desert of architectural intention everywhere else. Within superprime there appears to be no serious consideration of how meaningful innovation might address actual habitation. From the vantage of the early twenty-first century, it seems self-evident that housing for the very wealthy would be disinterested in investigating inhabitation and living; after all, those with a great amount of wealth are almost by definition less inclined to disrupt the status quo. But many earlier examples prove otherwise. In the early twentieth century, Manhattan, the emergent capital of industrial capitalism, witnessed remarkable experiments in the living spaces of the wealthy. The Waldorf Astoria, for example, tested new densities and scales for housing the wealthy collectively. Kitchens were eliminated from individual units; food was delivered, or residents ate together in shared dining halls. Another example is Indian architect Charles Correa's Kanchanjunga Apartments tower in Mumbai, completed in 1983 in a context of extreme inequality. It caters to that city's elite with thirty-two luxury apartments, yet it manifests considerable architectural innovation by terracing floor plates that generate landscapes of living inside the units. These were radical experiments in the possibilities of modern domesticity, and the spaces of the wealthy proved a fertile territory for exploration.

Except for a handful of projects in Japan and Western Europe, it is difficult to find recent market-based housing projects anywhere in the world that substantially and provocatively explore new possibilities for high-density housing in terms of unit interiors, unit organization, and questions of inhabitation—that type of thing is typically left to the occasional social housing project. This conveys the degree to which finance capitalism encourages architecture to abandon the domestic interior entirely. "This is also the moment that architecture and marketing become indistinguishable," Reinier de Graaf has observed.[37] The interior now appears little more than a space to frame a view, and a receptacle for appliances and fixtures that signify luxury and privilege. Marble countertops and expensive faucets embody wealth; that finishes and kitchen fixtures alone represent almost the entire apparatus of the interior conveys the remarkable efficiency of contemporary capital. The meager presence of actual physical wealth in the

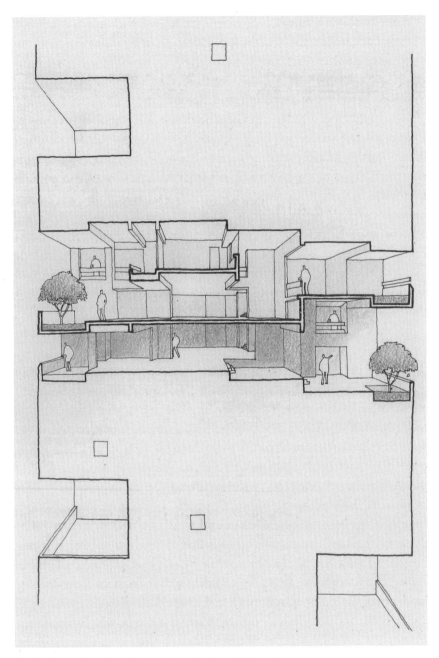

Charles Correa Associates, Kanchanjunga Apartments, Mumbai,
1983, section drawing showing two separate units.

architectural materiality of the interior, coupled with mind-bendingly stratospheric prices, conveys the sophistication of financialization's non-material emphasis.

Style Omnivores and Sheltered Taxes

The inequality measured by the Gini coefficient and described by Thomas Piketty is itself accelerated by the schism between more-affordable, use-based housing and superprime investment housing. Aureli's identification of the dyad of use and ownership plays out across the spectrum of UHNWI investing. Finance capitalism's wall of money has surged into material assets of many types. Architecture serves as a spatio-financial object alongside such things as paintings, wine, and antiques; all are being financialized. It is no coincidence that companies specialized in selling valuable items play an important role in the luxury housing market. Just as housing prices have dramatically escalated in much of the world, so has the value of many luxury investment commodities.

A compelling parallel to UHNWI investment in real estate can be found in what is called the storage free port—warehouses in which standard taxes and duties do not apply. As long as an artwork stays within a free port, the owner can indefinitely postpone value-added tax and customs duty payments on it. There are major art-focused free ports in Switzerland, Singapore, Monaco, Luxembourg, and Delaware. In the Geneva Free Port alone, there are more than one million art pieces worth more than $100 billion and said to include the world's most expensive painting, Leonardo da Vinci's *Salvator Mundi*.[38] By comparison, MoMA in New York City contains almost 200,000 works. But at the Geneva Free Port, the art remains unseen.

A tax-sheltering regime is often also at play in superprime architecture. In Manhattan, for instance, New York's property taxes result in luxury condo owners paying far fewer taxes than the occupants of more moderately priced condominiums and cooperative units. For example, the buyer of the ninetieth-floor penthouse of One57, which at the time of its sale was the most expensive home sale in New York's history, paid one-hundredth of the average property tax rate in the United States.[39] Superprime architecture is like a free port—units are sheltered from taxes, and, frequently, taken out of use.

In the current postideological condition, in which the logics of real estate have free rein, perhaps the true ideology is that of hyperbole—or, in other words, hype. While superprime is a distinct category, because of its tight relationship with elite architecture and the urban-multiplier effect of UHNWIs, its shadow is long. The architectural ideology of the now might represent nothing more than the maintenance of systems of wealth and power and the propagation of the inherent scarcities that they necessitate.

CHAPTER FIVE

SIMPLIFICATION AND POSTSOCIAL SPACE

T he financialization of architecture necessitates its simplification in order to make it easier to own and trade as an asset. This process standardizes, homogenizes, and physically disengages architecture, yet, paradoxically, attempts to render it unique and locally specific. This fabrication of locality and complexity is the means by which real estate keeps its stake in the "real," not entirely becoming another asset category. However, these invented forms of reality are more singular and simpler than versions that are not financialized, facilitating a higher degree of control, predictability, and stability.

Assets in Relation to Simplicity and Complexity

Investment portfolios are typically populated by ostensibly diverse assets. A portfolio might include stocks in a broad number of public companies alongside a range of government bonds. It also might include a selection of derivatives, such as options to purchase certain stock at a future date, and commodities like grain and soybeans. This form of diversity-based complexity coexists with the relative complexity of the assets themselves, such as credit default swaps and mortgage-backed securities possessing designs so esoteric that it is difficult for the average individual to understand them.

Leigh Claire La Berge, an assistant professor of English at City University of New York, has documented how descriptions of finance as *complicated* or *complex* proliferated in the 1980s. She writes:

> In its new instantiation, finance was conceived of as private in that it delimited a rich psychic interior, and as complicated or complex in that few could understand its exterior representation. Indeed, financial transactions became, in the discourse of the period, too complicated or complex to explain either to lay people or, increasingly, to the financial community in which the transactions originated.[1]

However, despite the apparent complexity of any given portfolio's collective holdings, each individual asset tends to be, in fact, relatively simple. Consider a company that is a complex economic formation in terms of its products, processes, and workforce. By comparison, its stock is simple. It is easy to purchase, own, and sell. It is an immaterial, low-cost way for an individual to own a portion of that much larger, more complicated entity from afar. Such a security radically simplifies ownership of the company and can be described as a simplification-of-ownership tool. This is in part because of what Karl Marx and others recognized as the separation of management from ownership. Of course, while securities make it simpler to own a portion of a corporation, there is nonetheless an array of information for an investor to digest: earnings and debt history, the composition of corporate leadership, and the larger market context in which these exist.

It is possible to invest directly in physical commodities. The most common investment commodities are incredibly simple—inherently standardized, homogeneous, and physically disengaged. Oil, for example, is by definition elemental and unchanging. One barrel of oil is essentially the same as any other barrel of oil. The lack of associated complexity allows the asset to function in a relatively pure supply-and-demand market that facilitates buying and selling. In other words, its simplicity enables liquidity.

Contrast this with urban and architectural space, where the classic credo "all real estate is local" reflects the widespread belief that the complexities associated with the built environment are so numerous and locally specific that any attempt to directly invest without deep local knowledge is foolish. And real estate is indeed highly diverse. Particularities of climate, neighbors, schools, transportation, noise, pollution, laws, regulations, building design, construction quality, and depreciation are just a sample of the considerations in a real estate purchase. While real estate and securities each have their own complexities, it can be argued that the sheer breadth of consideration is more extensive in real estate. And, crucially, there is no standardized way to access and organize this information easily. This contrasts sharply with publicly traded stocks, which require annual company filings providing standardized information to investors.

The relative complexity and opacity of real estate constrains architecture's performance as an asset; the necessity of local expertise limits buying and selling, and therefore liquidity. Thus, one of the critical operations of spatial financialization is to simplify and universalize architectural properties, making them into more standardized assets. A fundamental tension of real estate's role in finance capitalism is that real estate must become in many ways less real without relinquishing its defining realism: physicality. Financialization is how architecture acquires certain physical characteristics that approximate a universal immateriality.

Simplification through Mediation and the Law: REITs and Condominiums

The simplification of architecture occurs across a spectrum that spans legal-bureaucratic structures to material ornament. At the seemingly immaterial end of the spectrum sit real estate investment trusts (REITs) and the legal invention of the condominium. Real estate investment is a slow, cumbersome process with many participants; REITs essentially offer the same simplification function for real estate that stocks do for a business entity, separating ownership from management. A REIT is a company that owns, and typically operates, income-producing real estate. Through buying shares in a REIT, the investor is able to own a portion of real estate in a mediated and simplified manner, accessing the standardized information that publicly traded entities reasonably ensure.

The condominium also offers simplification, not through mediated ownership but rather through a new legal designation of ownership. Up until the 1960s in North America, direct individual ownership of housing was legally premised upon land ownership. In that model, an individual could possess legal title to a horizontal territory defined by vertically extruded parcel demarcations and, by extension, any building that occupied that territory. Therefore, it was possible to directly own only those housing types based upon single ownership in the vertical dimension: detached homes, duplexes, townhomes, and their variants. There was no common and easy way to directly own a vertically stacked unit in a multiunit housing project. The tenure for this type of unit was, for the most part, only possible as rental, cooperative, or subsidized social housing. In cooperative housing, a tenant-controlled corporation owns a building in which individuals occupy specific units upon mutual agreement—individuals do not possess direct legal title to specific units.

Starting with the Utah Condominium Act of 1960, jurisdictions throughout North America enabled a new form of direct ownership: the condominium. In the words of Canadian legal scholar Douglas C. Harris, the condominium is a "legal innovation without peer in its capacity to increase density of private ownership in land" because it "simplified the stacking of fee simple interests [absolute ownership] in land in a vertical column."[2] While 1960s legislation created the condominium, it was not until finance capitalism's rise in subsequent decades that condominiums became widespread.

The condominium facilitates the financialization of architecture, heightening architecture's investment asset function by increasing the liquidity of housing. One way an asset's liquidity can increase is via an enlarged market populated by active buyers and sellers, which increases trading activity. Another means is through reduced structural obstacles to ownership and exchange. The condominium achieves heightened liquidity through both. Because condominiums increase the number of tradable assets within the housing market, they amplify real estate trading activity. One way they increase the number of tradable assets is to change property that had typically been built as rental typologies into ownership assets. In some local markets, such as Vancouver, the construction of purpose-built rental housing mostly ceased with the advent of the condominium. Investor-owners now rent out roughly half of the city's condo units, which have become the de facto rental housing stock. At the same time, condominiums tend to be less costly than traditional real estate assets such as detached homes. The combined increase in market size and supply of lower-cost assets accelerates the ease of buying and selling and therefore liquidity.

More significant is the way in which condominiums change the structure of ownership and exchange by strategically individualizing and streamlining private financial interests while collectivizing operation and maintenance. As the architecture critic Paul Goldberger notes when comparing New York City's co-ops to that city's new crop of condominiums, "Everything about the city's co-op buildings…is structured to make it impossible to treat them as commodities. That, however, is precisely what the new condominiums are: tradable commodities, perfect for the speculatively inclined."[3] Occupying a unit in a co-op—possible only through buying shares in the co-op—requires a time-consuming interview process with a co-op board. In a condominium, individuals can freely buy, sell, and finance units at their own discretion, unencumbered by an entity like a co-op board. This individuation of direct ownership applies the ownership model of single-family detached housing to multiunit housing. At the same time, the condominium collectivizes operation and maintenance in a manner that significantly enhances the asset function. The vertical stacking of most condos minimizes maintenance concerns; what tasks remain fall under the responsibility of third parties hired by condominium strata councils. Removing key operation and maintenance responsibilities from individual owners makes ownership and, by extension, buying and selling easier, thereby increasing liquidity. This has a simple but profound implication: it enables ownership without occupation or even contact with a unit, propelling housing closer to intangible asset classes like stocks and bonds. As Harris states, "A 'condo' was self-contained and simple, could be owned from a distance, occupied or left vacant, and transferred in a market of highly fungible commodities."[4]

Condominiums can be found in most housing types. While they are most often associated with multiunit buildings, even single-family home subdivisions can be condominiums in which discrete homes are privately owned while the shared landscape and infrastructure is collectively owned and managed. These single-family subdivision condos have similarities to the homeowner association (HOA) subdivisions that have become popular in the United States since 1985. However, an HOA differs from a condo in relation to common property: in a condo, all owners jointly own common property, whereas in an HOA, the HOA association itself owns the common property. It is possible to trace how the logics of finance capitalism subtly manifest in the architectural form of condominiums. Condo subdivisions, for instance, often exhibit a compression of space between individual homes. It is as if they are multifamily buildings that have been pried apart and disaggregated just enough to provide a minimum semblance of detached housing.

Make It Secure

Parallel to the mediation and legal apparatuses that enhance liquidity are physical changes that simplify architecture by increasing security, decreasing maintenance, and ultimately reducing unpredictable social interaction. Three common tactics of spatial simplification are minimizing the necessity of physical contact, diminishing sociality, and abstracting locality. The simple necessities of security and maintenance problematize the asset function of real estate. Buildings can be understood on a security spectrum—total security at one end and total insecurity at the other. While some buildings are designed to be more secure than others, all are insecure when compared to an asset like oil. This is partly because systems of physically securing oil are so well established and operate at such magnitudes of scale that they are inconsequential to the individual investor. Oil as an asset is unseen, untouched, and entirely abstract in the mind of the investor—it might as well be immaterial. In contrast, real estate assets require proactive security at the scale of the investor to diminish the risk of vandalism, theft, and trespass. A certain level of security is an inherent by-product of occupancy, but because the optimal real estate asset can be owned remotely, its potential vacancy ushers in a heightened risk that requires a compensatory hardening. Buildings are thus pushed along the spectrum toward total security through such elements as strategically placed walls, gates, and controlled access points. But security is also ensured passively and far more discreetly through the grouping of multiple assets into architectural forms that offer the inherent protection of collectivity.

No Maintenance, No Repair

Unlike traded securities or common commodities, directly owned real estate physically degrades and requires routine firsthand inspection and ongoing material maintenance. These demands add to the complexity of real estate assets, heightening the friction of ownership. Just as buildings can be understood on a security spectrum, they can be placed on a maintenance and repair spectrum. Materials and assemblies deteriorate unevenly, some more rapidly than others. Similarly, some types of physical massing and form are more resilient than others. As architecture is simplified for investment purposes, it is propelled toward materials and forms that minimize the burdens of maintenance: those that minimize an individual real estate asset's contact with the weathering exterior.

Collective Disentanglement

The diversity and unpredictability of human behavior contributes to the "all real estate is local" credo; the simplification process seeks to minimize this complexity by diminishing the breadth of collective social life. This occurs in terms of how real estate assets are organized, in relation both to each other and to their surrounding public context. Assets are shielded or isolated from public space through various organizational and formal methods: walls, barriers, landscaping, and setbacks isolate assets from the nuisances and dangers of noise, pollution, and strangers. Perhaps even more significantly, certain building types and morphologies inherently provide this disengagement. Forms that limit public access and separate real estate assets from the public ground have flourished in the era of finance capitalism. In describing the marketing videos for London residential towers, the London-based architect Sam Jacob says:

> It's all part of the same narrative, the separation of the individual from collectivity, the fact that you rise above the city, the idea that the city is a kind of beast that is there to be beaten or to beat you. That of course means you're separated from society and the things that really make a city exciting.[5]

Just as asset-oriented housing units are shielded from the public, there is a parallel effort to minimize interaction among assets (units). To flourish, finance capitalism requires a large number of relatively inexpensive assets, which enable a liquid market. Producing a large number of units on a given plot of land, usually in the form of condominiums, can populate a market with a larger number of less expensive units than constructing single-family homes, increasing market liquidity by allowing more buyers and sellers to be active in the market. This produces tension within finance capitalist architecture. At the moment that a vast number of units are required in the relatively high densities that provide liquidity, those units need to be shielded from the very collective life they potentially generate.

This translates into strategies to diminish social contact within buildings. Unit organization and circulation are therefore primary concerns of finance capitalism. The territory through which one moves from the entrance of a building to an individual unit is vital for establishing the necessary lack of direct human encounter. At the same time, unit organization and materiality serve to limit sensory contamination—visual, acoustic, and olfactory—among units. In this manner, finance capitalism advances specific organization and massing that disentangle individual units from the messy unpredictability of collective life and thereby simplifies real estate assets.

The Ultra-Thin Pencil Tower as a Zenith of Simplification

The simplification of architecture through collective disentanglement, security, and minimization of maintenance can be found across building types, but the ultra-thin pencil tower exhibits these qualities in sharp relief and provides a useful illustration.

The slender tower minimizes repairs and maintenance. In comparison to the detached home, with its yard and its entirely exposed envelope that operates at the scale of the individual housing unit, the multiunit structure reduces the landscape-to-interior ratio while diminishing the amount of exterior envelope connected to any one unit. This is most evident with the roof—a major point of failure and concern in the single-family home. A tower, in contrast, can pack hundreds of units under one small roof area, which diminishes the per-unit responsibility for failure to a comparably minimal level. And the slender tower puts this into extreme terms. For example, Melbourne's first pencil tower, Collins House, has a roof area of roughly 4,500 square feet (420 square meters) that shelters 298 units. That is about 17 square feet (1.6 square meters) per unit.

The vertical envelope offers similarly radical benefits. Slender towers have unique sources of potential failure that are collectivized in the condominium structure, but these collected concerns come nowhere close to the individual repair and maintenance burden of the typical single-family home. In terms of security, the slender tower is also difficult to rival. Almost by definition, having one access point provides an ease of surveillance and control. Units are raised off the ground plane, and in more and more instances, the distance from the ground is vast. Furthermore, the collectivization of security responsibilities decreases the individual burden. Contrast this to a single-family home, in which the unit of investment is in direct contact with the hazards of the ground. Here, an intruder can easily survey the property and access it from multiple points. Any security measures tend to be the direct responsibility of the owner. These qualities of reduced maintenance and diminished security concern make units in the ultra-thin tower especially easy to own remotely. A buyer could essentially never visit an empty unit on the twenty-fifth floor of a typically functioning condominium and be reasonably sure that it was safe and sound. There would be no overgrown grass, broken windows, or leaks in the roof.

The pencil tower's most elemental operation removes the housing unit from the ground, where it is susceptible to the unpredictability of public space. In addition, the slenderness of the tower heightens social disentanglement through the simple but highly consequential reduction of the number of units on any given floor. Holding unit size constant, slender towers have fewer units per floor. Indeed, the apotheosis of the slender tower is one having a single unit per floor—with all the asociality of a detached home, but in the sky. The elevator deposits investors directly into their private real estate territory with minimal chance to encounter the unknown.

This configuration also reduces the multisensory evidence of neighbor proximity. It is more difficult to mitigate the transmission of sound and odor in the horizontal than the vertical dimension in multiunit housing, and therefore, minimizing the number of units on any given floor reduces this transmission. The slender tower helps inhabitants avoid the neighbor's noisy television and smelly meals or, heaven forbid, the sight of that neighbor in the hallway.

Uncoincidentally, the very form and organization that enervates sociality optimizes view production. Desirable views are achieved via small-floor-plate towers because of what they enable internally and imply urbanistically. Corners inherently maximize views through their multidirectionality, and a small floor plate uniquely offers a high corner-to-floor area ratio. Additionally, when combined with strategic spacing between towers at the urban scale, the repetition of small-floor-plate towers affords ample view lines between towers when compared to the repetition of other typologies such as slabs or mid-rise blocks.

Height itself maximizes the reproduction of these presumably desirable attributes. Taken collectively, these straightforward organizational and proportional tactics amount to an architectural form of dense isolation. The avoidance of social contamination effectively abstracts domestic space and removes it from collective entanglements, ultimately facilitating its postsocial role—that of a tradable financial asset. Housing in the era of finance capitalism can thus be thought of as postsocial housing.

The Ongoing Simplification of the Suburban Home

While the slender condominium tower exemplifies finance capitalist simplification, the same trajectory can be found in other building and tenure types—even at the opposite end of the spectrum, in the suburban single-family rental home. In a textbook example of how crises enable new forms of capital accumulation, starting at the peak of the US foreclosure crisis in 2010, institutional investors such as hedge funds and private equity groups, with the support of the federal government, invested billions in foreclosed properties. The rental of single-family homes had historically been highly fragmented and characterized by small-scale, mom-and-pop-type landlords; for the first time, large financial corporations became major players in the business. These corporations aimed to make profit from speculative investment in real estate, taking advantage of the low prices resulting from the crisis as well as from ongoing rental income streams.

By 2016, these corporations had invested more than $60 billion into owning more than two hundred thousand single-family rental homes in the United States. These vulture capitalists targeted neighborhoods with high foreclosure rates, like certain areas of Atlanta, where one in five houses is now owned by institutional investors. And there appears to be a racial aspect to this investment, with a higher proportion of Black residents in neighborhoods where institutional investors are especially active.[6]

Predictably, the management and maintenance of homes spread out over a metropolitan area has proved challenging. For the same reasons that the single-family home reduces liquidity for the individual investor, the financial corporations found challenges relating to maintenance and upkeep. In an effort to reduce ongoing operating expenses and increase profits, these firms sought to minimize maintenance expenses or pass them on to the renter, generating all manner of complaints and lawsuits that have been covered in the popular media.[7] Investment companies have been accused of reducing the frequency of maintenance and unfairly forcing renters to fix problems themselves in order to keep their own costs down. They have also sought to standardize their homes and streamline their operations, installing common flooring materials and appliances, and smart locks to allow remote access.

As the foreclosure crisis has subsided and property values have increased, these companies have increasingly had trouble buying existing homes at a desirable cost. In response, they have started developing their own built-to-rent single-family housing. The REIT American Homes 4 Rent was founded in 2012 to invest in single-family rental homes. It now owns more than fifty thousand homes, with the largest concentrations in Atlanta and Dallas–Fort Worth. In its earnings call in the fourth quarter of 2019, Chief Operating Officer Bryan Smith stated:

> Our expanded use of data and analytics, allows us to optimize our platform while listening to what our residents want....We are able to value engineer homes that closely match resident preferences and are efficient from a maintenance perspective. Our analytics drive both high-level decisions such as location selection in the ideal mix of three, four and five bedroom homes in the community, as well as lower level decisions like the types and features of appliances all the way down to the optimal horsepower of our garbage disposals.[8]

In both the acquired and newly built homes of these types of REITs, materials, appliances, and spatial dimensions are all optimized to minimize maintenance and operating expenses. But this occurs at a tremendous social cost that highlights how finance capitalism exacerbates racial inequality.[9]

Standardized Real Estate Products

There is a tendency in the investment community to favor assets that easily fit into simple and clear categories. For example, REITs overwhelmingly invest in standardized architectural products. As Christopher B. Leinberger, chair of the Center for Real Estate and Urban Analysis at George Washington University, has written, in order for real estate developers to fully participate in Wall Street, "they have had to commodify what they build, and this has meant ensuring that each unit of each product type was adequately similar to every other. Such a situation has very quickly led to what can be called the Nineteen Standard Real Estate Products."[10]

These "products" tend to be single-program and stand-alone. As Leinberger writes, "From an investment point of view, commodification has also resulted in extreme specialization. REITs today nearly all specialize in one product type or another."[11] One particular REIT will invest exclusively in power centers (large, big-box-oriented shopping centers, typically organized around a common outdoor parking area); another, in only commercial office space; and yet another, in only middle-income rental housing. The Simon Property Group, for example—the fifth largest REIT in the United States, with a market capitalization in 2020 of $44 billion—invests exclusively in malls and outlet centers, most of which are suburban.[12] Leinberger argues that REITs are habitually reluctant to invest in programmatically heterogeneous architecture, propagating the single-use landscape that defines much of the United States. While American REITs have recently embraced "mixed-use" developments, they are still remarkably homogeneous and effectively simplistic. REITs' bias against programmatic diversity exemplifies finance capitalism's preference for simple real estate assets. The clearly identifiable asset—urban housing, golf property, view unit—further diminishes social complexity and shifts "all real estate is local" toward "all real estate is global." The process of simplification thus seeks a postsocial condition for architectural assets at the same time that it pursues asset clarity. This parallel reduction of social complexity and heightened asset clarity allows built space to function more optimally according to the demands of finance capitalism.

Compensating with "Complexity"

Financialized space compensates for its simplified, standardized, and postsocial character by inventing new abstract localities that provide a semblance of specificity. Complex local conditions are replaced with simpler versions of reality. This is sometimes achieved with strategies that obscure homogeneity: Jane Jacobs–influenced podiums mask standardized condo towers rising above, and nostalgic, materially diverse skins conceal spatial homogeneity. But much more significant are the deployment of recreational leisure space, the emphasis on the semiotics of nature, and the obsessive provision of views. These abstract localities offer heightened predictability, stability, and therefore simplicity compared to other types of local complexity; they are postsocial versions of local specificity.

Recreational Leisure Space

Associating housing with recreational leisure activity is a long-standing practice that has flourished with the rise of finance capitalism. The reasons for this are numerous and include recreation's inherent appeal as well as, more importantly, its ability to lend a softened, universal identity to housing—delocalizing it, reducing social complexity, and thereby facilitating buying and selling liquidity.

While many recreational programs provide housing projects with clear identities and imbue them with sought-after postsocial attributes, one has played an outsize role in the era of finance capitalism: golf. Locations with a large amount of speculation-driven development, such as Spain's Mediterranean coast and the American Southwest, tend to incorporate a vast amount of golf-based housing. And since these golfscapes are highly sought after but significantly underused, a nonfunctional logic is operative. The increased value of residential property incorporating golf courses has been demonstrated in various studies and provides evidence that golf is primarily a real estate device that facilitates investment.[13]

Why golf in particular? The perception of golf as an activity for the wealthy gives it relatively broad aspirational appeal that is vital to its role in contemporary real estate. However, at least equally important from the perspective of finance capitalism and investment are its sociospatial qualities. While individual golf courses possess unique characteristics, they have more similarities than differences, which makes them a universal commodity. Their landscapes are easily synthesized with housing. The formulaic ingredients of greens, sand traps, and water features succeed in generating a simulacrum of nature. And as the primary public space within these developments, they help constrain social life to what is possible on a golf course—a highly limited sociality. Golf lends developments a sociospatiality that is removed from potential complications and imbued with the universalized character of a commodity. In this manner, golf-based housing functions as an easily identifiable and stable investment asset class that is primed for the market.

It is not a coincidence that golf-oriented housing projects flourished in some parts of the world most impacted by the 2008 crisis. Spain,

Florida, and the American Southwest, where speculative development coincided with incredibly lax lending capital, saw an explosion of golf-based housing during the boom. In the United States, developments of single-family homes often wrap around golf greens (or, sometimes, the golf course encircles a development). In Spain, it is more common to witness multiunit building complexes that are golf based.

While golf dominates this type of abstracted locality, housing projects identified with recreational programs are also centered around the beach, the garden, and the pool. If the golf green provides a simplified nature that is postsocial, the artificial lake accelerates this trajectory. For example, the Lakes at Rancho El Dorado in metropolitan Phoenix, with space for just over 1,500 single homes, is organized around an immense

The Fairways housing development, shown in 2015, in Beaumont, California.

serpentine water feature. The eponymous lakes are a series of 100-foot-wide (30-meter) water-filled trenches that were carved out of the desert to form an overall length of two and a half miles (four kilometers). As a car-oriented synthesis of waterworks and a maximized number of housing plots, the project exemplifies the drive to produce a nature that heightens returns. The Lakes is developed by the Meritage Homes Corporation, one of the top ten largest home builders in the United States, whose profits derive from both developing and financing their products. The Lakes started construction in 2006 and fifteen years later is about one-quarter complete—largely because of the massive overbuilding in the years leading up to 2007–8 and the ensuing crisis. Its unfinished landscape and the no-go zone of the artificial lake form a highly postsocial version of simplified reality.

The Construction of Nature

Because much of what constitutes local complexity is related to human behavior, as opposed to "nature," it is often construed as artificial. Human factors such as a population's age, class, race, sexual orientation, and religion, as well as quality of schools, noise, traffic, transit, pollution, and safety, all dynamically coexist to produce a local milieu. Overcoming the investment limitations of such complex conditions engenders a move away from perceived human artificiality toward an ostensible nature.

The perception of nature offers finance capitalism a preferred form of universal abstraction that sits alongside recreational leisure programming. As human social complexity bound within the idea of local specificity is stripped away, it is replaced by an ersatz presentation of what appears to be natural. A perceived contrast between the iniquity of the urban environment and the wholesomeness of nature is widespread. In Western culture it can be found in narratives that go back at least to Sodom and Gomorrah, as the artificial and urban antitheses to the innocence of the Garden of Eden. Finance capitalism intensifies and exacerbates this binary. Today nature functions as the softener of all things urban, but it is a constructed and controlled nature that offers value that is simple and singular. While wild nature consists of dynamic and complex ecologies, the constructed nature of contemporary real estate is comparably lethargic and singular. The nature within a golf course excludes much of any social life at all. Floridian housing

TOP In 2015, a golf course wrapping around a housing subdivision in Corona, California.

MIDDLE Multiunit housing shown in 2014 at Calanova Golf, Mijas, Málaga, Andalusia, Spain.

RIGHT A golf-focused urbanization shown in 2014, Mijas, Málaga, Andalusia, Spain.

estates project gangly fingers into forests in a proximity that greatly diminishes their working ecology but maintains the appearance of raw nature. Naturalistic landscaping at the perimeter of condominium towers detaches them from the public intensity of the street while cloaking them in an image of purity. Shrubs and artificial lakes can be found on the roofs of podiums—offering an Edenic escape for the condominiums above. The forest, the beach, the lake, and the mountain all provide clear asset identities and stabilize housing products as postsocial assets.

It is not surprising that nature takes on a heightened role in finance capitalist architecture. Marketing strategies that leverage popular concern for the environment are an everyday feature of contemporary life, sometimes garnering accusations of "greenwashing." Architecture's ecological pretensions, from green roofs to recycled building products, are often aligned with real estate marketing strategies regardless of what meaningful environmental benefits they may offer.

A 2015 aerial image of the incomplete Lakes at Rancho El Dorado in metropolitan Phoenix.

The constructed waterfront at the Lakes at Rancho El Dorado, shown in 2015.

The architectural deployment of nature for capitalist purposes has a long history that accelerated with the ascent of finance capitalism. Manfredo Tafuri recounted how the roof gardens at New York City's Rockefeller Center, for example, were specifically intended to achieve higher profits.[14] By the twenty-first century, as noted by Reinhold Martin, nature had come to play a central function in how architecture that in reality channels power has become perceived as "happy and pleasant."[15] Martin argues that the neo-naturalist interior atriums of the Atlanta-based architect and developer John Portman that emerged in the United States in the 1970s are symptomatic of a novel architectural deployment of nature in relation to capital: "We can call this new regime, this new nature grown up in cities like Atlanta and San Francisco but exported worldwide, 'the regime of the potted plant.'"[16] In Portman's Hyatt Hotel in San Francisco, with its cave-like atrium with thousands of potted plants from which vines descend, the interiors of global travel and business began to replace complex exterior and public downtown spaces with a new nature of capitalism. While this was incubated alongside the framework of finance capitalism (such as the elimination of the gold standard in 1971), it became more widespread from the 1980s to the present. It jumped from the commercial office and hotel atrium to the architectural environment at

TOP Shown in 2020, boulders and waterfall at the base of the Palisades condominium towers in Vancouver.

ABOVE Rock outcroppings at the base of the Pointe condominium tower in 2020 in Vancouver.

LEFT A forest floor at the base of the Residences on West Georgia condominium towers, as seen in 2020 in Vancouver.

large and in the 2010s began its climb into high-density housing and large mixed-use projects in the most literal of ways.

A milestone in the explicit merger of nature with the high-density housing market can be found in architect Stefano Boeri's Bosco Verticale, a pair of luxury residential towers in the Porta Nuova area of Milan. These two towers, roughly 250 feet (76 meters) and 370 feet (113 meters) high, hold 800 trees, 15,000 perennials and ground covering plants, and 5,000 shrubs in a series of deep balconies. As the architect states, the project is "a home for trees that also houses humans and birds."[17] In subsequent years, more new housing projects around the world have foregrounded plants. Amsterdam-based UNStudio's winning competition proposal for Southbank by Beulah in Melbourne, which will be Australia's tallest building upon completion, is organized around what the architects and developer call the Green Spine. This space is a twisting vertical array of terraced verandas containing shrubs and trees that front the residential units. Here Bosco Verticale meets the parametric style, as touted by Patrik Schumacher, to produce a green icon.

While Southbank by Beulah is an extreme example of an artificial nature simulating a sense of local complexity, similar projects have recently been completed or are in the works in many cities. The Danish architect Bjarke Ingels's King Toronto condominium complex resembles a shrub-covered hillside in renderings. For Henriquez Partners' Oakridge Centre, under construction in Vancouver, each unit is ringed with planters. On the Sky Green tower in Taichung, Taiwan—completed in 2019 and designed by Singapore-based WOHA—single-tree planters cantilever beyond condominium units. In the era of finance capital, increasing numbers of residential projects include plants as major programmatic elements.

Nature is itself an important sector of financialization. Political ecologists Alex Loftus and Hug March argue, "The truly distinctive aspects of the political economy of nature in the present moment lie not in an apparent shift to neoliberalism, nor in a new stage in capitalist social relations but rather in increasing financial influences on the contemporary production of nature."[18] From weather derivatives to carbon trading, nature is increasingly within the operational purview of finance. But while nature is financialized, the aesthetics of nature play an important role in the financialization of architecture. Constructed perimeters of green, podium rooftops with arrays of shrubs, and vertical walls functioning as the backdrops of planting terraces all provide an appearance of complexity that mitigates the simplification that architecture's heightened liquidity requires. Perhaps when Boeri says that Bosco Verticale is first and foremost a home for trees, not humans, he unwittingly references a new type of financialized tree that helps provide liquidity to the architectural investments of the financialized human subject?

Boeri Studio, Bosco Verticale, Milan, Italy, 2014.

View Machines

Architecture that emphasizes the exterior view plays a heightened role in finance capitalism. The view is an asocial attribute that generates the powerful perception of local specificity while offering asset classification. Although a view is a sensory experience that requires emplacement in physical space, it tends to be relatively incorporeal. Unlike a collective social experience in real time and space, it is a singular sensory experience, stripped of touch, smell, sound, and the body in motion. It is constructed as a simplified and abstract experience on the verge of disembodiment, most often experienced in solitude. This absence of physicality is about as abstract a way as possible to engage with the particularities of context. Since a view is premised upon looking upon something that is proximate to but not exactly where one is, it is irreducibly relational but in a manner that relies on a single sense, and this singularity is its power. This incorporeality of the situated view makes it one of the most representable architectural qualities: "Look at this photograph: Apartment 3X has this exact view." It is almost impossible to capture an apartment's smells, light, or other ambient ingredients. It is equally challenging to represent its embeddedness in the community. Representations of the view, both photographic and digital, offer the sense that one does not have to physically inhabit the space to understand the experience of it. This allows the view to accelerate finance capitalism's drive toward incorporeal architecture and the commodification of architectural space as asset. Images that can easily be circulated and viewed may not offer the exact same depth as a publicly traded corporation's annual report, but they facilitate a similar standardization of information that is acquired without firsthand experience.

A foreground view renders certain qualities—things like individual human presence and particularities of flora—in sharp relief. A midground view can emphasize group social behavior or the detailed mixing of difference: plants, people, and buildings. Finance capitalism is not so interested in these views. It favors the long, epic, distant view—the sublime view. Of course, the inherent scarcity of this type of view from most residences associates it with privilege and power. But in many ways, finance capitalism proliferates the sublime view. The same way that "luxury" apartments seem to be everywhere, so do "views." City views, lake views, downtown views, ocean views, historic district views, river views, city lights views, park views—the offerings are abundant.

UNStudio, Southbank by Beulah, Melbourne, Australia, 2018 (proposed), rendering. Looking up at the terracing of the Green Spine.

Just as strategies to minimize maintenance and heighten security are influencing development patterns and form, so too does the inclination for views. Their provision has deep impact on physical forms, from the siting of buildings to their morphology. As Chicago-based architect Gordon Gill describes the logic for the design of Central Park Tower to *New York* magazine:

> Everyone wants a view of Central Park, but we had a big building [220 Central Park South] right in front of us. It's like being at the theater; if everyone's in rows trying to see the stage, nobody can see anything at all. The solution is to stagger the seats. When we moved the tower off-center to get better retail spaces, we discovered an opportunity to capture incredible direct and oblique views. That's why the building is stepped and staggered in every direction—north, south, east, and west—walking all the way up to 1,550 feet. If you look at this building from a distance, it has a strong ethos and a sense of stability. On the other hand, there's a lot of movement. The trick was managing all that activity without getting overly effusive.[19]

The Financial Good Life?

Finance capitalism traffics in a long-standing conception of the good life—recreation, nature, and views—and does so to make it easier to invest in architectural assets. When considered alongside finance capitalism's inherent emphasis on investment over production, an illusory promise comes into sight—one in which everyone is an investor, everything is an asset, and life is spent golfing, swimming, taking in a view, and periodically tending to an investment portfolio via a seamless mobile app. This investment playscape has echoes of the 1960s optimism of *homo ludens*, in which *ludens* (playing) is celebrated, as witnessed in projects like the Dutch artist Constant Nieuwenhuys's anti-capitalist city, New Babylon.[20] Of course, that era's collective radicalism is now entirely absent, leaving only an alienated pursuit of pleasure. "What does New Babylon signify at this moment, when reality seems to indicate that the imagined *homo ludens*, being part of a nonworking community, has not brought about a daily life of invention and action but of leisure and consumption?" asked the art historian Catherine de Zegher in 2001.[21] In the years since, finance capitalism has become much more pronounced; it is no longer only a question of leisure and consumption.

In 1900 sociologist Georg Simmel commented, "The fact that money is detached from all specific contents and exists only as a quantity earns for money and for those people who are only interested in money the quality of characterlessness."[22] The proliferation of investment heightens this quality of characterlessness. The absence of character is perhaps the height of the postsocial. In this absence, architecture is without the collective, and the new complexities are to be experienced alone.

WOHA, Sky Green, Taichung, Taiwan, 2019. Single-tree planters
cantilevering from condominium units.

CHAPTER SIX

RESIDENTIAL AVATARS AND LIFE SURROGATES

V ancouver House is a Bjarke Ingels–designed condominium tower in Vancouver that was ready for occupation in 2019. For every unit sold in the tower, a house is built and donated to an impoverished family. It is thus, through what its creators describe as "the world's first one-for-one real-estate gifting model," that the project's 388 condominium units, ranging from $225,000 lower-floor studios to $15 million penthouses upon initial offering, translate into a small armada of rudimentary homes in a Cambodian slum.[1] This philanthropic scheme forms part of Vancouver House's intensely wrought marketing accoutrements, sitting alongside such requisites of luxury as an on-demand fleet of BMWs and the Fairmont Hotels concierge service.

Like many of the world's magnet cities for international real estate investment, Vancouver experienced a period of sustained and dramatic real estate price escalation for much of the early twenty-first century, resulting in a major affordability crisis. In 2019, Vancouver was reported to have the fourth most expensive housing market in the world.[2] As the market is increasingly decoupled from the local economy, salaries are outstripped by soaring housing costs, and the majority of condominiums in central Vancouver are purchased by investors who rent them out, with a subset allowing their units to sit empty. The city has become a preferred destination for global capital pouring into real estate as a complement to stocks, bonds, and other more historically dominant assets.

Vancouver House is among a new crop of superprime towers that are exacerbating these conditions in their explicit campaigns to attract wealthy global investors. The tower was marketed globally through a range of tools and techniques, including multilanguage websites, billboards in cities such as Taipei, and physical sales centers in major cities across Asia.

Own a Living Sculpture

The marketing campaign and promotional website for Vancouver House were organized around a list, "20 Reasons to Own a Living Sculpture." The number one reason was the building's superprime status. Number twelve was the BMW fleet. Number sixteen was the home-gifting program. Number nineteen was ocean and mountain views. The word *sculpture* conveys the self-conscious formalism of the Ingels design. *Living*, of course, refers to the fact that this sculpture is actually a building composing a series of residential units. The primacy of the superprime rationale captures the double logic of the building as both a status property and an investment vehicle. But perhaps a living sculpture in the context of finance capitalism and the age of superprime is a dangerous oxymoron?

Nobody Has to Be Vile

In describing the various dimensions of postpolitical culture, the Slovenian philosopher Slavoj Žižek discusses the ways in which the social awareness and activism historically associated with the left have merged with the capitalist interests of the right. This mutation of previously opposing ideologies has generated new characters such as the "liberal communist," who "claim[s]...we can have the global capitalist cake (thrive as entrepreneurs) and eat it (endorse the anti-capitalist causes of social responsibility, ecological concern, etc.)."[3] In this synthesis of left and right, the liberal communist is a fervent philanthropist whose acts of charity provide cover and ethical comfort in the context of overwhelming exploitation. Žižek states:

Bjarke Ingels Group, Vancouver House, Vancouver, 2020.

According to liberal communist ethics, the ruthless pursuit of profit is counteracted by charity: charity is part of the game, a humanitarian mask hiding the underlying economic exploitation. Developed countries are constantly "helping" undeveloped ones (with aid, credits etc), and so avoiding the key issue: their complicity in and responsibility for the miserable situation of the Third World.[4]

Philanthropy plays an integral role in the postpolitical era. It is a vehicle by which one hand takes a lot while the other returns a little, affording the enviable ultra-luxury of feeling socially responsible and pursuing deeper meaning while propelling a system of overarching self-benefit. Within this schema, as Žižek says, "nobody has to be vile."[5]

At Vancouver House, buyers receive respite from feeling overly burdened with the effects of their speculative activities on the lower- and middle-income residents who are being priced out of the city. Even more anesthetic is their ethical insulation from the practices of wealth generation that enable their superprime real estate purchase in the first place. After all, buyers are donating a home to those in need. At Vancouver House, one witnesses liberal communists enacting postpolitics with every purchase. Vancouver House's one-for-one home-gifting scheme was inevitable. Why would the liberal communist ethical agenda not touch every transaction and every market segment? That it now operates within luxury real estate is no surprise, but what were less expected are the ways in which it propels emerging conceptions of occupancy and the role of architecture.

Philanthropy has a long history in capitalism, with many of the most renowned capitalists well known for their large donations. The steel magnate Andrew Carnegie donated the bulk of his enormous wealth and started the Carnegie Foundation. John D. Rockefeller gave away roughly $10 billion in today's dollars. This type of large-scale philanthropy continues, with the likes of Warren Buffet and Bill and Melinda Gates funneling vast sums into an array of global causes. Today, a list of the world's biggest philanthropists aligns fairly closely with the world's wealthiest billionaires. Philanthropy is strongest in the United States; in countries with more robust government social support systems it tends to play a smaller role. Nonetheless, as capitalism has intensified globally, so has the scope and scale of philanthropy, offering apparently heightened ethical opportunities at the moment of transaction. Everyday

Sid Landolt (left) and Peter Dupuis (right), pictured in 2015, showing off a model of the typical housing unit built in Cambodia as part of their one-for-one home-gifting program with Vancouver House.

Inside a housing project completed by World Housing, as seen in 2017, in Phnom Penh, Cambodia.

Shown in 2017, housing built by World Housing in Phnom Penh, Cambodia.

examples include the chance to purchase carbon offset when buying a plane ticket and the AmazonSmile web platform's donation of 0.5 percent of an item's purchase price to a charitable organization. At some locations of the US-based supermarket Whole Foods (an Amazon subsidiary), customers are given a philanthropic opportunity at checkout if they bring their own bags: "Would you like to donate your bag savings to charity or have the refund?" Some of the donated money goes to social housing.

"One-for-One" and Spatial Philanthropy

Southern California–based TOMS started selling shoes in 2006. For every pair sold, the company promised to donate one pair to an impoverished child. In 2018, its website declared, "TOMS has given away 86 million pairs of new shoes to children in need. One for one."[6] This charity is a key component of the company's brand identity and has been vital to its success. TOMS has even trademarked the phrase *one for one*. In 2014, Bain Capital, one of the world's largest private equity firms, acquired 50 percent stake in TOMS, cementing high finance's support of the model.

Vancouver House's one-for-one model is directly modeled on TOMS. After a chance meeting with Blake Mycoskie, the founder of TOMS, Peter Dupuis and Sid Landolt decided to apply TOMS's one-for-one model to luxury real estate. Vancouver House became the first project of their new company, World Housing. Each donated home that World Housing constructs costs between $4,000 and $6,000, a fraction of the sales price for a Vancouver House condominium. According to Dupuis, Vancouver House's one-for-one program was a large success, attracting investors while "[saving] our client a lot of money on marketing."[7] Some condo buyers even flew to Cambodia to meet the recipients of their charity and personally hand them the keys to their new homes.[8]

For all the commercial success of TOMS, its shoe-gifting program has experienced considerable criticism. In 2012 the company commissioned two separate academic groups to study the impact of its free shoes. These studies found that the shoes had no meaningful benefit and increased the likelihood of aid dependency over self-sufficiency.[9] A prominent 2015 article by the former human rights lawyer Amanda Taub in *Vox* declared:

TOMS and the many other companies like it are the charitable equivalents of yes men. They're telling you what they think you want to hear in order to get what they want (for you to purchase trendy, pricey accessories), not what you need to hear in order to do what you want (to have your purchase to do as much good in the world as it can).[10]

Seemingly in response to this criticism, TOMS revised their model for giving in 2019. Now, customers are offered a choice of causes and money is directed to nonprofits working on specific issues such as ending gun violence. But giving shoes remains as an option.

It is reasonable to extend this type of scrutiny to World Housing, given its use of TOMS's philanthropic model. It is likely that it has similar problems. But giving away free shoes is a far cry from giving away free homes. Since the latter is spatial and incorporates all the sociocultural attributes that a home entails, is there particular architectural or urban significance in the one-for-one spatial formula beyond a marketing gimmick? Žižek writes, "The ultimate liberal communist dream is to export the entire working class to invisible Third World sweat shops."[11]

In its own way, the Vancouver House formula accelerates this exportation. Unlike standard philanthropic practices, the spatial version of one-for-one gifting directly propels a geographic order of vast segregation. As superprime towers increase in Vancouver, the city empties of lower-income individuals just as spaces are made for a separate impoverished class on the other side of the globe. While Vancouver's working class is not migrating to Cambodia, the trajectory manifest in Vancouver House is not far off: the Vancouvers of the world are transformed into enclaves of seemingly frictionless capital in which no one visibly labors and only the edifices of the global investor class exist. All work and suffering hide in the slums. After all, the majority of what Karl Marx calls the industrial proletariat currently lives outside of the world's most developed countries.[12] As the promotional material for Vancouver House states, "The sense of citizenship for the residents…extends past the project's walls, even the borders of Canada."

In his 2006 book *Planet of Slums*, American historian Mike Davis argues that "rapid urban growth in the context of structural adjustment, currency devaluation, and state retrenchment has been the inevitable recipe for the mass production of slums."[13] The United Nations defines slum living conditions as existing in a household lacking one or more of the following: improved water, improved sanitation, sufficient living area, durable housing, and secure tenure.[14] According to its statistics for 2001, just under one billion people, 31.6 percent of the world's urban population, lived in slums.[15] While establishing accurate statistics on slum populations is next to impossible, the UN's first "global assessment of slums," which was issued in 2003, stated, "It is almost certain that slum dwellers increased substantially during the 1990s. It is further projected that in the next 30 years, the global number of slum dwellers will increase to about 2 billion, if no firm and concrete action is taken."[16] The 2010 revision to this report was more upbeat, maintaining that efforts to curtail slum growth were having positive results; while the absolute number of world slum dwellers had increased, as a percentage of urban population they had decreased.[17]

While the reasons for slum growth are manifold and complex, it is important to recognize that slum growth has occurred alongside finance capitalism's ascendancy. As Mike Davis notes, the UN report bluntly declares that the rise of the informal economy, which is intimately connected with the function of slums, is a direct result of liberalization.[18] From Davis's perspective, the forces that propel the construction of wealthy enclaves at various scales, from gated communities to entire city-states like Dubai, are those that also result in the large-scale proliferation of slums. From this vantage, the neoliberal policies of deregulation and privatization and the practices of finance capitalism, which propel the increasing inequality that Thomas Piketty describes, enable the wealthy to construct their speculative wealth-storage edifices while the poor are left behind. The superprime towers of New York and Vancouver are the flip side of the same coin as the slums of Nairobi and Mexico City.

Think of Vancouver House as a Giant Curtain

According to Bjarke Ingels, we should "think of Vancouver House as a giant curtain, at the moment of being pulled back to reveal the world to Vancouver and Vancouver to the world."[19] The magician Harry Houdini had a well-known trick, the Metamorphosis, that relied on a curtain to achieve its effect. Houdini's wife, Bess, would close a curtain around Houdini, who was tied up in a box. She would clap three times, and on the third clap, to the audience's shock, Houdini would open the curtain, revealing himself while showing that his wife had disappeared.

The box would then be opened to show her tied up inside. The more technical name of this illusion: the Substitution Trick. The illusionism of Vancouver House's ethical operation is similarly a substitution trick, by which small benevolence helps conceal large exploitation.

Does the tower's form play a role in this substitution? The curtain in Houdini's trick provides the necessary cover for substitution to occur. What cover does architectural form provide here? This top-heavy building transforms from a triangular plan at its base to a rectangular plan up top—a formal metamorphosis that increases the most expensive and profitable floor area at its apex. While enhancing profitability, the sculptural dynamism masks an absence of lived vitality. If its usage follows existing patterns, its upper units will be owned but will sit empty for much of the time, while the form itself minimizes the more modestly priced units that are most likely to be regularly inhabited. It is a dead space masquerading as dynamic—a kind of animated zombie.

The slum homes built by World Housing are occupied, and Vancouver House will probably be significantly vacant (owned but underoccupied), lending a perverse dimension to the one-for-one gifting model's dream of exporting poverty and the working class to invisible locations—it expands this export to include the act of bodily domesticity itself. The exportation of the working class alone is just one aspect of the dream; Vancouver House demonstrates that the full scope includes a long-standing notion of use value in architecture, namely, that it provides shelter. From this vantage, shelter is for the poor, and a dwelling for actual regular bodily inhabitation is a working-class anachronism. Merging the words *living* and *sculpture* underscores this aspect of the substitution trick. What is supposedly conceived as art—a banal sculpture—offers the guise of living to a silent investment tool. Investing happens in Vancouver, while real living happens far away, in a Cambodian slum.

As Mike Davis writes, since "1980…economic informality has returned with a vengeance, and the equation of urban and occupational marginality has become irrefutable and overwhelming."[20] He conceptualizes the resulting marginalized population as "surplus humanity." While Vancouver House seemingly helps this surplus humanity, it in effect maintains it as a reservoir of ethical fuel for the superrich to draw upon to fortify their moral sense of self while continuing to propagate the systems that support their own existence and expansion. The building's dynamic and illusory physical form works in concert with this reservoir of surplus humanity by producing its own version of "living." Each does its own substitution trick—replacing living with something else. Here it is tempting to recall Marx: "Capital is dead labour which, vampire-like, lives only by sucking living labour, and lives the more, the more labour it sucks."[21]

Secrets and Intermediaries

The investor class that purchases properties like the more expensive units in Vancouver House often practices tactics intended to cloak their actions in secrecy—using shell companies and chains of intermediaries to conceal their identities and generally obfuscate.[22] Purchasing real estate through a corporation, trust, or limited partnership is a convenient and well-used tactic to conceal the identity of ownership. The limited liability company (LLC), for example, is widely used as a shell company for expensive real estate purchases in the United States.[23] The shell company sits alongside intermediary networks that liberate the superrich from the entanglements of owning real estate; these intermediaries include commercial agents such as consultants, lawyers, fund managers, credit raters, and auditors.[24] "Converting simple property rights (which are unavoidably political and normative in nature) into lengthy chains of subsidiarity is a means of avoiding public accountability in general and escaping taxation in particular," writes the English sociologist and political economist William Davies in his exploration of the role of intermediaries in urban real estate.[25] These insulating strategies are an extreme manifestation of the general drive of finance capitalist architecture to extricate itself from engagements with local specificity. They are postsocial simplification in the extreme.

In using intermediaries, wealthy investors "seek a form of representation which absolves them of the need to become involved in matters of public concern or controversy. Rather than a democratic representation, which seeks the power of voice, it is a form of delegation which secures the power of exit," writes Davies.[26] Not only are superprime condominium towers scarcely inhabited in a literal sense, but this absence extends to ownership itself. The superprime condo tower thus generates multiple paradoxes of being present while being absent. It is owned but empty, a trophy that is held anonymously. Intermediaries fulfill an almost shamanic role of facilitating *exit*—a multidirectional exit that allows for a wholly new financial capitalist dynamism based in architecture and urbanism, what might be called avatar architecture. In this condition the superrich can jump in and out of architectures they never fully inhabit. The shell companies and intermediaries of superprime real estate are a form of postpolitics. After all, "politics" means "affairs of the cities," and it is in architectural and urban space that postpolitics finds one of its most potent formations.

Philanthropic Urbanism

Interestingly, the one-for-one house-gifting program is perhaps a perverse outgrowth of the kind of urban development policies that Vancouver pioneered in the late 1990s and that now can be found in many luxury avatar supercities around the world. A host of spatio-financial exchanges—all aimed at leveraging community benefits from private development—have become embedded in development in Vancouver. Development cost levies (DCLs), started in 1992, are a flat per-square-foot fee that applies to all development in the city. Community amenity contributions (CACs) started in 1999 and apply only to development involving rezoning. Both take capital, either in cash or in kind, from developers and apply it to community amenities such as libraries, childcare facilities, and public art. From 2010 to 2017, the biggest allocations from CACs went toward affordable housing.[27] The result is a dense spatio-financial web connecting donor and recipient sites in the city; a mid-rise building here supports a new park over there. Sometimes the contributions fund an amenity (like a public art gallery at the base of condo tower) directly within the donor development site, other times something specific on the other side of town; in many instances, cash is pooled from many contributing developments and used at a later date.

A new condo tower named 8X on the Park, marketed as "the new benchmark for luxury living in Vancouver," contributed $20 million to a social housing project across the street.[28] But the relationship between donor and recipient in a scenario like this is often discreet and not overtly advertised. Indeed, in most DCL and CAC scenarios, it is difficult to trace the relationships between donor and recipient projects unless they are components of the same site. Nevertheless, it can be argued that the process works toward an effective privatization of social housing in a schema of apparently ethical capitalism in which developers

Rodney Graham, *Spinning Chandelier*, Vancouver, 2019. This 14-by-21-foot (4.25-by-6.4-meter) re-creation of an eighteenth-century chandelier hangs from the Granville Street Bridge adjacent to Vancouver House.

are guaranteed requisite profits and city governance achieves its aspirations through ongoing condominium development.[29]

While investors in individual condominium units at Vancouver House are provided moral insulation through the one-for-one gifting program in a manner that does not disrupt and arguably increases the gap between wealthier and lower-income nations, the internal urban philanthropy of cities like Vancouver can also be understood to accelerate these dynamics. The amenities that increase Vancouver's perceived livability (like public art, daycare centers, and park space) also increase its ranking on livability indexes, generating the city's prestige as a magnet site for international capital. Somewhat paradoxically, this international capital propels the escalating real estate prices that compromise many people's ability to afford living in the city at all. Developer Westbank bundled its development contributions for public art from Vancouver House and three other buildings to pay for a $3.5 million sculpture that hangs under a bridge directly adjacent the tower. Created by Rodney Graham, *Spinning Chandelier* is a more-than-7,000-pound (3,200-kilogram) enlarged replica of a French chandelier. Twice a day it lights up, descends, and spins in an urban spectacle. Needless to say, it has become a source of controversy in a city beset with housing affordability challenges and homelessness—an aesthetic trope of luxury transforming the immediate environs of a self-consciously superprime tower, delivered through governmental mechanisms that are supposedly intended for broad community benefit. The in-city philanthropy of Vancouver often transforms the urban experience to conform to the standards of global investment capital, creating a safe, green, livable, and ultimately anodyne spectacle. At Vancouver House it is so brazen, it veers into parody. Vancouver House contributes to the safe amenities at its doorstep but consigns its less luxurious contributions to the other side of the globe.

Avatars and Surrogates

Vancouver House's one-for-one gifting program is a disheartening development at the frontiers of the ethical compromises that contemporary capital encourages. At the same time, a sober assessment of the architecture of neoliberal excess and finance capitalism renders a stranger-than-fiction reality in which mass overbuilding is normalized, growth and decay are collapsed upon each other, owned vacancy is widespread, and market volatility destabilizes communities. From this surreal vantage, everything begins to appear as fiction. Maybe the most important category of fiction today is what has be called financial fiction: fi-fi. In the financial fictions that form our reality, it is not only that Vancouver House's Houdini-like illusion (a lie) is a problem, it is also that it furthers a dystopian fiction: a small collection of richly constructed but sparsely inhabited superprime avatar cities existing in tandem with a larger and distant group of surrogate, bodily slum cities. Buildings such as Vancouver House are akin to avatars—figures or icons—that possess the possibility of animation on the part of wealthy investors. Shamanic intermediaries are hired to maintain a network of avatar structures in which secretive "animations" periodically occur. While these avatars sit in suspended animation, in the "most deserving areas," surrogates do the real living. Places like Vancouver, Manhattan, and Melbourne glitter in contrast to Kibera, Nairobi or Dharavi, Mumbai. Surplus humanity remains all too human, while the superrich perform spatial rituals in the quest to overcome both space and time.

CHAPTER SEVEN

CONSTANT OBJECT

The underoccupied, ultra-thin condominium tower is the apotheosis of finance capitalist architecture, and no project so perfectly embodies this phenomenon as New York City–based architect Rafael Viñoly's 432 Park Avenue in Midtown Manhattan. With its epic proportions and rigorous use of the square and grid, 432 Park Avenue can be understood as a transhumanist totem. The building marks the emergence of a new form of monumentality that is devoted to a spirituality inherent in finance capitalism.

432 Park Avenue

432 Park Avenue is a 93 ½-by-93 ½-foot (28 ½-by-28 ½-meter) square in plan. Rising eighty-five stories to a 1,396-foot (426-meter) roof height, it has a 1:15 slenderness ratio. It is ultra-thin. And it is remarkably pure. It is common for tall buildings to meet the ground in a particular way—often through a podium, a widened base, or a change in material. Similarly, towers often meet the sky in unique ways—they taper, point, or wear a hat. 432 Park Avenue appears to do none of these things.[1] It is a pure extrusion of its perfect square footprint, unchanging through eighty-five floors. It meets the ground in exactly the same way it meets

Rafael Viñoly Architects, 432 Park Avenue, New York City, 2015.

the sky. The building's form seems completely disinterested in where exactly it starts and stops; it could be flipped upside down or it could continue forever—nothing would change. And the building's four sides amplify this basic formal characteristic by being exactly identical: a grid of immense, 110-square-foot (10-square-meter), square-shaped windows. The only semblance of differentiation is that the extrusion is subtly divided into seven vertical segments, separated by recessed spaces that expose the building core behind the continuous concrete grid. The bottom segment contains amenities for condominium owners, such as staff accommodations, conference facilities, a swimming pool, and wine cellars, while the upper six segments are devoted to condominium units. This programmatic distinction is impossible to discern from the exterior.

The building has 104 units that range from a 350-square-foot (33-square-meter) studio to full-floor apartments just over 8,000 square feet (740 square meters). According to CityRealty, a New York real estate website that tracks sales data, the average cost of units sold in 432 Park is more than $5,500/square foot ($59,200/square meter).[2] The total value of all closed sales in the building exceeds $2 billion. Because of the opacity of real estate ownership generally and the secrecy of superprime buildings specifically, it is difficult to acquire accurate data on occupancy. But by all reports, 432 Park is largely empty most of the time.[3]

A Brief History of Towers and Inhabitation

While the vacancy rates of slender condominium towers in certain housing markets appear unprecedented, it is useful to recall that, in premodern times, towers were almost never conceived as shelter. While early towers did accommodate some bodily inhabitation, they were not intended for human occupation in any meaningful sense. They were designed instead to fulfill functions that required, at most, short-term and intermittent occupancy or to satisfy human needs that were simply incorporeal. For example, current archaeological theories suggest that the Tower of Jericho, sometimes referred to as the world's first skyscraper, was built not as a defensive watchtower, as long believed, but rather as a vertical symbol of power and a celestial marker that connected "the early Neolithic inhabitants of Jericho to their immediate landscape and the cosmos."[4] The ninth-century Towers of Silence, built in Persia by the Zoroastrians to elevate corpses for excarnation, function as the

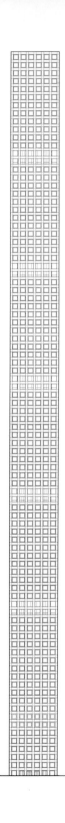

Rafael Viñoly Architects,
432 Park Avenue,
elevation drawing.

interface between bodily existence and immaterial afterlife. The purpose of Irish Round Towers is debated, with theories ranging from watchtowers to bell towers to royal chapels. Medieval Bologna is thought to have had more than one hundred towers, some reaching up to 200 feet (60 meters), which may have simultaneously defended the families that built them and indicated their owners' social prestige. As these examples illustrate, the tower's premodern history is dominated by two entwined operations: the representation and protection of wealth on one hand and spiritual mediation on the other.

It was not until the full entrenchment of industrial capitalism that the occupied shelter tower spread from its nineteenth-century origins in Chicago and New York to dominate much of global urbanization. As a distinctly capitalist operation, whereby the ground is replicated for exponential profit, the occupied tower took on new forms and roles. That many early American towers assumed a language drawn from Gothic cathedrals reinforces the implicit spirituality of these capitalist devices, echoing the role of the earliest towers as mediators between material and immaterial worlds. The neo-Gothic Woolworth Building, the world's tallest building for seventeen years after its completion in 1912, was called the Cathedral of Commerce. These command and control centers of industrialism normalized the use of vertical structures for accommodating vast numbers of people. And what began as an extruded shelter primarily for the corporate workplace eventually came to shelter domestic life as well.

The era of deregulation, privatization, and market liberalization that arose in the 1980s saw finance capitalism overtake industrial capitalism as the West's primary economic mode, displacing the human body and physical habitation as the central and unquestioned concerns of architecture. If it is possible to say that industrial capitalism witnessed the rise of the occupied tower, then finance capitalism has engendered a return to the nonsheltering, unoccupied tower. But while early towers were purposefully intended for sparse or intermittent occupation, the new unoccupied towers of finance capitalism masquerade as housing. This posthousing form of housing can be seen not only as an outgrowth of finance capitalism but also as indicating a shift toward a disembodied state of capitalism—toward what could be called spiritual capitalism.

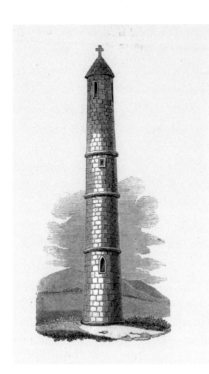

LEFT Illustration of an Irish Round Tower in Ardmore, Ireland, from Henry O'Brien, *The Round Towers of Ireland: Or, The History of the Tuath-de-danaans*, 1898.

MIDDLE Speculative depiction of Zoroastrian Towers of Silence, from Edward Ives, *A Voyage from England to India*, 1773.

BOTTOM Toni Pecoraro, speculative depiction of medieval Bologna, etching, 2012.

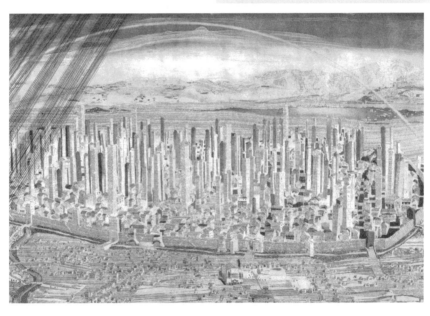

Contemporary Capitalism and Disembodiment

The FIRE economy, with its interconnected market sectors of finance, insurance, and real estate, occupies a central position in contemporary capitalism, rivaled only by the technology industry. Differences notwithstanding, what these dominant market domains share is a telling barometer of the ideology of contemporary capital; both offer parallel trajectories toward disembodiment in the service of capital accumulation.

Silicon Valley's dematerialized worldview is best understood through its advocacy of transhumanism—a movement to transform the human condition through technologies that radically enhance human capabilities. The British-born philosopher and futurist Max More provided in 1990 the first-known definition of "transhumanism" in the contemporary sense:[5]

> Transhumanism differs from humanism in recognizing and
> anticipating the radical alterations in the nature and possibility
> of our lives resulting from various sciences and technologies
> such as neuroscience and neuropharmacology, life extension,
> nanotechnology, artificial ultraintelligence, and space habitation,
> combined with a rational philosophy and value system.[6]

While transhumanism shares similarities with posthumanism, the two diverge significantly. Posthumanism incorporates a range of positions but tends to emphasize a critical assessment of humanism and associated notions of humanity, human nature, and the human condition. The New York–based philosopher Francesca Ferrando writes, "While posthumanism comes out of postmodernism, transhumanism seeks its origins in science and technology, especially early ideas about human evolution....It suggests that diversity and multiplicity will replace the notion of existing within a single system, such as a biological body."[7]

These ideas currently enjoy mainstream prominence, propagated by people at the center of corporate power. Summoning a variety of once-peripheral science-fiction fantasies, the leaders of some of the world's largest tech corporations—including Elon Musk, CEO of Tesla and SpaceX, and Ray Kurzweil, Google's director of engineering—herald the imminent metamorphosis of the human species. Kurzweil promises the real possibility of immortality arising from the synthesis of human and machine: "We're going to be able to overcome disease and

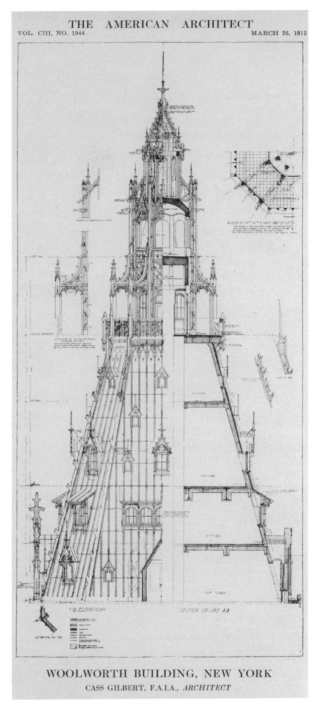

WOOLWORTH BUILDING, NEW YORK

CASS GILBERT, F.A.I.A., *ARCHITECT*

Cass Gilbert, Woolworth Building, New York City, 1912, half-elevation and section of spire, from *The American Architect*, 1913.

aging. Most of our thinking will be nonbiological....And we will be able to extend our lives indefinitely."[8]

According to transhumanists, ultra-high-powered nanotechnology, once it has been inevitably integrated into the body, might allow humans to sprint for fifteen minutes without taking a breath, remain underwater for hours, or sleep outside unprotected in a blizzard. But such transformations are small steps toward the major leap of leaving the body entirely, becoming pure electromagnetic energy. In this vision, humans will alter their biological systems and ultimately move beyond them, changing the human relationship with the environment dramatically. Liberated from the limited range of temperature, humidity, and oxygen in which humans can find comfort, let alone survive, what remains of the need for shelter? How would architecture operate within this context?

A phase shift in which humanity achieves a postmaterial, postcorporeal state of pure electromagnetic energy — called the singularity by transhumanists — is ultimately a spiritual vision. Tellingly, Max More's defining text from 1990 was largely concerned with questions of religion, as he proposed transhumanism as a replacement for theism. He wrote, "God was an oppressive concept, a more powerful being than we, but made in the image of our crude self-conceptions. Our own process of endless expansion into higher forms should and will replace this religious idea."[9] The spiritual and religious aspects of transhumanism continue unabated; one of Kurzweil's books exploring the singularity is titled *The Age of Spiritual Machines*.

The science fiction author Vernor Vinge influenced the form of transhumanism popular in the technology industry. Vinge wrote that "immortality would be achievable"; the American religious and cultural critic Mark C. Taylor notes:

> With this comment, it becomes clear that, for many influential people, the vision shaping our technological future is in important ways religious. What appears to be a radically new understanding of what once was called human being is really the latest version of the ancient quest to escape time by fleeing decaying bodies and a confining world and gaining immortality in a transcendent otherworldly realm that is not plagued by the pain, suffering, and boredom of life on earth. Mathematical formulas and algorithms become the new gnosis that promises liftoff.[10]

This religiosity sits squarely within the logical nebulae of contemporary capitalism. "Transhumanism is a philosophy that is well suited to Silicon Valley's neoliberalism," says the Italian philosopher Giorgio Griziotti regarding his work on the emergence of new forms of technologically driven capitalism." And Taylor continues, "It is no accident that the most enthusiastic supporters of the singularity are the tech billionaires whose financial assets are as virtual as the realities in which they traffic."[12] The fact that corporate leviathans such as Google are actively pursuing this future makes the stakes clear. After all, which entities will produce and maintain the technology and power the electromagnetic continuum through which this new technospiritual domain operates? It is not hard to envision a fee-based spiritual domain, generating vast profit for corporate shareholders.

Capitalism and Spirituality

Many have argued that capitalism has always been at least somewhat spiritual. Adam Smith, the eighteenth-century political economist and philosopher who is sometimes called the father of capitalism, used the metaphor of the "invisible hand" to describe the unseen forces of the free market. The phrase conveys a spiritual impetus in Smith's writing that has generated interpretations that vary from secular to theological. One of Smith's most important interpreters, the early twentieth-century Chicago School economist Jacob Viner, argued that it is impossible to understand Smith's *The Wealth of Nations* outside the context of his earlier book *The Theory of Moral Sentiments*, where he developed a system of ethics premised upon a harmonious state of affairs guided by God. Viner points out that Smith posited that laissez-faire capitalism works to the benefit of humankind because of a beneficent force that Smith variously terms "the great Director of Nature," "the final cause," "the Author of Nature," "the great judge of hearts," "an invisible hand," "Providence," "the divine Being," and, in rare instances, "God."[13]

Others have examined, beyond the role of divinity in this primary capitalist text, metaphysical and spiritual aspects of capitalism. Georg Simmel, in *The Philosophy of Money*, explored the metaphysics of money:

> The unearned increment of the ownership of money is nothing but
> a single instance of what one might call the metaphysical quality of
> money; namely, to extend beyond every particular use and, since it is

the ultimate means, to realize the possibility of all values as the value of all possibilities.[14]

The German sociologist Max Weber famously argued that Protestantism influenced the development of capitalism.[15] Walter Benjamin, the German philosopher, wrote a short text titled "Capitalism as Religion" that states, "Capitalism is a pure religious cult, perhaps the most extreme there ever was. Within it everything only has meaning in direct relation to the cult: it knows no special dogma, no theology."[16] The Italian philosopher Giorgio Agamben builds on Benjamin in an essay of the same title in which he explores the possibility of capitalism as a religion in which credit/debt is a faith-based system that is substituted for God, enabling the purest form of credit, which is money, to function as God.[17]

Mark C. Taylor has written extensively on the religious dimensions of capitalism, touching on everything from the first paper money, invented in China to be used in ritual sacrifices, to the adoption of the dollar sign ($) from a Christian numismatic sign, to the "bull" market's reference to sacrificial animals.[18] While demonstrating that capitalism has possessed a religious aspect from its inception, Taylor argues that the advent of finance capitalism marks the transition of capitalism to a dominant global mode of religious activity. For Taylor, since the end of the gold standard, after which money became speculative and free-floating and has been electronically traded, finance has displaced art as a dominant mode of spiritual communion.[19] He writes, "In the late twentieth century, something approximating the Hegelian Absolute appears in global networks of exchange where money is virtually immaterial. When read through [G. W. F.] Hegel's logical analysis of Spirit, it becomes clear that money is God in more than a trivial sense."[20]

The capitalist utopian spirituality manifest in transhumanism's popularity foretells a radical form of emptiness: the vacant body. What if the architecture of finance capitalism is unwittingly preparing for a disembodied future by building the vacant city now? What if the financialization of architecture—its role as a pure financial instrument that is left unoccupied—is an early foray into a disembodied transhumanism in which physical shelter is anachronistic? Not only has money become immaterial, but those beings so devoted to its godlike role are becoming less material themselves and in turn are changing architecture.

The Downtown Athletic Club and the Corporeal Tower

In examining spiritual capitalism and its vacancies, it is useful to revisit an icon of corporeal occupancy that can be understood in relation to capitalism before the current ascent of finance. In Rem Koolhaas's 1978 recounting in *Delirious New York*, the Downtown Athletic Club in Lower Manhattan's financial district was a stacked machine for the perfection of bachelors' bodies. Opened in 1930, this body machine was the perfect tower for the era's industrial capitalism. When goods are produced and sold, there is an insistence on material production that ontologically extends to the physical body. "Eating oysters with boxing gloves, naked, on the *n*th floor" is Koolhaas's social conclusion of the vertical stacking of bodies. For Koolhaas, the Downtown Athletic Club, this bodily "incubator," is "at once spiritual and carnal."[21] The tower as a machine for bodily modification also propels a parallel proto-spirituality in the form of the cult of bachelorhood. As Koolhaas writes, "The only price [Downtown Athletic Club] graduates have to pay for their collective narcissism is that of sterility. The self-induced mutations are not reproducible in future generations. The bewitchment of the Metropolis stops at the genes; they remain the final stronghold of Nature."[22]

432 Park as the Apotheosis of Finance

Just as the Downtown Athletic Club is an ideal tower for industrial capitalism, 432 Park Avenue is the perfect tower for finance capitalism. Koolhaas argues that the skyscraper was the rare invention that was perfect at the moment of its inception, and that, as it marched toward the present, it steadily degenerated, losing its programmatic heterogeneity and therefore its potential as a social condenser.[23] The evacuation enacted in 432 Park Avenue and other investment condominiums only accelerates this trajectory toward an extreme endpoint.

With social and bodily performance devitalized, 432 Park Avenue functions as a machine at the interface between material and immaterial forces. From this conceptual vantage, its formal and aesthetic character is particularly significant. The structure's relentless repetition of the square, from its plan shape to the grid of its elevations, allows it to achieve a monolithic abstraction unrivaled by recent towers. Viñoly said he wanted the building to "read like a constant object."[24] By *constant*, he seems to mean an unchanging formal totality, a complete isotropic homogeneity—an object devoid of differentiation. But *constant*

Rafael Viñoly Architects, 432 Park Avenue, New York City.

also suggests an object that is in every place and in every time. In other words, the word evokes a double transcendence: omnipresent purity. The Downtown Athletic Club's proto-spirituality is thus replaced with outright spirituality.

Religious buildings and monuments, such as temples and churches, are at the core of architectural history. What is unique now is that finance capitalism is the faith that more and more buildings operate within. Reinhold Martin has written that architecture now "complements and even reproduces the rush of religious fervor generated by—and generating—worldwide financialization."[25] And he has asked, "What does it mean to understand the relationship between architecture and capital as, at least in part, a *religious* one?"[26] The answer resides in how buildings like 432 Park Avenue are at once simplified, abstracted, and made incorporeal. Like the Zoroastrian Towers of Silence or the monolith in Stanley Kubrick's *2001: A Space Odyssey*, 432 Park Avenue is a totemic object—all spirituality and no carnality—teetering between

LEFT Rafael Viñoly Architects, 432 Park Avenue, concept sketch by Rafael Viñoly.

BELOW Aldo Rossi, San Cataldo Cemetery, Modena, Italy, 1984, study.

different worlds and different times as an avatar of capitalism's spiritual drive to move us all into deadened worlds of perpetual profit without even the pleasure of our bodies.[27]

Aldo Rossi and the Ossuary at San Cataldo Cemetery

By the late 1990s, Fredric Jameson had sensed that a defining formal characteristic of finance capitalism was "extreme isometric space." Although derived from the modernist free plan, "modernism to the second power no longer looks like modernism at all, but some other space altogether," Jameson wrote.[28] The supremely monumental isometry of 432 Park has antecedents that precede this "modernism to the second power." The modern capitalist office tower offers an almost endless repertoire of isometric forms, and much of that particular isometry is found in curtain walls (often glass and sometimes mirrored). Jameson identified these walls and the building forms they wrapped as a second key characteristic of finance capitalist architecture in the 1980s: the "enclosed skin volume."[29]

The load-bearing concrete grid of 432 Park's elevations is more solid than the enclosed skin volumes described by Jameson, and reminiscent of a more rigid and elemental architecture. The most celebrated practitioner of this rigidity was Italian architect Aldo Rossi, whose approach was formed within the vibrant leftist intellectualism particular to 1960s Italy.[30] Joining the Italian Communist Party in 1956, he was influenced by the politics of the party and debates on how to construct an alternative to the capitalist city.[31] Rossi's answer was a simple, rationalist, autonomous architecture that challenged "the open-ended space of the capitalist city-territory."[32]

In light of 432 Park's stark monumentality, concrete solidity, grid of punched window openings, and relative unoccupancy, it is tempting to think of the project in aesthetic, formal, and functional relation to Rossi's ossuary building at the San Cataldo Cemetery in Modena, Italy. Construction at San Cataldo started in 1978, in the context of neoliberalism's debut on the world stage and the early stirrings of finance capitalism's current ascent.[33]

Rossi placed an ossuary building in a prominent focal point on the cemetery's central axis.[34] Square in plan with four identical facades, the structure is close to a perfect cube. Its elevations are defined by a grid of equidistant square openings. These attributes offer an isotropic homogeneity similar to 432 Park Avenue. But while 432 Park can be described as

Aldo Rossi, the ossuary cube at San Cataldo Cemetery, Modena, Italy, 1984.

a largely unoccupied space voided of use, the ossuary is a space literally voided: its exterior mass encloses an empty interior that is open to the sky. The bones of the dead are stored in niches within the four exterior walls. The ossuary cube thus offers two starkly contrasting experiences, presenting a solid heavy mass of the exterior only to reveal a complete void of the interior.

Rossi's views on architecture are illuminated by his interest in the French architect Étienne-Louis Boullée. In Rossi's introduction to Boullée's "Architecture, Essay on Art," he quotes Boullée: "Temple of Death! Your aspect should freeze our hearts."[35] This comment summarizes Boullée's attitude toward architectural character in general. It signifies the importance that memorials and monuments hold for architecture as its elemental type. Rossi referred to the San Cataldo cemetery as a city for the dead, and, as the American architectural historian Eugene J. Johnson has written, the basic architectural type for the entire project is housing. And Rossi described the ossuary cube as "an abandoned or incomplete house, with empty windows, unroofed." This residential form and character fulfill the ultimate purpose of the cemetery, which Johnson calls "an arena of time, of death, and of regeneration."[36] The empty housing project, by being both housing and not housing, serves as a monument at the interface between corporeal and incorporeal worlds. The formal similarities between the ossuary cube, with its overt and necessary spirituality, and 432 Park, with its ostensible secularism, serve to underscore the spiritual aspects of both. But whereas Rossi sought to make his cemetery like a city, contemporary capital appears intent on making the city like a cemetery.

The Spanish architect Rafael Moneo writes of the ossuary:

> One enters through the ambiguous double access to find a house stripped of all the elements that once made it inhabitable: a desolate, roofless cube.…But the house doesn't hide the path. The path stretches between gaps that speak of the infinitude of eternity, of the loss of the value of time that death implies.[37]

That Rossi's ossuary cube is designed as an abandoned apartment building underscores a significant ideological difference between today's spiritual capitalism and its precursors. For Rossi, the exterior that signifies housing is appropriate to his purposes because there is no possibility of

Adolf Loos, Max Dvořák mausoleum, Vienna, 1921, photograph of model.

reincarnate living; the dead are not returning to life to make use of kitchens or living rooms. 432 Park, on the other hand, maintains its interior
in full; it can be occupied on demand. This suggests the contrasting radical utopianism of the nexus between finance capitalism and transhumanism. 432 Park is a monument to life that never ends. It is outside of
time because it transcends death. Nothing could be more different from
Rossi's cemetery.

The influential early modernist Austrian architect Adolf Loos was
deeply important to Rossi—his impact "ever present" in Rossi's work.[38]
Loos wrote in his 1910 essay "Architecture," "Only a very small part of
architecture belongs to the realm of art: the tomb and the monument.
Everything else that fulfils a function is to be excluded from the domain
of art."[39] Perhaps somewhat surprisingly, the building of the unoccupied
city that finance capitalism and transhumanism inch toward amounts to
a new deployment of Loos's position. "Function" equates with corporeal
occupation, and the incorporeal practices of investment surely amount
to its absence. Thus, as investment logics eclipse those of shelter, it might
be possible to say that buildings move toward Loos's true realm of art,
which paradoxically approximates an essence of architecture for Loos:

When we come across a mound in the woods, six feet long by three feet wide, raised to a pyramidal form by means of a spade, we become serious and something in us says: somebody lies buried there. *This is architecture*.[40]

Is it possible then that industrial capitalism and its modernities, in which "form follows function," were an aberration from the modalities of the tomb, the monument, and the burial mound—just as the occupied towers of industrial capitalism might be aberrations from the long-standing incorporeality of the tower type?

A Tomb for the Immortal

The Downtown Athletic Club is architecture as program—an architecture premised entirely on physical human occupancy. The intensity of its function as a social condenser makes it something close to an antimonument. In the early twenty-first century, the tomb and the monument have returned. As finance capitalism displaces (not replaces) the role of physical human occupation in architecture, the role of the monument increases. 432 Park Avenue's reformulation of the San Cataldo ossuary illuminates the emergent role of architecture in the era of finance capitalism and this new significance of the monument. Built at the turning point between industrial and finance capitalism, San Cataldo is a humanist tomb; the remains of the dead occupy the architecture, which conceptually relies on the finitude of human existence. 432 Park is, by contrast, a tomb for humans who do not want to "stay within the limitations of our biology," as Google's Kurzweil puts it.[41] 432 Park is therefore a tomb for the immortal—or a cemetery for the living. Where the ossuary is premised upon the value of time that death implies, 432 Park, in being *constant*, is a monument that seeks to transcend the limitations of time and place. The reformulation of attributes of Rossi's leftist architecture into that of finance capitalism also demonstrates capitalism's seemingly unending capacity to absorb challenges into its own means of reproduction. It is also a reminder to recall what Rossi himself wrote: "There are no buildings of opposition because the architecture that is going to be realized is always an expression of the dominant class."[42]

One of the more memorable marketing images of 432 Park is a digital rendering of a luxurious bathtub looking south over Manhattan from one of the building's ten-by-ten-foot (three-by-three-meter) windows.

The Chrysler Building, the Empire State Building, and One World Trade Center (the Freedom Tower) are all visible. Given the incorporeality of 432 Park and its spiritual role, it is no coincidence that the project's imagery both foregrounds and negates the body. The sumptuously empty bathtub, promising the luxury of being naked in the center of the city, is a twenty-first-century sarcophagus for the absent body of finance.

Rafael Viñoly Architects, 432 Park Avenue, New York City, 2015, rendering. Interior view of a bathtub adjacent to one of the building's 10-by-10-foot (3-by-3-meter) windows.

CHAPTER EIGHT

FROM SCI-FI TO FI-FI

F
inance capitalism forces a reconsideration of buildings not only as shelters but also as physical entities. While the practice of architecture and its irreducible necessity of representation has always foregrounded the relationship between representation and actuality, the technologies and practices of investment are exerting novel pressure on this relationship.

The increased role of presales (the marketing and selling of housing units before a building has been completed) is indicative of these new forces. Physical solidity has long been one of architecture's defining attributes, but the advent of digital representation and mass computing has challenged this definition for decades, and the potential of augmented and virtual realities has only further destabilized it. The investment practices around presales demonstrate that there is already a vibrant market for what can be called virtual architectural assets. As the current era of finance capitalism has arisen, an increasingly intermediated architecture has emerged in which the virtual and the real are tethered to each other in a new formation. Perhaps as finance capitalism accelerates, the extension and morphology of this tethering will further mutate, generating even more novel hybrids of the real and the virtual.

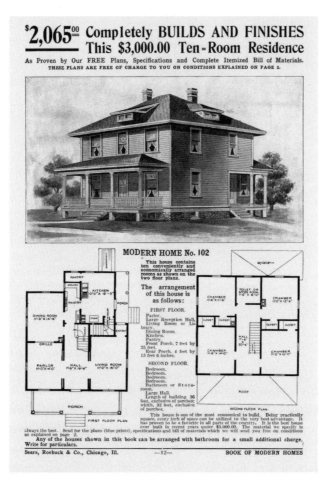

Sears, Roebuck & Co., the Hamilton, model home number 102,
Sears catalog, 1911.

Presales: Buying and Selling Buildings before They Exist

Presales can occur prior to construction or during construction. While
the specific character of contemporary presales is unique to finance capitalism, the practice of buying housing before construction is not unique
to the era of finance capitalism. Predecessors can be found in the nineteenth century and became widespread in the early twentieth. It is not
a stretch to describe the phenomenon of purchasing not yet physically
existing homes as a fundamental trait of modern capitalist housing markets. Sears, the American department store, sold more than seventy
thousand catalog homes between 1908 and 1940.[1] These homes, which

were purchased from plans and images in the company's mail-order catalog, played a key role in the transition of housing from home to consumer item. While these houses popularized a new buying, shipping, and construction method, they did not significantly initiate the transition of the house to an investment product.

Prior to World War II, it was uncommon to purchase buildings or parts of buildings without first directly experiencing them; the market for buildings had been predicated on their physical presence in the world. The suburbanization of the postwar United States began to change that, as large-scale housing projects, in a for-profit context, demanded the assurances that presales provided. William J. Levitt was the largest developer in the United States by 1950, and his eponymous suburban Levittown communities relied on presales. Prospective buyers could visit a model house that offered a full-scale simulation of their future home. As the American architectural historian Gwendolyn Wright reported, "When sales opened in March 1949 for the new homes to be constructed that year, the firm signed fourteen hundred contracts in one day on the basis of their reputation and one model house."[2] The model home or "show home" continues to be a vital ingredient of suburban tract housing across the United States.

The phenomenon of home buyers being asked to envision their future purchases has been encouraged by Western governments' active promotion of homeownership. (Renters tend to rely upon existing properties, and therefore simulation is a moot issue for them.) Homeownership in the United States increased from 46 to 65 percent between 1900 and 2020.[3] In England and Wales, it grew from 23 percent in 1918 to 64 percent in 2011.[4] In Australia, ownership grew from 53 percent in 1947 to 67 percent in 2016.[5] With more people buying housing, more people are pulled into the orbit of projections of architecture.

Presales have flourished alongside the popularity of condominiums. The first presales in the Chinese-speaking world appear to have occurred in the late 1960s with a condominium in Taiwan.[6] The method has since become especially popular in North America, Hong Kong, Singapore, Taiwan, and Mainland China.[7] In 2004, it was reported that "nearly all" residential projects in Hong Kong and Singapore were presold.[8] In numerous North American condominium markets, it is now standard practice for marketing and selling to commence years before construction.

More than one hundred people, some camping overnight for days, waited in line for presales of Montrose Square condominiums in Port Coquitlam, a suburb of Vancouver, 2017. The photographer of this image was paid $325 to wait in line for a real estate professional—a common practice in Metro Vancouver.

The presales buyer does not technically purchase a unit, but rather enters an agreement to purchase a particular dwelling for a specific price at a future date when it is complete. Legally, the presales contract is not a real estate transaction but rather the transaction of a financial instrument, meaning that it falls under regulations that are distinct from those for real estate. The closest comparison among existing financial instruments is a futures derivative, in which the buyer agrees to purchase a stock, for example, at a future date for a specified price. And just as there is a market for stock derivatives, there is a market for presales contracts; a presales contract might be bought and sold multiple times between initial purchase from the developer and the unit's completion.

Sales centers facilitate preselling by displaying representations of the building and its units. In cities with a lot of condominium construction, the sales center itself has become a prominent feature of the urban environment. Centers are organized around architectural representation: floor plans, renderings, a building model, sample finishes, and in some cases a typical unit interior at full scale, complete with simulated views. In markets with high demand, long lines form at sales centers at the premiere, with potential buyers eager to have first dibs. It is not uncommon for people to camp outside sales centers for three or four days. Condominium debuts begin to join the ranks of rare fashion drops and consumer technology releases—where, for example, the early adopters of a new iPhone receive an extra thrill by lining up early to be one of its first buyers.

Presales are a risk-sharing technique, permitting developers and construction finance lenders to shift some of their risk to the condominium buyer. Developers reduce the likelihood of amassing unsold inventory at the same time that lenders reduce the likelihood of developers being unable to repay their loan. As compensation for assuming some risk, the presales buyer receives a lower purchase price than the buyer of a completed project would. Every presales purchaser assumes a heightened investment role within the project, which in itself proliferates and magnifies the asset function.

Often, a developer will not move forward with construction until a certain minimum percentage of units are presold. In many instances, developers need to achieve a minimum threshold of presales to acquire financing; in North America, that minimum is often 70 percent.[9] While developers typically want to start construction as quickly as possible, when that happens depends on a number of factors, including the permitting process, the size and complexity of the project, and the speed of presales purchases. Presales contracts vary from project to project, and each real estate market has particular norms. In Toronto, for example, contracts often allow for a four-and-a-half-year delay beyond the agreed-upon occupancy date.[10] A many-year wait between making a presales deposit and occupation is common; while the typical duration between presales and completion is roughly four years, the time varies. Some projects reach completion in three years, and some take up to eight. Bjarke Ingels's Vancouver House incurred a five-year gap between preselling and occupation.

In North America, preselling is now so widespread and normalized, it is difficult to register just how remarkable it is, considering that housing is by far the largest purchase that most individuals and families make, that it requires a substantial faith in architectural representation, and that it involves a protracted wait. This is a sizable feat for architectural simulation and represents the profound embrace of computer visualization in the real estate market.

A Market for Architectural "Futures"

The market for presales assignments is an intensified arena of finance capitalism—its emphasis on profit making from the speculative exchange of financial instruments is perfectly manifested in this market. Arguably, the most speculative activity in real estate occurs when a buyer assigns a unit to another buyer at a higher price before the unit has been completed and the underlying real estate transaction has been closed. In many instances, the developer receives a percentage fee for each of these assignment flips—an amount reported to be between 1 and 5 percent of the purchase price.[11] The activity within this market varies from region to region, and its lack of transparency makes it hard to clearly assess; there are no methods of tracking or recording presales contracts because they are not legally considered real estate transactions. The developer is legally bound to the assignee and therefore is the only entity other than the buyer and seller with knowledge of the transaction.

Therefore, one has to rely on the imperfect evidence found in the media, online, and in popular discourse for data on assignment flips. Given the amount of conversation devoted to the topic, it seems likely that flips are happening to a significant degree. For example, a 2018 investigative report by one of Canada's two national newspapers, the *Globe and Mail*, includes an interview with a real estate agent who describes how he and his clients bought 120 units during presales in one suburban Vancouver development. That real estate agent is quoted as saying:

> Half were investors and half people who want to live there, but most of them came back [later] to resell....They made the most money in the last two years. Three hundred to four hundred thousand [Canadian dollars] they are making on their flips.[12]

In markets with rapidly escalating prices, a staple urban legend is of the person in a presales line at the sales center who purchases her assignment only to walk to the back of the line and sell it at a profit. The suspected role these practices play in housing affordability challenges facing some cities has prompted increased scrutiny and debates around whether to curtail the activity. The degree to which any regulation would be effective is anyone's guess. But what is remarkable is that this market—a housing market for units that do not physically exist in the world, in essence the speculative exchange of architectural representation—occurs at all.

Fredric Jameson thought "futures" were critical to understanding how speculation was transforming architecture, writing in 1998:

> One can certainly begin a properly aesthetic exploration of these issues with a question about the way in which specific "futures"—now in the financial as well as the temporal sense—come to be structural features of the newer architecture: something like planned obsolescence, if you like, in the certainty that the building will no longer ever have any aura of permanence, but will bear in its very raw materials the impending certainty of its own future demolition.[13]

While it may be the case that much of capitalist architecture does not possess the material permanence of earlier architecture, the full force of finance capitalism had not yet come into being when Jameson considered futures. At that time, any physical obsolescence within architecture was just the foothills of the ultimate transition. What does it mean that there is a robust market for housing units that do not yet exist? It is not that the market favors the planned obsolescence of any given building, but rather that there does not need to be a building at all. The presales market can thus be thought of as a postmaterial housing market. Of course, this market is predicated on eventual physical structures. In its current form, the market works because the developer owns the land and is contractually obligated to build; thus, the postmaterial market is temporary and tethered to material reality.

Representing the Future

In the 2002 Rem Koolhaas–led Harvard Project on the City publication *Great Leap Forward*, graduate student Nancy Lin wrote of the presales market in Shenzhen, China:

> Because people...do not see what they are buying during the pre-sale phase, advertisements become indispensable....The sheer number of billboards on streets and construction sites for frantic developments turn billboards into public art works by which architecture is visualized.[14]

These billboards worked in tandem with architecture vendors "found almost everywhere: streets, atria and lobbies of office buildings, and department stores."[15] The images adorning these billboard advertisements relied heavily on computer renderings, and in the years since Lin wrote they have been augmented by increasingly sophisticated online and app-based marketing. This demonstrates the degree to which financialization may move architecture to a newly virtual condition. If units are exchanged through only virtual representation and this is coupled with increasing numbers of units sitting empty, perhaps it suggests a transformation in architectural production—one in which architectural production is merging with financial technology (FinTech) to establish entirely postmaterial worlds of architectural exchange value.

Real Virtuality

The virtualization of architecture via the real estate market should come as no surprise, for the entire economic system is becoming increasingly virtual. As Mark C. Taylor writes, "With the movement from industrial through consumer to financial capitalism, there is a progressive dematerialization or virtualization of tokens of exchange."[16] As buildings become financialized, they are necessarily virtualized. But, of course, since this virtuality is tethered to a possible reality, it is not a question of the virtual replacing the real. Taylor comments:

> The globalization of the economy and the electrification of currency
> transforms the hierarchy of infrastructure/suprastructure into
> lateral extensions of information networks. While so-called material
> production does, of course, continue, the forces driving the economy
> are increasingly virtual. The theoretical challenge we now face is not
> to reduce superstructure to infrastructure but to reread what once
> appeared to be surface and depth in terms of complicated surfaces
> where materiality and immateriality are thoroughly reconfigured.[17]

A thoroughly reconfigured materiality and immateriality is the key point here. This reconfiguration sometimes presents odd paradoxes. Buildings themselves may not appear physically less material; in many instances they appear even more monumental. Yet as monuments—defunctionalized in terms of traditional architectural purpose and electronically mediated as investment imagery—they operate immaterially.

There are numerous virtual territories in which it is possible to buy and sell virtual property. These forms of property are untethered to physical reality and occur within online environments such as Second Life, Entropia Universe, and Decentraland.

Since 2003, it has been possible to rent and own virtual land and buildings in the online virtual world Second Life; transactions are facilitated through a virtual currency. In 2006, Anshe Chung, the avatar of Ailin Graef, a Chinese woman who became a virtual real estate entrepreneur, was reported to have become the first "virtual millionaire," primarily through buying, renting, and selling real estate in Second Life. She appeared on the cover of *BusinessWeek* magazine on May 1, 2006.

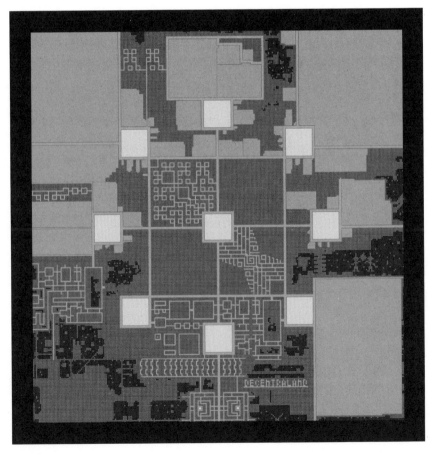

Map of Genesis City, Decentraland.

Although Second Life is past its prime, it is still reported to have between five hundred thousand and one million users.

Entropia Universe was released in 2003 and has had a series of record-setting virtual real estate transactions. In 2010, Yan Panasjuk reportedly purchased a portion of an Entropia destination called Club Neverdie, "including eight bio-domes, space docks, a stadium, club and mall" for $335,000 in actual US dollars.[18]

The advent of blockchain technology has helped propel new forms of virtual worlds. Decentraland is a "blockchain-based virtual reality world" that was released in 2017.[19] Developers within Decentraland are creating Genesis City, which has a finite area of land. In a 2018 article titled "Making a Killing in Virtual Real Estate," *Bloomberg Businessweek* reported that 1,100-square-foot (100-square-meter) plots in Genesis City were selling for up to $200,000.[20]

Foliage almost entirely eclipsing architecture in a sample rendering from Lumion's web showcase, 2020.

While the market capitalization of virtual real estate within these online platforms is minute in comparison to that in the nonvirtual, its existence lends credence to the hypothesis that the mainstream real estate market is moving toward virtuality, making first life more like Second Life. These virtual environments demonstrate that entirely immaterial architecture can have financial value. As these markets converge with the real real estate market, a wholly new worldview emerges—one in which all real estate, and by extension architecture, is a hybrid of the real and the virtual.

It is a common lament among North American architects of market-based housing that marketers are now more powerful than architects. In Vancouver, for example, architectural fees on condos with 150 or more units are approximately 2.5 percent of construction costs.[21] This translates into approximately $4,000/unit in architectural design fees.[22] Marketers are also typically paid a percentage fee, but on the (far higher) sales price of the unit. Since these percentage fees are almost always confidential and change from project to project, it is difficult to determine a precise number, but a reasonable estimate appears to be 2 percent of the sales price.[23] In December 2017, the benchmark price for an apartment in Vancouver was $424,500, providing an approximately $8,500 marketing fee per unit—112 percent higher than the per-unit architectural design fee.

This fee hierarchy translates to the decision-making process, where marketing firms specializing in condo sales are part of the project team from day one and can have more input than architects. In this context, the architect's role can seem little more than to provide a rote container that facilitates the representation of a marketable lifestyle. The digital rendering is the unrivaled device to communicate the marketing aspirations of a project. In many ways, it is the entire project. As London-based architect Jack Self says, "Contemporary rendering engines employed by developers and commercial architects conceal the brutality of capital at work by dissimulating the world into impossibly glorious realities."[24]

A rendering software like Lumion allows for a drag-and-drop dispersion of the elements of lived reality from its library: furniture, people, vehicles, plants, and atmospheric and weather conditions. Its promotional material states, "Lumion instantly breathes life into your designs with realistic landscapes and urban context, stylish effects, and thousands of objects and materials from the content library."[25] The synthesis of marketing intelligence with rendering software has generated a social milieu in which architecture is constituted in the production of investment images.

The English political economist William Davies writes, "The only resource on which financialization is necessarily dependent…is the future."[26] Transhumanist monuments are already a feature of finance capitalism, but what about the next step: an investment-oriented architecture that moves further and further away from materiality itself? As the vibrant presales market suggests, it is already happening. What will be left of architecture in this emergent condition could be what is already the essential fact of architectural production: representation and its potential realization. If one imagines the duration of presales increasing to ten years, to twenty years, to fifty years, to perpetuity, where only the investment image exists as the medium of investment, then one can glimpse one possible outcome of the financialization of nonfinancial entities.

From this vantage point, it is possible to conceptualize rendering software as not only an architectural tool, but also a type of FinTech. For through it, architecture sublimates into the financial electrosphere—all that is solid is now all that could possibly be solid. Virtual and augmented reality now achieves a sophistication that indicates an imminent role in everyday life. In this version of representational agency, current truisms of architecture give way to a form of representation that is less virtual reality and more real virtuality. Reinhold Martin recognized this when he wrote of architecture, "It has become a kind of real virtuality, in which, from the point of view of the markets and those who manipulate them, the actual, tangible existence of anything that can plausibly be called a useful object (i.e., a real building) has been superseded by a set of representations."[27]

Science Fiction and Architecture

"City lights receding." The science fiction author William Gibson's metaphor for cyberspace, the term he coined in 1985, conveys immediately its affinity with actual space. Gibson's *Neuromancer*—and the entire sci-fi genre—establishes a strong urban-architectural sensibility; it is hard to imagine science fiction without its highly particular architectural settings. At the same time, the practice of architecture can be understood as a type of fiction that draws heavily upon science and technology. Buildings are themselves a type of technology, even as they incorporate particular technologies and scientific knowledge—from the steel beams first used in the late nineteenth century to the electronic sensors of the late twentieth.

In a broader cultural and aesthetic sense, buildings are influenced by scientific knowledge. As Antoine Picon and Alessandra Ponte say in the introduction to their book *Architecture and the Sciences*, "Since the time of Vitruvius and Leonardo, the sciences have served as a source of images and metaphors for architecture and have had a direct influence on the shaping of built space."[28] Not only does Vitruvius address the importance for an architect to be knowledgeable in meteorology, astronomy, and medicine, but he also devotes roughly a third of his *The Ten Books on Architecture* to describing Roman technology, ranging from dewatering machines to force pumps. The symbiosis between architecture as a projective future-inventing act and science fiction allows one to consider architecture as sci-fi and sci-fi as architecture.

There is, of course, a strong relationship between scientific and technological advances and economic systems. Technological change is a major aspect of economic development, since technology is a powerful component of any given mode of production.[29] The advent of agrarian capitalism is associated with technological improvements to the plow in the seventeenth and eighteenth centuries in the Netherlands and England. The steam engine and other innovations of industrialization worked in concert with the rise of industrial capitalism. As Mark C. Taylor states, "While modernity and industrial capitalism would have been impossible without fossil fuels and print, postmodernity and consumer capitalism would have been impossible without electricity and revolutionary changes in the production and distribution of images."[30]

As technologies and economic structures mutate over time, so does architecture. Early modernism is symbiotic with industrial capitalism. Le Corbusier was famously fascinated with the artifacts of industrial capitalism: grain silos, trains, automobiles, ocean liners. What Corbusier is to industrial capitalism, Rem Koolhaas is to consumer capitalism. Koolhaas's firm, the Office for Metropolitan Architecture (OMA), was founded in 1975, and its first major project, the Netherlands Dance Theatre, was completed in 1987. OMA's mashups of Miesian and Corbusian aesthetics and program-driven hyperfunctionalism resonate with larger characteristics of consumerism. But it is in the eclectic material palette of OMA where this interest is most evident. The firm's exploration of paint, carpets, curtains, and appliquéd textures resonates with the world of consumerist interior design. As Andy Warhol experimented with the aesthetics of advertising and celebrity culture, OMA repositions and modulates the objects and atmospheres of consumerist interiors.

OMA's 1995 book *S,M,L,XL* was a radical departure from the typical firm monograph or architect's manifesto. The introduction declares it "an amalgam that makes disclosures about the conditions under which architecture is produced." One of the dominant means by which this disclosure occurs is literary text—a series of stories that blur fiction and nonfiction. Images of the OMA project Nexus World Housing are presented with a story titled "Learning Japanese," which begins, "A desperate call to Tokyo." The project Villa dall'Ava is prefaced by an enigmatic tale that starts, "It was handwritten in blue ink, obviously by someone who was very passionate about architecture. Reading it, you knew immediately that this was going to be a mythological enterprise."[31] The drawings of Très Grande Bibliothèque sit above a series of fictional diary entries. By so thoroughly integrating OMA's architectural projects into this series of texts, *S,M,L,XL* conflates buildings and text in a realm that blurs fiction and nonfiction.

Koolhaas commences the *S,M,L,XL* essay "Singapore Songlines" with a critique of William Gibson's thoughts on Singapore. While conveying a difference between Koolhaas and Gibson, the essay signals the former's interest in the latter. There are moments in *S,M,L,XL* where Koolhaas addresses the conceptual overlaps of cyberspace and real space, writing, for example, that "the Generic City is what is left after large sections of urban life crossed over to cyberspace."[32] More important than any literal references, the overall tone of *S,M,L,XL*'s fiction has significant commonalities with that of Gibson's cyberpunk. The basic literary mechanism of cyberpunk is the juxtaposition of high-tech futurism with banal, quotidian social conditions through a kind of hard-boiled, film noir style. The genre explores utopian and dystopian tensions while representing cultural transformation and unorthodox uses of technology. Cyberpunk also tends to make significant reference to architectural and urban space in establishing its milieu.

The essays and fictions of *S,M,L,XL* portray architecture mutating under the influence of technology and globalization in ways that are simultaneously dystopian and utopian but always rich in agitation.

Newly empowered by the ease of global communication and transportation, the architect is portrayed as a nomad of worldwide urbanization. Yet, at the same time, the architect is also a banal and impotent figure, sentenced to an empty glamour of endless travel. Fredric Jameson hinted at the resonance between Koolhaas and cyberpunk in writing on urbanist discourse: "Cyberpunk seems to be a reference to grasp at here, which—like Koolhaas...—seems positively to revel in its own (and its world's) excess."[33]

The science fiction quality of *S,M,L,XL* situates the book's architectural content in a cyberpunk vein that derives its amalgam from the sociotechnological preoccupations of the early 1990s: fax machines, cheap air travel, personal computing, and consumer culture. What might be some contemporary corollaries? The most technologically oriented architecture practices of the past two decades have been focused on the new possibilities of the digital—with parametric design at the center. Parametric design, in its most basic sense, emphasizes algorithmic thinking in the design process. It stretches back at least a century; building on its analog beginning, computers performing algorithmic equations have facilitated the ascent of its processes and their formal possibilities, helping to usher in a wave of iconic forms. If the Koolhaasian project can be understood in relation to consumer capitalism, parametric design can be understood in relation to finance capitalism.

But perhaps parametric design's emphasis on style, as championed by Patrik Schumacher, misses the most important point. Because of its basis in financial algorithms, finance capitalist architecture is already algorithmic in a manner that absorbs a range of styles, not adhering only to the curvilinear exoticism of the parametric style. The formal myopia of Schumacher's version of parametric architecture is that it eclipses other major shifts in architecture that do not necessarily look parametric. The architecture of contemporary capitalism is not primarily about bending and warping physical forms (although that is a significant aspect). Rather, the technologies of finance are propelling architecture toward something much more radical than what Schumacher envisions: a postshelter and postmaterial formation that serves the spirituality that is finance capitalism.

The Technologies of Finance

The integration of advanced computing with finance was early, comprehensive, and transformative. The New York Stock Exchange switched to a computerized trading system in 1966, and the NASDAQ became the world's first electronic stock exchange when it opened in 1971. A 2016 analysis by the McKinsey Global Institute showed that, outside of the technology sector itself, finance was one of the three most highly digitized sectors in the US economy, alongside media and professional services.[34] It is impossible to imagine anything that even remotely resembles the current economy without digital technology.

Contemporary globalized capitalism necessitates the near-instantaneous transfer of financial information and is itself remarkably algorithmic. While there are debates on what portion of global stock trading volume is algorithmically based, there is a broad consensus that it is the vast majority—from 70 to 90 percent.[35] These algorithms enable high-frequency trading in which stocks are bought and sold in nanoseconds, a speed at which no human can operate. When it was first introduced, high-frequency trading was highly lucrative, since the technique permitted traders to take advantage of momentary oscillations in stock value and offered a competitive advantage to any who wielded it. Algorithmic trading is an extreme form of finance capitalism because of the intensity of its focus on earning profit without production. Given that this extremity is possible only with artificial intelligence, perhaps finance capitalism is an economic modality uniquely predisposed to AI.

FinTech seeks to maximize the finance industry's integration with advanced computing. According to the World Economic Forum, FinTech "companies harness mobile technologies, big data and superior analytics to tailor products for various customer segments."[36] Examples of FinTech range from services like TransferWise, which allows money to be moved around the world easily with "borderless accounts," to decentralized cryptocurrencies such as Bitcoin and Ethereum. Many business analysts argue that finance is highly susceptible to continued disruption by software because financial services, in common with music, television, and publishing, are made of information rather than physical goods. The FinTech sector is growing significantly: according to a report by the global accounting firm Deloitte, 2008 global investment in FinTech was around $1 billion and by 2017 had reached $22 billion.[37]

The Rise of PropTech

Since real estate occupies a central position in the finance industry, as to be expected, a subcategory of FinTech is devoted to real estate. In the current era's penchant for catchy abbreviations, this domain is known as either RE Tech or PropTech. While FinTech targets the finance industry generally, PropTech focuses on the array of market actors specific to real estate, including developers, marketers, renters, investors, and various real estate professionals. PropTech addresses how people design, construct, market, discover, transact, and operate real estate. Examples of PropTech include online real estate databases such as Zillow, which offers a mobile interface for residential real estate that provides geographic and financial data on homes for sale, custom loan quotes provided anonymously, and real estate advice boards. Perhaps the most disruptive PropTech to date is Airbnb, which has transformed how people operate their homes. Some see a large potential for blockchain technology and its distributed ledger to transform the process of real estate transactions, essentially streamlining them in terms of both time and cost.[38]

Beyond FinTech and PropTech, the overarching inventions of financial instruments and practices have generated the first truly global real estate market. These inventions have been among the most influential technological transformations of the last forty years, although they are rarely thought of as technologies. At the dawn of the twenty-first century, technological changes increased the speed at which real estate information could be gathered, analyzed, and communicated. These changes include the availability of local and dwelling-specific data on the internet and the emergence of big real estate data, with its incorporation into online real estate systems.

The Australian urban geographer Dallas Rogers demonstrates that a key technology for wealthy investors is what he calls the "investor-focused mediating technologies" that came into existence after 2000. These technologies provide global investors access to closed networks of small data about local real estate and even local financial institutions. As an example, Rogers offers the Chinese website Juwai ("home overseas"), which provides an integrated platform linking Chinese buyers with Australian, Canadian, and American real estate markets.[39] A similar set of mediating technologies have focused on the real estate professional. From this vantage, such things as REITs and mortgage-backed securities and their generalized electronic mediation can also be understood as a technological regime.

Architecture as Financial Fiction

S,M,L,XL's approach to architectural discourse reminds readers of the utility of assuming a speculative, fictional lens in order to conceptually organize contemporary conditions. This approach seems equally relevant today. However, its particular genre of speculation—cyberpunk— is less potent than it was twenty-five years ago.

A revised speculative mode of architectural thought necessitates a shift to the novel condition that is hegemonic but little discussed in architecture: finance capitalism. The degree to which finance is technological and technology is financial underscores the potential for reimagining architecture's utilization of science fiction as a means to envision domains of architectural operation. An approach to generating new architectural knowledge might be to simply place financial technology at the center of the "science" in science fiction—in other words, to make the shift from science fiction to financial fiction, from sci-fi to fi-fi.

Jameson wrote, "Without wishing to belabor the point, it strikes me that the abstract dimension or materialist sublimation of finance capital enjoys something of the same semi-autonomy as cyberspace."[40] Karl Marx's description of credit and the joint-stock system, the primary elements of today's finance capitalism, as involving a type of capital he called fictitious is motivated by a similar sense of semiautonomy. For Marx, fluctuations of the stock market in absence of any correlative fluctuations in physical production and the doubling of capital that occurs in accounting practices signified that semiautonomous and hence fictitious character. As Rudolf Hilferding developed Marx's initial thoughts into a more thorough articulation of what he explicitly labeled finance capitalism, a thread of conceiving finance as fiction was extended, and this continues in varying degrees to the present. As architecture has come to be a preferred medium of finance capitalism, it too has become fictitious, regarded from the vantage points of Marx, Hilferding, Lenin, and others. Perhaps a better way to say it is that architecture's inherently fictional character has been accelerated. It is thus that the market for condominium presales, the primacy of digital rendering, and PropTech algorithms amount to the semiautonomy of fictitious capital.

The genre of financial fiction is typically understood to include literature, film, and "the expanse of horizontal, textual space"—from business journalism to self-help guides to investing—that Leigh Claire La Berge calls "financial print culture."[41] Examples range from the movie *Wall Street* to Thomas J. Stanley's 1996 book *The Millionaire Next Door: The Surprising Secrets of America's Wealthy*. As surplus money fueled the creation of new financial instruments and practices, for scholars like La Berge it also established new "channels for the production and contestation of literary meaning and narrative form."[42] These new channels do not merely represent finance, but also are a component of financialization, just as architecture is integral to financialization. La Berge has identified abstraction, complexity, and simplicity as prominent organizing tropes of academic discourse on finance, as well as of financial fiction vernaculars.[43] But a persistent tension exists between abstraction/complexity and experienced human conditions because finance is always both abstract and material. La Berge writes:

> Real abstraction seems to me a potentially useful concept for critical studies of finance in that it necessarily links actions such as exchange or the giving of credit (which includes both the immediacy of exchange and a potentially unlimited duration) to a larger social structure that appears divorced from the actions that constitute it. As such, finance may appear abstract, but as a real abstraction, it is concrete as well.[44]

The architecture of finance capitalism is a real abstraction—a real virtuality. It functions as a device at the liminal space between material, concrete existence and the seemingly mystical, abstract, complex, and immaterial realm of finance. Of course, this is exactly where finance capitalism operates. The rise of finance capitalism has diminished the traditional conception of architecture as human shelter and replaced it with a postshelter financial functionality that is comparably abstract and immaterial—comparably fictitious. By continuing to inhabit this relatively abstract and dematerialized yet real city of finance, the human subject becomes a fictional character in its own financialized reality.

Epilogue

T he final manuscript for *Icebergs, Zombies, and the Ultra Thin* was
nearing completion when COVID-19 emerged. During the editing
and layout process, the world seemed exceptionally destabilized
on multiple fronts: a global pandemic, widespread protests against
racist police brutality in North America and Europe, numerous extreme
weather events related to climate change, and political devolution in the
United States as the November election neared. As I sit alone inside my
apartment, typing this epilogue, I am wearing an N95 mask—not to
protect me from the virus but as a reprieve from the thick, throat-and-
nose-burning wildfire smoke that has blanketed Vancouver and the rest
of North America's West Coast for about a week now. I own two N95
masks (a chance leftover from a pre-COVID project), and I'd been sav-
ing them in case the virus became much, much worse. Well, this seemed
like as opportune a time as any to break them out.

Amid the fear, turmoil, and loss of life unleashed by the novel coronavirus is, from the perspective of architecture, at least, a remarkable
nexus of public health, economics, and architectural space. Dominant

discourse posits the central concern of managing COVID-19 as balancing economics with health, while the chief tactic of mitigating the virus is spatial: *social distancing*. During initial lockdowns in much of the world, people were asked to stay home, and now millions of people are repurposing domestic interiors for sustained work. And the incorporeal tendencies of today's finance capitalism, as described in this book, have been intensified in the context of the coronavirus. The more time we spend on Zoom instead of interacting in person, ordering things from Amazon instead of shopping in brick-and-mortar stores, and maintaining a closed "social bubble," the further we move away from our bodies and toward becoming more devout followers of totems of dematerialized finance capitalism such as Manhattan's 432 Park Avenue.

The architectural investment portfolios that finance capitalism has engendered have played a particular role in the era of COVID-19. Investors with multiple properties have been able to relocate with relative ease to locations perceived to be safer.[1] Manhattan feels too risky? Head to the Hamptons. The Hamptons just isn't far enough away…then what about that fourth property in the Colorado Rockies? This privilege exemplifies the inequality that finance capitalism generates, which COVID-19 and the response to it have both highlighted and accelerated.

Real estate and architecture have often served as potent mediums of racism. There is no question that the inequality manifest in the spaces of finance capitalism has a racist dimension—discernible in everything from the predatory tactics of institutional investors scooping up single-family homes in predominantly Black neighborhoods to the spatial philanthropy of Vancouver House, which propagates segregation at a global scale. As the American geographer Ruth Wilson Gilmore has said, "Capitalism requires inequality and racism enshrines it."[2] The Black Lives Matter movement seeks the end of racially motivated violence against Black people not only at the hands of the police but everywhere racist violence takes place—and this can extend to violence at the hands of architects and through the strictures of financialization.

Will substantial change arise from current instability? Will unprecedented wildfires prompt collective action to halt climate change? Will Black Lives Matter meaningfully reduce racism? Will the changes brought on by COVID-19 result in permanent transformation in housing markets? It's anyone's guess. However, there's ample reason to believe that no significant, monumental change will occur. The 2008 financial crisis laid bare the problems of positioning buildings at the center of speculative financial markets. Yet following what was roundly described as the worst financial crisis since the Great Depression, no significant change has occurred. Indeed, the world's financial system and the built environment through which it operates are in an even more precarious position than in 2007. Here in Vancouver, which suffers from a deep affordability crisis and where announcements that a massive housing bubble is about to burst have long been part of the city's ambient soundscape, housing prices have continued to climb during the pandemic. Recently, a mortgage specialist told me, "The market is hot!" The only change is that searching for properties has become even more incorporeal, with "virtual viewings" becoming de rigueur.

Yet, it seems that things can't continue on their current trajectory forever. How extreme does the wealth gap have to become for the entire system to break apart? The protests in the streets of Minneapolis and elsewhere are one manifestation of the inequalities that capitalism requires. I, for one, am hoping that things never return to the pre-COVID-19 state of affairs.

Architecture has long grappled with how to respond to the shortcomings of capitalism. But capitalism's rapacious capacity to absorb all manner of attack is legendary. Because architecture is now finance, an effective critical architect must practice a form of critical finance. This doesn't mean architects should become bankers, but rather that architects might consider collaborating with financiers in a manner that is similar to how they currently work with structural engineers. Architecture has no meaningful autonomy from finance capitalism, and to claim so only perpetuates the inequalities that are played out across buildings and cities. Architecture as a critical and creative act must expand its operational milieu to reassert its purpose in the twenty-first century. Perhaps it is from within the instability of the present that architecture can find its place in the future. No return!

Acknowledgments

Icebergs, Zombies and the Ultra Thin grew out of research that was funded by the Social Sciences and Humanities Research Council of the Government of Canada. I am thankful for the exceptional contributions of research assistants Lőrinc Vass and Josimar Dominguez, who were graduate students at the University of British Columbia's School of Architecture and Landscape Architecture (SALA) when this project started.

I am thankful to the many people who have contributed in diverse ways. Here are a few: the photographer Anthony Haughey for touring me around Irish ghost estates. Leslie Van Duzer for supporting the FIRE Lecture Series that I co-organized with my colleague Sara Stevens. Masha Hupalo for her research assistance during my time at the Southern California Institute of Architecture (SCI-Arc). Jay Wollenberg for sharing his insights regarding British Columbia's real estate industry. David Ruy, for opening up new avenues for my work. And an especially deep gratitude to George Baird, John Bass, Peggy Deamer, Alex Duval, Geoff Mann, Sherry McKay, and Sara Stevens for their feedback on various aspects of the manuscript.

And a big thank-you to all at Princeton Architectural Press who have supported this project and brought it to fruition, not least of whom is expert editor Sara Stemen. Finally, I would like to recognize all the students I have taught at SALA, the Harvard University Graduate School of Design, and SCI-Arc. The insights of these students have informed this book in innumerable ways.

Notes

Translations from the Spanish throughout are by Josimar Dominguez.

Preface

1. Leilani Farha, UN Human Rights Council, *Report of the Special Rapporteur on Adequate Housing as a Component of the Right to an Adequate Standard of Living, and on the Right to Non-Discrimination in This Context,* A/HRC/34/51, January 18, 2017, https://digitallibrary.un.org/record/861179.

2. The Social Sciences and Humanities Research Council (SSHRC) is the primary grant-funding agency for social sciences and the humanities in Canada. It is administered by the Canadian government.

3. K. Michael Hays, *Architecture Theory since 1968* (Cambridge, MA: MIT Press, 1998), 3.

4. Fredric Jameson, *Postmodernism, or, The Cultural Logic of Late Capitalism* (Durham, NC: Duke University Press, 1992), 5.

5. Jameson, *Postmodernism, or, The Cultural Logic,* 38.

6. Jameson, *Postmodernism, or, The Cultural Logic,* 44.

7. Fredric Jameson, "The Brick and the Balloon: Architecture, Idealism and Land Speculation," *New Left Review* 228 (March–April 1998): 26.

8. Fredric Jameson, "Culture and Finance Capital," *Critical Inquiry* 24, no. 1 (1997): 260.

9. Jameson, "Brick and Balloon," 44.

10. Jameson is borrowing this terminology from the architectural historian Charles Jencks. See notes in "Brick and Balloon," 44.

11. Reinhold Martin, "Financial Imaginaries: Toward a Philosophy of the City," *Grey Room* 42 (Winter 2011): 65.

12. Martin, "Financial Imaginaries," 65.

13. Martin, "Financial Imaginaries," 64.

14. Martin, "Financial Imaginaries," 77.

15. For instance, Reinhold Martin, *Utopia's Ghost: Architecture and Postmodernism, Again* (Minneapolis: University of Minnesota Press, 2010) discusses primarily corporate office towers when considering 1980s finance capitalism. See chapter 5, "Materiality."

16. Douglas Spencer, in his work on neoliberalism, uses such architects as Zaha Hadid and Foreign Office Architects to develop his conceptual position. See *The Architecture of Neoliberalism: How Contemporary Architecture Became an Instrument of Control and Compliance* (London: Bloomsbury, 2016).

17. Giovanni Arrighi, *The Long Twentieth Century: Money, Power, and the Origins of Our Times* (1994; repr., New York: Verso, 2010), 6. Citations refer to the 2010 edition.

18. See Sara Stevens, *Developing Expertise: Architecture and Real Estate in Metropolitan America* (New Haven, CT: Yale University Press, 2016).

Introduction

Epigraph: Fredric Jameson, "The Brick and the Balloon: Architecture, Idealism and Land Speculation," *New Left Review* 228 (March–April 1998): 32.

1. Giovanni Arrighi wrote in the opening line of his 1994 book *The Long Twentieth Century,* "Over the last quarter of a century something fundamental seems to have changed in the way in which capitalism works." Giovanni Arrighi, *The Long Twentieth Century: Money, Power, and the Origins of Our Times* (New York: Verso, 2010), 1.

2. Greta R. Krippner, "The Financialization of the American Economy," *Socio-Economic Review* 3, no. 2 (2005): 174.

3. See Karl Marx, "Part Eight: Primitive Accumulation," in *Capital: A Critique of Political Economy,* vol. 1 (1867; repr., London: Penguin Books in association with New Left Review, 1981).

4. See Krippner, "Financialization of American Economy."

5. "Listed Domestic Companies, Total," World Federation of Exchanges Database, World Bank, accessed March 7, 2020, https://data.worldbank.org/indicator/CM.MKT.LDOM.NO.

6. "Stocks Traded, Total Value (Current US$)," World Federation of Exchanges Database, World Bank, accessed March 7, 2020, https://data.worldbank.org/indicator/CM.MKT.TRAD.CD.

7. "Stocks Traded, Total Value (% of GDP)," World Federation of Exchanges Database, World Bank, accessed March 7, 2020, https://data.worldbank.org/indicator/CM.MKT.TRAD.GD.ZS.

8. Costas Lapavitsas, *Profiting without Producing: How Finance Exploits Us All* (London: Verso, 2013), 7.

9. Bernard Lietaer, *The Future of Money: A New Way to Create Wealth, Work, and a Wiser World* (London: Century, 2001), 312.

10. Lietaer, *Future of Money,* 314.

11. "Triennial Central Bank Survey of Foreign Exchange and Over-the-Counter (OTC) Derivatives Markets in 2019," Bank of International Settlements (Basel), December 8, 2019, https://www.bis.org/statistics/rpfx19.htm.

12. David M. Kotz, *The Rise and Fall of Neoliberal Capitalism* (Cambridge, MA: Harvard University Press, 2015), 33.
13. Krippner, "Financialization of American Economy."
14. David M. Kotz, *Neoliberalism, Globalization, Financialization: Understanding Post-1980 Capitalism* (paper, Department of Economics, University of Massachusetts Amherst, August 2015), 24, https://www.umass.edu/economics/sites/default/files/Kotz.pdf. This paper is a revised version of chap. 2, "What Is Neoliberalism?," in Kotz, *Rise and Fall*.
15. "Business: Stockholders," *The First Measured Century*, PBS, December 2000, http://www.pbs.org/fmc/book/14business6.htm.
16. Lydia Saad, "What Percentage of Americans Owns Stock?," Gallup, September 13, 2019, https://news.gallup.com/poll/266807/percentage-americans-owns-stock.aspx.
17. Randy Martin, *Financialization of Daily Life* (Philadelphia: Temple University Press, 2002), 3.
18. Karl Marx, *Capital: A Critique of Political Economy* (1894; repr., London: Penguin Books in association with New Left Review, 1991), 3:566.
19. Marx, *Capital*, 3:601.
20. Marx, *Capital*, 3:526.
21. Marx, *Capital*, 3:596, 3:600.
22. Marx, *Capital*, 3:572, 3:568.
23. Rudolf Hilferding, *Finance Capital: A Study of the Latest Phase of Capitalist Development* (1910; repr., trans. Tom Bottomore, London: Routledge and Kegan Paul, 1981), 6.
24. Hilferding, *Finance Capital*, 115, 112, 104.
25. Hilferding, *Finance Capital*, 133, 134, 138.
26. Vladimir Lenin, *Imperialism: The Highest Stage of Capitalism* (1916; repr., London: Junius, 1996), 102.
27. Arrighi, *Long Twentieth Century*, 6.
28. Arrighi, *Long Twentieth Century*, 6.
29. Fredric Jameson, "Culture and Finance Capital," *Critical Inquiry* 24, no. 1 (1997): 249–50.
30. Jameson, "Culture and Finance Capital," 251.
31. Lapavitsas, *Profiting without Producing*, 44.
32. Lapavitsas, *Profiting without Producing*, 106, 103, 168.
33. Lapavitsas, *Profiting without Producing*, 29.
34. Jameson, "Brick and Balloon," 26.
35. Kotz, *Neoliberalism, Globalization, Financialization*, 1.
36. Kotz, *Neoliberalism, Globalization, Financialization*, 23, 9, 25.
37. Jeremy Clift and Elisa Diehl, eds., *Financial Globalization: The Impact on Trade, Policy, Labor, and Capital Flows* (Washington, DC: International Monetary Fund, 2007), 8.
38. Susan Lund and Phillipp Härle, "Global Finance Resets," *Finance and Development* 54, no. 4 (December 2017): 43.
39. Lapavitsas, *Profiting without Producing*, 14.

40. Reinhold Martin, *Utopia's Ghost: Architecture and Postmodernism, Again* (Minneapolis: University of Minnesota Press, 2010), 106.
41. Timothy Mitchell, "Rethinking Economy," *Geoforum* 39 (2008): 1120.

Chapter 1: Finance Capitalism and Architecture

Epigraph: Rem Koolhaas, "Beijing Manifesto," *Wired*, June 2003, 124.
1. Fredric Jameson, "Culture and Finance Capital," *Critical Inquiry* 24, no. 1 (1997): 260.
2. Michael Hudson, "The Transition from Industrial Capitalism to a Financialized Bubble Economy" (working paper 627, Levy Economics Institute, 2010): unpaginated.
3. Prequin, *Prequin 2019 Global Real Estate League Tables*, accessed May 29, 2020, https://docs.preqin.com/reports/2019-Preqin-Global-Real-Estate-League-Tables.pdf.
4. Amy Whyte, "The Biggest Investors in Real Estate," *Institutional Investor*, August 3, 2018, https://www.institutionalinvestor.com/article/b19c23gdjjkvn9/The-Biggest-Investors-in-Real-Estate.
5. Christopher B. Leinberger, "The Need for Alternatives to the Nineteen Standard Real Estate Product Types," *Places* 17, no. 2 (2005): 25.
6. Vladimir Lenin, *Imperialism: The Highest Stage of Capitalism* (London: Junius, 1996), 54.
7. Giovanni Arrighi, *The Long Twentieth Century: Money, Power, and the Origins of our Times* (London: Verso, 2010), 184.
8. David Harvey, *The Limits to Capital* (London: Verso, 2018), 347.
9. Costas Lapavitsas, *Profiting without Producing: How Finance Exploits Us All* (London: Verso, 2013), 4.
10. Manuel B. Aalbers, *The Financialization of Housing: A Political Economy Approach* (London: Routledge, 2016), 2, 83.
11. Aalbers, *Financialization of Housing*, 3.
12. World Bank, *World Development Report 2009: Reshaping Economic Geography* (Washington, DC: World Bank, 2009), 206.
13. Hudson, "Transition from Industrial Capitalism," unpaginated.
14. "Households and Nonprofit Organizations; One-to-Four-Family Residential Mortgages; Liability, Level," Economic Research, Federal Reserve Bank of St. Louis, accessed May 30, 2020, https://fred.stlouisfed.org/series/HHMSDODNS.
15. "Household Debt, Loans and Debt securities," IMF DataMapper, International Monetary Fund, accessed May 30, 2020, https://www.imf.org/external/datamapper/HH_LS@GDD/AUS/USA/GBR/CAN.
16. Thomas I. Palley, *From Financial Crisis to Stagnation: The Destruction of Shared Prosperity and the Role of Economics* (New York: Cambridge University Press, 2012), 58.

17. International Monetary Fund, *Global Financial Stability Report, April 2018: A Bumpy Road Ahead* (Washington, DC: International Monetary Fund, 2018), 93.

18. Alex Blumberg and Adam Davidson, "The Giant Pool of Money," May 5, 2009, in *This American Life*, podcast, MP3 audio, 59:00, https://www.thisamericanlife.org/355/the-giant-pool-of-money; Aalbers, *Financialization of Housing*, 3.

19. PwC, *Asset & Wealth Management Revolution: Embracing Exponential Change* (2017), 7, https://www.pwc.com/gx/en/industries/financial-services/asset-management/publications/asset-wealth-management-revolution.html.

20. Aalbers, *Financialization of Housing*, 84.

21. David Harvey, "Right to the City," *New Left Review* 53 (September–October 2008): 24.

22. Blumberg and Davidson, "Giant Pool of Money."

23. David Harvey, "Foreword: The Urban Roots of the Financial Crisis," in *Subprime Cities: The Political Economy of Mortgage Markets*, ed. Manuel B. Aalbers (Chichester, UK: Blackwell, 2012), xv.

24. Harvey, "Right to the City," 24.

25. Lapavitsas, *Profiting without Producing*, 260.

26. Aalbers, *Financialization of Housing*, 83.

27. Arrighi, *Long Twentieth Century*, 184.

28. The Penthouses, Pentominium, accessed May 10, 2020, http://pentominium.com.

29. Arindam Dutta, "Marginality and Metaengineering: Keynes and Arup," in Aggregate Architectural History Collective, *Governing by Design: Architecture, Economy, and Politics in the Twentieth Century* (Pittsburgh: University of Pittsburgh Press, 2012), 257.

30. Catherine Yoshimoto, "Yield-Seekers Embrace Emerging Market Real Estate," FTSE Russell, accessed May 31, 2020, https://www.ftserussell.com/blogs/yield-seekers-embrace-emerging-market-real-estate.

31. "History," Colliers International, accessed January 30, 2018, http://www.colliers.com/en-us/about/history.

Chapter 2: Ghosts and Zombies, Growth and Decay

Earlier versions of this chapter's content were presented at the 102nd and 103rd annual meetings of the Association of Collegiate Schools of Architecture and published as "Asset Urbanism: Ghosts, Zombies, and the Simultaneity of Amplified Growth and Decay," in *Globalizing Architecture: Flows and Disruptions: Paper Proceedings, ACSA 102nd Annual Meeting, Miami Beach, 2014*, ed. John Stuart and Mabel Wilson (Washington, DC: Association of Collegiate Schools of Architecture, 2015), 686–94 and "Spain Is Everywhere: Asset Urbanism and the Spatial Avatars of Neoliberalism," in *The Expanding Periphery and the Migrating Center:*

Paper Proceedings, 103rd ACSA Annual Meeting, Toronto, 2015, ed. Lola Sheppard and David Ruy (Washington, DC: Association of Collegiate Schools of Architecture, 2015), 421–30.

1. US Government Accountability Office, *Vacant Properties: Growing Number Increases Communities' Costs and Challenges*, GAO-12-34 (Washington, DC: GAO, 2011), 12.

2. Michael Hudson, "The Transition from Industrial Capitalism to a Financialized Bubble Economy" (working paper 627, Levy Economics Institute, 2010): 7 (unpaginated).

3. US Census Bureau, "Rental and Homeowner Vacancy Rates by Area," Housing Vacancies and Homeownership, Annual Statistics: 2018, https://www.census.gov/housing/hvs/data/ann18ind.html.

4. US Census Bureau, "Rental and Homeowner Vacancy."

5. Daniel A. Hagen and Julia L. Hansen, "Rental Housing and the Natural Vacancy Rate," *Journal of Real Estate Research* 32, no. 4 (2010): 413–33.

6. J. W. R. Whitehead, "The Settlement Morphology of London's Cocktail Belt," *Tijdschrift voor economische en sociale Geografie* 58 (January–February 1967): 20–27.

7. Julie Satow, "Pied-à-Neighborhood," *New York Times*, October 24, 2014, https://www.nytimes.com/2014/10/26/realestate/pieds-terre-owners-dominate-some-new-york-buildings.html.

8. Jeffrey C. Mays and Jesse McKinley, "Lawmakers Support 'Pied-à-Terre' Tax on Multimillion-Dollar Second Homes," *New York Times*, March 11, 2019, https://www.nytimes.com/2019/03/11/nyregion/mta-subways-pied-a-terre-tax.html.

9. Population Division—New York City Department of City Planning, Selected Housing Characteristics, 2017 American Community Survey 1-Year Estimates, New York City and Boroughs, https://www1.nyc.gov/assets/planning/download/pdf/planning-level/nyc-population/acs/hous_2017acs1yr_nyc.pdf.

10. Elyzabeth Gaumer, *Selected Initial Findings of the 2017 New York City Housing and Vacancy Survey* (New York: New York City Department of Housing Preservation and Development, 2018), 17.

11. *Atelier Parisien d'urbanism, recueil thématique 1er, 2e, 3e et 4e arrondissements de Paris* (Paris: Paris Urbanism Agency, 2017), 18.

12. Evie Burrows-Taylor, "Paris: 26 Percent of City Centre Homes Lie Empty," *The Local*, August 18, 2017, https://www.thelocal.fr/20170818/paris-26-percent-of-city-centre-homes-empty.

13. Sarah Lyall, "A Slice of London So Exclusive Even the Owners Are Visitors," *New York Times*, April 1, 2013, http://www.nytimes.com/2013/04/02/world/europe/a-slice-of-london-so-exclusive-even-the-owners-are-visitors.html.

14. Savills World Research, *Spotlight: The World in London* (London: Savills Research, 2012), 4.

15. "Population and Dwelling Count Highlight Tables, 2016 Census," Statistics Canada, accessed May 19, 2020, https://www12.statcan.gc.ca/census-recensement/2016/dp-pd/hlt-fst/pd-pl/Table.cfm.

16. *Measuring the Presence of Absence: Clarifications and Corrections in the Reportage of the BTAworks' Foreign Investment in Vancouver Real Estate*, March 25, 2013, accessed November 15, 2013, http://www.btaworks.com/2013/03/25/measuring-the-presence-of-absence- clarifications-and-correctionsin-the-reportage-of-the-btaworks-foreign- investment-invancouver-real-estate/.

17. Jan Nijman, *Miami: Mistress of the Americas* (Philadelphia: University of Pennsylvania Press, 2011), 168.

18. Katrin Kandlbinder, Norman G. Miller, and Michael Sklarz, "Leveling the Playing Field: Out-of-Town Buyer Premiums in US Housing Markets over Time," *International Journal of Housing Markets and Analysis* 12, no. 3 (June 2019): 387.

19. "Narco-A-Largo: Money Laundering at the Trump Ocean Club, Panama," Global Witness, November 2017, https://www.globalwitness.org/en/campaigns/corruption-and-money-laundering/narco-a-lago-panama.

20. Catherine Cashmore, *Speculative Vacancies 8: The Empty Properties Ignored by Statistics* (Melbourne: Prosper, 2015), 18.

21. "The Housing Crisis in Cities: Causes, Effects and Responses: Summary of the Talks Given at the Barcelona Housing and Renovation Forum," MACBA auditorium, Barcelona, March 19–21, 2019, 15.

22. Scott Bollens, "An Island in Sectarian Seas? Heritage, Memory and Identity in Post-War Redevelopment of Beirut's Central District," in *Urban Heritage in Divided Cities: Contested Pasts*, ed. Mirjana Ristic and Sybille Frank (London: Routledge, 2019), 179.

23. Feargus O'Sullivan, "Paris Is Tripling Its Tax on Second Homes," Bloomberg CityLab, January 26, 2017, https://www.citylab.com/equity/2017/01/paris-france-property-taxes-vacation-homes/514496/.

24. Satow, "Pied-à-Neighborhood."

25. Joseph Schumpeter, *Capitalism, Socialism and Democracy* (New York: Harper & Brothers, 1942).

26. David Harvey, *The Urbanization of Capital: Studies in the History and Theory of Capitalist Urbanization* (London: Basil Blackwell, 1985), 16.

27. DEHLG (Department of Housing, Local Government and Heritage), as referenced by Rob Kitchin et al., *A Haunted Landscape: Housing and Ghost Estates in Post-Celtic Tiger Ireland* (Maynooth, Ireland: National Institute for Regional and Spatial Analysis, 2010), 17.

28. DEHLG (Department of Housing, Local Government and Heritage), as referenced by Kitchin et al., *Haunted Landscape*, 17.

29. Kitchin et al., *Haunted Landscape*, 10.

30. *Retail Space Europe: Yearbook 2010* (Amsterdam: Europe Real Estate Publishers, 2010), 23.

31. Andrew MacLaran, Katia Attuyer, and Brendan Williams, "Changing Office Location Patterns and Their Importance in the Peripheral Expansion of the Dublin Region 1960–2008," *Journal of Irish Urban Studies* 7–9 (2008–10): 60.

32. Peter Bacon & Associates, *Over-Capacity in the Irish Hotel Industry and Required Elements of a Recovery Programme*, November 2009, 12, http://www.ihf.ie/documents/HotelStudyFinalReport101109.pdf.

33. DKM Economic Consultants, *Review of the Construction Industry 2007 and Outlook 2008 to 2010* (September 2008), ii, https://www.housing.gov.ie/sites/default/files/migrated-files/en/Publications/StatisticsandRegularPublications/ConstructionIndustryStatistics/FileDownLoad%2C18630%2Cen.pdf.

34. Kitchin et al., *Haunted Landscape*, 11, 12.

35. Morgan Kelly, "The Irish Credit Bubble" (working paper 09/32, UCD Centre for Economic Research Working Paper Series, University College Dublin, December 2009), 9, https://www.ucd.ie/t4cms/wp09.32.pdf.

36. See Barend Wind, Caroline Dewidle, and John Doling, "Secondary Property Ownership in Europe: Contributing to Asset-Based Welfare Strategies and the 'Really Big Trade-Off,'" *International Journal of Housing Policy* 20, no. 1 (January 2020): 25–52. See also Manuel Aalbers et al., *Buy-to-Let: gewikt en gewogen* (Leuven, the Netherlands : KU Leuven and University of Amsterdam, 2018), https://www.sp.nl/sites/default/files/onderzoek_buy_to_let_0.pdf.

37. Anne McGuinness, "The Distribution of Property Level Arrears," *Economic Letter Series, Central Bank of Ireland* 6 (2011): 3.

38. John FitzGerald, in discussion with the author, Dublin, July 23, 2013.

39. "House Price Statistics," Department of Housing, Local Government and Heritage, Ireland, accessed November 16, 2020, https://www.housing.gov.ie/housing/statistics/house-prices-loans-and-profile-borrowers/house-price-statistics.

40. "Housing Stock and Vacant Dwellings 2006 and 2011," Central Statistics Office (CSO), Ireland, accessed November 16, 2020, https://statbank.cso.ie/px/pxeirestat/Statire/SelectVarVal/Define.asp?maintable=CDP07.

41. *Annual Housing Statistics Bulletin 2006* (Dublin: Government of Ireland, 2007), 41, https://www.housing.gov.ie/sites/default/files/migrated-files/en/Publications/StatisticsandRegularPublications/HousingStatistics/FileDownLoad%2C14648%2Cen.pdf.

42. Mark Scott, Craig Bullock, and Karen Foley, "Design Matters: Understanding Professional, Community and Consumer Preferences for the

Design of Rural Housing in the Irish Landscape,"
Town Planning Review 84, no. 3 (2013): 338.

43. Department of Housing, Planning and Local
Government (Republic of Ireland), *Resolving
Unfinished Housing Developments: 2017 Annual
Progress Report on Actions to Address Unfinished
Housing Developments* (February 2018).

44. "Forty Ghost Estates Targeted
for Demolition," The Journal.ie,
November 18, 2013, http://www.thejournal.ie/
ghost-estates-demolish-1180225-Nov2013/.

45. Housing Agency, Department of Environment,
Community, and Local Government (Republic of
Ireland), *National Housing Development Survey:
Summary Report*, November 2012, 8.

46. Isabel Concheiro, "Interrupted Spain" in *After
Crisis: Contemporary Architectural Conditions*, ed.
Josep Lluís Mateo (Baden, Switzerland: Lars Müller
Publishers, 2011), 13.

47. William Chislett, "Is Spain Different? The
Political, Economic and Social Consequences of Its
Crisis," *International Journal of Iberian Studies* 28,
nos. 2–3 (June 2015): 258.

48. Christopher Marcinkoski, *The City That Never
Was* (New York: Princeton Architectural Press,
2015), 81.

49. Paco Segura, "Infraestructuras de transporte,
impacto territorial y crisis," in *Paisajes devastados.
Despues del ciclo inmobiliario: impactos regionales y
urbanos de la crisis* (Madrid: Traficantes de Sueños,
2013), 85.

50. "Gross Domestic Product," Organization
for Economic Cooperation and Development,
accessed May 8, 2020, http://stats.oecd.org/index.
aspx?queryid=9185.

51. Angel Bergés and Emilio Ontiveros, "La nueva
Ley de Suelo desde la perspectiva económica.
Sostenibilidad y eficiencia en los Mercados del
Suelo." *Ciudad y territorio: Estudios territoriales*
no. 152–53 (2007): 260; Ministerio de Transportes,
Movilidad y Agenda Urbana, "Precios del suelo,"
accessed November 9, 2020, https://apps.fomento.
gob.es/BoletinOnline2/?nivel=2&orden
=36000000.

52. Ministerio de Transportes, Movilidad y Agenda
Urbana, "Valor tasado de vivienda libre" accessed
November 9, 2020, http://www.fomento.gob.es/
BE2/?nivel=2&orden=35000000.

53. Asociación Hipotecaria Española, *Indicadores
del coste de la deuda hipotecaria*, 2010, http://www.
ahe.es/bocms/images/bfilecontent/2006/04/26/93.
pdf.

54. José García-Montalvo, "Deconstruyendo la
burbuja. Expectativas de revalorización y precio
de la vivienda en España," *Papeles de economía
española* 109 (2006): 49.

55. Banco de España, "Indicadores del mercado de
la vivienda," accessed November 9, 2020, https://
www.bde.es/webbde/es/estadis/infoest/sindi.html.

56. Isidro López and Emmanuel Rodríguez, *Fin
de ciclo. Financiarización, territorio y sociedad de
propietarios en la onda larga del capitalismo hispano
(1959–2010)* (Madrid: Traficantes de Sueños, 2010),
292.

57. Isidro López and Emmanuel Rodríguez, "The
Spanish Model," *New Left Review* 69 (May–June
2011): 10.

58. Tomás Mazón, Elena Delgado Laguna, and José
A. Hurtado, "Mortgaged Tourists: The Case of the
South Coast of Alicante (Spain)," in *Second Home
Tourism in Europe: Lifestyle Issues and Policy
Responses*, ed. Zoran Roca (Farnham, UK: Ashgate,
2013), 36.

59. Aitana Alguacil Denche et al., *La vivienda en
España en el siglo XXI* (Madrid: Cáritas Española
Editores, 2013), 104.

60. Quoted in Concheiro, "Interrupted Spain," 19.

61. Professor Fernando Gaja i Díaz, University of
Valencia, in discussion with the author, Valencia,
Spain, July 7, 2014.

62. Concheiro, "Interrupted Spain," 19.

63. Fernando Gaja i Díaz, "Una desamortización a
finales del siglo xx: el 'urbanizador' en la legislación
urbanística valenciana," in *Ordenación del territorio
y urbanismo en Castilla-La Mancha*, ed. Francisco
Blázquez Calvo (Toledo, Spain: Almud, Ediciones
de Castilla-La Mancha, 2008), 138.

64. Gaja i Díaz, "Una desamortización," 139.

65. Marcinkoski, *City That Never Was*, 73.

66. Tom Allet, "The 'Ghost' Comes to Life," *Airports
International* 52, no. 2 (March 2019): 18.

67. Eugenio L. Burriel, "Empty Urbanism:
The Bursting of the Spanish Housing Bubble,"
Urban Research & Practice (2015): 7, doi:
10.1080/17535069.2015.1110196.

68. Eugenio L. Burriel de Orueta, "El estallido de la
burbuja inmobiliaria y sus efectos en el territorio,"
in *Geografía de la crisis económica en España*,
ed. Juan M. Albertos Puebla and José Sánchez
Hernández (Valencia, Spain: University of Valencia,
2014), 136.

69. José María Ezquiaga Domínguez uses the
phrase *post-metropolitan archipelagos* to describe
aspects of Madrid's urbanization.
I have derived *postmetropolitan islands* from his
phrase, although I define it differently. To read his
use of the phrase, refer to "Archipiélagos post-
metropolitanos," *Cuestiones Urbanas* 1 (2010):
46–56.

70. Jorge Salido Cobo, "Venta de pisos a
contrarreloj," *El Mundo*, October 10, 2007,
https://www.elmundo.es/elmundo/2007/10/02/
suvivienda/1191338644.html.

71. "Cuatro bancos se quedan con 2,000 pisos
de El Pocero," *El País*, January 15, 2009,
https://elpais.com/economia/2009/01/15/
actualidad/1232008383_850215.html.

72. Ramón Fernández Durán, "El Tsunami
urbanizador español y mundial,"
El Ecologista 48 (2006): 22.

73. Concheiro, "Interrupted Spain," 23.

74. See "About," Phantom Urbanism, accessed May 29, 2019, http://www.phantom-urbanism.com/about.html.

75. Kaiji Chen and Yi Wen, *The Great Housing Boom of China* (working paper 2014-022C, St. Louis: Federal Reserve Bank of St. Louis, 2014; revised 2016), 1.

76. Marcinkoski, *City That Never Was*, 46.

77. Max D. Woodworth and Jeremy L. Wallace, "Seeing Ghosts: Parsing China's 'Ghost City' Controversy," *Urban Geography* 38, no. 8 (2017): 1272.

78. Max D. Woodworth, "Ordo Municipality: A Market-Era Resource Boomtown," *Cities: The International Journal of Urban Policy and Planning* 43 (March 2015): 127.

79. Uchralt Otede, "Kangbashi: The Richest 'Ghost Town' in China?," in *Prosperity*, ed. Jane Golley and Linda Jaivan (Canberra: Australian National University Press, 2018), 79.

80. People and Society, China, The World Factbook, Central Intelligence Agency, accessed September 20, 2020, https://www.cia.gov/library/publications/the-world-factbook/geos/ch.html.

81. Marcinkoski, *City That Never Was*, 47.

82. "A Fifth of China's Homes Are Empty. That's 50 Million Apartments," *Bloomberg News*, November 8, 2018, https://www.bloomberg.com/news/articles/2018-11-08/a-fifth-of-china-s-homes-are-empty-that-s-50-million-apartments.

83. "Beijing Issues New Rules to Limit House Purchase," *China Daily*, February 16, 2011, http://www.chinadaily.com.cn/china/2011-02/16/content_12028324.htm.

84. "More Chinese Cities Restrict House Purchases," *Xinhua Net*, March 29, 2017, http://www.xinhuanet.com/english/2017-03/29/c_136167353.htm.

85. "China's Home Vacancy Rate Is over 20 Percent," China Scope, December 30, 2018, http://chinascope.org/archives/17144.

86. "Housing Should Be for Living In, Not for Speculation, Xi Says," *Bloomberg News*, October 18, 2017, https://www.bloomberg.com/news/articles/2017-10-18/xi-renews-call-housing-should-be-for-living-in-not-speculation.

87. Tamsin McMahon, "Return of the Housing Bubble," *Macleans*, March 4, 2013, https://www.macleans.ca/economy/business/return-of-the-bubble-2/.

88. David Castillo and William Egginton, "Dreamboat Vampires and Zombie Capitalists," *New York Times*, October 26, 2014, https://opinionator.blogs.nytimes.com/2014/10/26/dreamboat-vampires-and-zombie-capitalists/.

Chapter 3: The Forms of Finance

1. Rodrigo Fernandez, Annelore Hofman, and Manuel B. Aalbers, "London and New York as a Safe Deposit Box for the Transnational Wealth Elite," *Environment and Planning A* 48, no. 12 (December 2016): 2456.

2. Geoffrey DeVerteuil and David Manley, "Overseas Investment into London: Imprint, Impact and Pied-à-Terre Urbanism," *Environment and Planning A* 49, no. 6 (June 2017): 1309.

3. Oliver Wainwright, "Billionaires' Basements: The Luxury Bunkers Making Holes in London Streets," *The Guardian* (Manchester), November 9, 2012, https://www.theguardian.com/artanddesign/2012/nov/09/billionaires-basements-london-houses-architecture.

4. The Royal Borough of Kensington and Chelsea, *Basements: Supplementary Planning Document*, April 2016, https://www.rbkc.gov.uk/sites/default/files/atoms/files/01%20160414%20Final%20Basements%20SPD.pdf.

5. Sophie Baldwin, Elizabeth Holroyd, and Roger Burrows, "Mapping the Subterranean Geographies of Plutocratic London: Luxified Troglodytism?," May 2018, https://www.researchgate.net/publication/325046741_Mapping_the_Subterranean_Geographies_of_Plutocratic_London_Luxified_Troglodytism.

6. Baldwin et al., "Mapping Subterranean Geographies."

7. Landmass London Property Development, *Millionaire Basement Wars*, BBC Documentary, 2015, directed by James Dawson, May 28, 2015, YouTube video, 1:21:07, https://www.youtube.com/watch?v=sLJozZQb9xo.

8. Alexander Robertson, "Nice Little Fixer-Upper!," *Daily Mail*, October 1, 2017, https://www.dailymail.co.uk/news/article-4939090/Foxtons-founder-wins-10-year-mega-basement-battle.html.

9. Sam Greenhill, "Tycoon's Underground Ferris Wheel to Show Off His Ferraris," *Daily Mail*, November 27, 2015, https://www.dailymail.co.uk/news/article-3336344/Foxtons-estate-agents-billionaire-founder-wins-battle-French-government-London-mega-basement-plans.html.

10. "New 'Sub Squad' to Stop Nuisance Basement Developments," City of Westminster, February 9, 2016, https://www.westminster.gov.uk/new-sub-squad-stop-nuisance-basement-developments.

11. Wainwright, "Billionaires' Basements."

12. Royal Borough of Kensington and Chelsea, *Basements*.

13. "New 'Sub Squad.'"

14. "Digging Deep for More Space," Glenigan, accessed October 12, 2019, https://www.glenigan.com/digging-deep-for-more-space/.

15. George W. Bush, "Remarks to the National Association of Home Builders in Columbus, Ohio, October 2, 2004," *Public Paper of the Presidents of the United States, 2004, Book III—October 1 to*

December 31, 2004 (Washington, DC: United States Government Printing Office, 2007), 2323.

16. Gareth A. Jones and Peter M. Ward, "Privatizing the Commons: Reforming the Ejido and Urban Development in Mexico," *International Journal of Urban and Regional Research* 22, no. 1 (March 1998): 77.

17. Richard Marosi, "A Failed Vision," *Los Angeles Times*, November 26, 2017, https://www.latimes.com/projects/la-me-mexico-housing/.

18. Alfonso Valenzuela Aguilera and Sasha Tsenkova, "Build It and They Will Come: Whatever Happened to Social Housing in Mexico," *Urban Research & Practice* 12, no. 4 (2019): 497.

19. Alfonso Valenzuela Aguilera, "The Crisis in the Private Production of Social Housing in Mexico," *Latin American Perspectives* 44, no. 2 (March 2017): 39.

20. Aguilera and Tsenkova, "Build It," 497.

21. Marosi, "Failed Vision."

22. Liette Gilbert and Feike De Jong, "Entanglements of Periphery and Informality in Mexico City," *International Journal of Urban and Regional Research* 39, no. 3 (2015): 39.

23. Tatiana Bilbao, "A House Is Not Just a House," *Architect*, October 17, 2018, https://www.architectmagazine.com/design/a-house-is-not-just-a-house_o.

24. Christopher DeWolf, "James Cheng: Vancouver's Point Man," *Maisonneuve*, October 24, 2012, https://maisonneuve.org/post/2012/10/24/james-cheng-vancouvers-point-man/.

25. Paul Goldberger, "Too Rich, Too Thin, Too Tall?," *Vanity Fair*, May 2014, https://archive.vanityfair.com/article/2014/5/too-rich-too-thin-too-tall.

26. Feng Fu, *Design and Analysis of Tall and Complex Structures* (Oxford: Butterworth-Heinemann, 2018), 129.

27. Juliet Chung and Alyssa Abkowitz, "Ackman Leads Group Paying $90 Million for Manhattan Penthouse," *Wall Street Journal*, May 16, 2013, https://blogs.wsj.com/moneybeat/2013/05/16/ackman-leads-group-paying-record-price-for-manhattan-penthouse/.

28. Arindam Dutta, "Marginality and Metaengineering: Keynes and Arup," in Aggregate Architectural History Collective, *Governing by Design: Architecture, Economy, and Politics in the Twentieth Century* (Pittsburgh: University of Pittsburgh Press, 2012), 237.

29. Dutta, "Marginality and Metaengineering," 257.

30. Nadia Alaily-Mattar et al., "Public Real Estate Development Projects and Urban Transformation: The Case of Flagship Projects," in *Routledge Companion to Real Estate Development*, ed. Graham Squires, Erwin Heurkens, and Richard Peiser (New York: Routledge, 2017), 49.

Chapter 4: UHNWIs and the Superprime

Epigraph 1: Joshua Brown, "Meet the House That Inequality Built: 432 Park Avenue," *Fortune*, November 24, 2014, http://fortune.com/2014/11/24/432-park-avenue-inequality-wealth/.

Epigraph 2: Michael Kimmelman, "Seeing a Need for Oversight of New York's Lordly Towers," *New York Times*, December 22, 2013, https://www.nytimes.com/2013/12/23/arts/design/seeing-a-need-for-oversight-of-new-yorks-lordly-towers.html.

1. OECD's member nations include countries in Europe and North America, along with Japan, South Korea, Colombia, Chile, Turkey, Israel, Australia, and New Zealand.

2. OECD, *Divided We Stand: Why Inequality Keeps Rising* (Paris: Organisation for Economic Cooperation and Development, 2011), 24; OECD, *A Broken Social Elevator? How to Promote Social Mobility* (Paris: Organisation for Economic Cooperation and Development, 2011), 66.

3. "Inequality," Organisation for Economic Cooperation and Development, accessed May 31, 2020, http://www.oecd.org/social/inequality.htm.

4. Thomas Piketty, *Capital in the Twenty-First Century* (Cambridge, MA: Harvard University Press, 2014).

5. Merrill Lynch and Cap Gemini Ernst & Young, *World Wealth Report 2001* (2001): 3, https://web.archive.org/web/20120617005805/http://www.in.capgemini.com/m/in/tl/pdf_2001_World_Wealth_Report.pdf.

6. Capgemini, *World Wealth Report 2018* (2018), 8, https://www.capgemini.com/wp-content/uploads/2018/06/Capgemini-World-Wealth-Report.pdf.

7. *World Wealth Report 2001*, 3.

8. Capgemini, *World Wealth Report 2012* (2012): 7, https://www.capgemini.com/resources/world-wealth-report-2012/.

9. Capgemini, *World Wealth Report 2018*, 8.

10. Vincent White et al., *World Ultra Wealth Report 2018* (New York: Wealth X, 2018), 10.

11. White et al., *World Ultra Wealth Report 2018*, 10.

12. Capgemini and RBC Wealth Management, *World Wealth Report 2013* (2013): 7, https://www.capgemini.com/se-en/wp-content/uploads/sites/29/2017/07/wwr_2013_1.pdf.

13. White et al., *World Ultra Wealth Report 2018*, 11.

14. White et al., *World Ultra Wealth Report 2018*, 13.

15. Knight Frank Research, *The Wealth Report: The Global Perspective on Prime Property and Wealth* (London: Think, 2014), 61.

16. Knight Frank, *Wealth Report*, 11, 61.

17. Savills World Research, *Around the World in Dollars and Cents: How Private Money Moves around the Real Estate World* (2014), 2, 3, https://pdf.euro.savills.co.uk/residential---other/private-wealth.pdf.

18. Erik Weinbrecht, "Sotheby's International Realty Brand Exceeds Record $112 Billion in Global Sales Volume for 2018," Extraordinary Living Blog, Sotheby's International Realty, February 27, 2019, https://www.sothebysrealty.com/extraordinary-living-blog/sothebys-international-realty-brand-exceeds-record-112-billion-in-global-sales-volume-for-2018/; "At a Glance," Christie's International Real Estate, accessed July 29, 2020, http://www.profusionimmo.ca/documents/Christies_International_Real_Estate_-_Metrics_20161.pdf.

19. "Luxury Real Estate—Redefined," Sotheby's International Realty, accessed May 29, 2019, https://www.sothebysrealty.com/eng/luxury-real-estate.

20. Christie's International Real Estate, *Luxury Defined: An Insight into the Luxury Property Market* (Toronto: August Media, 2013), 4.

21. Reinier de Graaf, "Architecture Is Now a Tool of Capital, Complicit in a Purpose Antithetical to Its Social Mission," *Architectural Review*, April 24, 2015, https://www.architectural-review.com/essays/viewpoints/architecture-is-now-a-tool-of-capital-complicit-in-a-purpose-antithetical-to-its-social-mission/8681564.article.

22. Rupert Neate, "UK's Most Expensive Home Valued at £160m," *The Guardian* (Manchester), October 9, 2018, https://www.theguardian.com/uk-news/2018/oct/09/record-160m-paid-for-uks-most-expensive-home-ever-sold.

23. "One Hyde Park," Rogers Stirk Harbour + Partners, accessed April 25, 2020, https://www.rsh-p.com/projects/one-hyde-park/.

24. "One Hyde Park."

25. Patrik Schumacher and Peter Eisenman, "I Am Trying to Imagine a Radical Free-Market Urbanism," *Log* 28 (Summer 2013): 39–52.

26. Patrik Schumacher, "In Defense of Capitalism," European Graduate School Video Lectures, YouTube video, 55:00, November 17, 2015, https://www.youtube.com/watch?v=Ai5nnnc1kyk.

27. Douglas Spencer, *The Architecture of Neoliberalism* (London: Bloomsbury, 2016), 64.

28. Patrik Schumacher, "The Concept of Style and Parametricism as Epochal Style," Patrick Schumacher website, 2016, http://www.patrikschumacher.com/Texts/The%20Concept%20of%20Style%20and%20Parametricism%20as%20Epochal%20Style.html.

29. Spencer, *Architecture of Neoliberalism*, 67.

30. "520 West 28th," Zaha Hadid Architects, accessed April 25, 2020, https://www.zaha-hadid.com/design/520-west-28th-street/.

31. "520 West 28th," Zaha Hadid Architects, video, accessed April 25, 2020, https://www.zaha-hadid.com/design/520-west-28th-street/.

32. Pier Vittorio Aureli, "A Room against Ownership," in *Real Estates: Life without Debt*, ed. Jack Self and Shumi Bose (London: Bedford Press, 2014), 42.

33. Aureli, "Room against Ownership," 44.

34. Pier Vittorio Aureli and Martino Tattara, "Barbarism Begins at Home: Notes on Housing," in *Dogma: 11 Projects* (London: AA Publications, 2013), 92.

35. Aureli and Tattara, "Barbarism Begins at Home," 90.

36. Aureli and Tattara, "Barbarism Begins at Home," 89.

37. de Graaf, "Architecture Is Now a Tool."

38. Hélyette Geman and Tara Velez, "On Rarity Premium and Ownership Yield in Art," *Journal of Alternative Investments* 18, no. 1 (Summer 2015): 14, https://jai.pm-research.com.

39. Kriston Capps, "Why Billionaires Don't Pay Property Taxes in New York," Bloomberg CityLab, May 11, 2015, https://www.citylab.com/equity/2015/05/why-billionaires-dont-pay-property-taxes-in-new-york/389886/.

Chapter 5: Simplification and Postsocial Space

1. Leigh Claire La Berge, "Introduction," *Scandals and Abstraction: Financial Fiction of the Long 1980s* (New York: Oxford University Press, 2014), 10, Oxford Scholarship Online, 2014, doi: 10.1093/acprof:oso/9780199372874.003.0001.

2. Douglas C. Harris, "Condominium and the City: The Rise of Property in Vancouver," *Law and Social Inquiry* 36, no. 3 (2011): 695.

3. Paul Goldberger, "Too Rich, Too thin, Too Tall?," *Vanity Fair*, May 2014, https://archive.vanityfair.com/article/2014/5/too-rich-too-thin-too-tall.

4. Harris, "Condominium and City," 714.

5. Oliver Wainwright, "'American Psycho' Property Promo Pulled after Twitterstorm," *The Guardian* (Manchester), January 5, 2015, https://www.theguardian.com/artanddesign/architecture-design-blog/2015/jan/05/american-psycho-redrow-property-promo-pulled-after-twitterstorm.

6. Robert Call, "Post-Crisis Investment in Single-Family Homes in Fulton County, Georgia" (master's thesis, MIT, 2017).

7. Alana Semuels, "When Wall Street Is Your Landlord," *The Atlantic*, February 13, 2019, https://www.theatlantic.com/technology/archive/2019/02/single-family-landlords-wall-street.

8. "American Homes 4 Rent, Q4 2019 Earnings Call Transcript," *Motley Fool*, February 28, 2020, https://www.fool.com/earnings/call-transcripts/2020/02/28/american-homes-4-rent-amh-q4-2019-earnings-call-tr.aspx.

9. See Paul Heideman, "To Fight Racial Inequality, We Have to Attack the Power of Corporations," *Jacobin*, July 23, 2020, https://jacobinmag.com/2020/07/private-equity-blackstone-anti-racism-housing.

10. Christopher B. Leinberger, "The Need for Alternatives to the Nineteen Standard Real Estate Product Types," *Places* 17, no. 2 (2005): 25.

11. Leinberger, "Need for Alternatives," 25.

12. Matthew Frankel, "The 10 Largest REITs by Market Cap in 2020," *Motley Fool*, January 11, 2020, https://www.fool.com/millionacres/real-estate-investing/reits/10-largest-reits-market-cap-2020/.

13. Armando Ortuño Padilla, María Hernández Hernandez, and Sergio Civier Planelles, "Golf Courses and Land Use Patterns in the South-East of Spain," *Land Use Policy* 51 (February 2016): 207.

14. Manfredo Tafuri, "The Disenchanted Mountain: The Skyscraper and the City," in *The American City: From the Civil War to the New Deal*, ed. Giorgio Ciucci, Franceso Dal Co, Mario Manieri-Elia, and Manfredo Tafuri, trans. Barbara Luigia La Penta (Cambridge, MA: MIT Press, 1979), 469.

15. Reinhold Martin, "Money and Meaning: The Case of John Portman," *Hunch* 12 (2009): 37.

16. Martin, "Money and Meaning," 40.

17. "Vertical Forest," Stefano Boeri Architetti website, accessed May 1, 2020, https://www.stefanoboeriarchitetti.net/en/project/vertical-forest/.

18. Alex Loftus and Hug March, "Financialising Nature?," *Geoforum* 60 (March 2015): 172.

19. Justin Davidson, "The Challenges of Constructing New York's Tallest Apartment Building," *New York Magazine Intelligencer*, September 16, 2019, http://nymag.com/intelligencer/2019/09/nyc-tallest-building-central-park-tower.html.

20. Catherine de Zegher and Mark Wigley, eds., *The Activist Drawing: Retracing Situationist Architectures from Constant's New Babylon to Beyond* (New York: Drawing Center, 2001), 9. The phrase *homo ludens* originates from Dutch historian and cultural theorist Johan Huizinga.

21. Catherine de Zegher, "Introduction," in *The Activist Drawing*, 10.

22. Georg Simmel, *The Philosophy of Money* (1900; repr., London: Routledge, 2004), 232.

Chapter 6: Residential Avatars and Life Surrogates

An earlier version of this chapter was published as "Residential Avatars & Life Surrogates," *Real Review* 5 (Winter 2017): 74–78.

1. Barry Newman, "TOMS for Houses, *New Yorker*, February, 2014, https://www.newyorker.com/business/currency/toms-for-houses.

2. CBRE, *Global Living 2019*, April 2019, 4–5, https://www.cbreresidential.com/uk/sites/uk-residential/files/property-info/FINAL%20REPORT.pdf.

3. Slavoj Žižek, "Nobody Has to Be Vile," *London Review of Books* 28, no. 7 (April 6, 2006), https://www.lrb.co.uk/v28/n07/slavoj-zizek/nobody-has-to-be-vile.

4. Žižek, "Nobody Has to Be Vile."

5. Žižek, "Nobody Has to Be Vile."

6. TOMS website, accessed October 16, 2019, https://www.toms.com/what-we-give-shoes.

7. Frances Anderton, "Buy a Condo, Gift a House," October 16, 2018, in *Design and Architecture*, podcast, MP3 audio, 16:00, https://www.kcrw.com/culture/shows/design-and-architecture/scooter-wars-gifting-houses-puppets-on-the-move buy-a-condo-gift-a-house.

8. Anderton, "Buy a Condo."

9. "Free Two Shoes," *The Economist*, November 5, 2016, https://www.economist.com/finance-and-economics/2016/11/05/free-two-shoes.

10. Amanda Taub, "Buying TOMS Shoes Is a Terrible Way to Help Poor People," *Vox*, July 23, 2015, https://www.vox.com/2015/7/23/9025975/toms-shoes-poverty-giving.

11. Žižek, "Nobody Has to Be Vile."

12. Mike Davis, *Planet of Slums* (London: Verso, 2006), 13.

13. Davis, *Planet of Slums*, 17.

14. United Nations Human Settlements Programme (UN-Habitat), "Chapter 1: Development Context and the Millennium Agenda," in *The Challenge of Slums: Global Report on Human Settlements 2003* (revised and updated version April 2010), 16, https://mirror.unhabitat.org/downloads/docs/GRHS_2003_Chapter_01_Revised_2010.pdf.

15. United Nations Human Settlements, *Challenge of Slums*, xxv.

16. United Nations Human Settlements, *Challenge of Slums*, xxv.

17. United Nations Human Settlements, *Challenge of Slums*, 17.

18. Davis, *Planet of Slums*, 175.

19. Hadani Ditmars, "Vancouver House by BIG Gears Up for Completion," *Wallpaper*, April 25, 2019, https://www.wallpaper.com/architecture/vancouver-house-big-canada.

20. Davis, *Planet of Slums*, 176.

21. Karl Marx, *Capital: A Critique of Political Economy* (1867; repr., London: Penguin Books in association with *New Left Review*, 1990), 1:342.

22. Louise Story and Stephanie Saul, "Stream of Foreign Wealth Flows to Elite New York Real Estate," *New York Times*, February 7, 2015, https://www.nytimes.com/2015/02/08/nyregion/stream-of-foreign-wealth-flows-to-time-warner-condos.html.

23. The first state to pass a law allowing limited liability companies was Wyoming in 1977. Thus, the LLC came into being around the same time as the federal regulatory changes associated with neoliberalization.

24. William Davies, "Elites without Hierarchies: Intermediaries, 'Agency' and the Super-Rich," in *Cities and the Super-Rich: Real Estate, Elite Practices and Urban Politics*, ed. Ray Forrest,

Sin Yee Koh, and Bart Wissink (New York: Palgrave Macmillan, 2017), 21.

25. Davies, "Elites without Hierarchies," 30.

26. Davies, "Elites without Hierarchies," 26.

27. "Community Amenity Contributions (CAC) Policy Update," City of Vancouver, accessed May 1, 2020, https://vancouver.ca/home-property-development/cac-guidelines.aspx.

28. 8X on the Park, accessed April 30, 2020, https://www.8xonthepark.com/the-building/.

29. For discussion of Vancouver's community contribution policies as a developer strategy of accumulation, see Zachary Hyde, "Giving Back to Get Ahead: Altruism as a Developer Strategy of Accumulation through Affordable Housing Policy in Toronto and Vancouver," *Geoforum* (July 2018), https://doi.org/10.1016/j.geoforum.2018.07.005.

Chapter 7: Constant Object

An earlier version of this chapter was published as "Constant Object," *Log* 40 (Spring–Summer 2017): 101–6.

1. 432 Park Avenue incorporates a very small podium-like extrusion to its north that houses retail, as well as a tiny protrusion to its west for parking access. A freestanding retail "cube" sits at the corner of Park Avenue and Fifty-Sixth Street. Each of these elements has its own distinct architectural character, maintaining the purity of the tower.

2. "The CityRealty 100," CityRealty, accessed March 15, 2019, https://www.cityrealty.com/nyc/building-indices/the-cityrealty-100/building-list/1.

3. Real estate journalists in New York City have tried to determine the amount of occupancy in superprime condominium buildings, including 432 Park Avenue. For a report that uses a combination of US Census data, information from the New York City Department of Housing and Development, New York City Department of Finance tax rolls, and interviews with industry professionals, to support the widely held belief that 432 Park Avenue is largely empty at any given moment, see E. B. Solomon, "NYC's Ghost Towers: Just How Many of Manhattan's Luxury Condos Are Owned by People Who Don't Live There?," *The Real Deal: New York Real Estate News*, April 1, 2019, https://therealdeal.com/issues_articles/ghost-towers-new-york-city/.

4. Roy Liran and Ran Barkai, "Casting a Shadow on Neolithic Jericho," *Antiquity* 85, no. 327 (March 2011), http://antiquity.ac.uk/projgall/barkai327.

5. Nick Bostrom, "A History of Transhumanist Thought," *Journal of Evolution and Technology* 14 (April 2005): 12.

6. Max More, "Transhumanism: Towards a Futurist Philosophy" (1990, revised 1996). This article was hosted on Max More's personal website but is not currently available there. It can be accessed at https://web.archive.org/web/20051029125153/http://www.maxmore.com/transhum.htm.

7. Francesca Ferrando, "The Body," in *Post- and Transhumanism: An Introduction*, ed. Stefan Lorenz Sorgner and Robert Ranisch (Frankfurt: Peter Lang, 2014), 221.

8. "Inventor Ray Kurzweil Sees Immortality in Our Future," PBS News Hour, March 24, 2016, https://www.pbs.org/newshour/show/inventor-ray-kurzweil-sees-immortality-in-our-future.

9. More, "Transhumanism."

10. Mark C. Taylor, *Abiding Grace: Time, Modernity, Death* (Chicago: University of Chicago Press, 2018), 61; Vernor Vinge, "The Coming Technological Singularity: How to Survive in the Post-Human Era," (lecture, NASA Vision 21 symposium, 1993): 19, https://ntrs.nasa.gov/citations/19940022856.

11. Giorgio Griziotti, "What Is Neurocapitalism and Why Are We Living in It?," interview by Antonella Di Biase, *Vice*, October 18, 2016, https://www.vice.com/en_us/article/qkjxaq/what-is-neurocapitalism-and-why-are-we-living-in-it.

12. Taylor, *Abiding Grace*, 64.

13. Jacob Viner, "Adam Smith and Laissez Faire," *Journal of Political Economy* 35, no. 2 (April 1927): 201–2.

14. Georg Simmel, *The Philosophy of Money* (1900; repr., London: Routledge, 2004), 237.

15. Max Weber, *The Protestant Ethic and the Spirit of Capitalism* (London: Routledge, 1930).

16. Walter Benjamin, "Capitalism as Religion" (1921), in *The Frankfurt School on Religion*, ed. Eduardo Mendieta (New York: Routledge, 2005), 259.

17. Giorgio Agamben, "Capitalism as Religion," in *Agamben and Radical Politics*, ed. Daniel McLoughlin (Edinburgh: Edinburgh University Press, 2017), 18.

18. Mark C. Taylor, *About Religion* (Chicago: University of Chicago Press, 1999), 149–54.

19. Mark C. Taylor, *Confidence Games* (Chicago: University of Chicago Press, 2004), 3.

20. Taylor, *About Religion*, 158.

21. Rem Koolhaas, *Delirious New York* (1978; repr., New York: Monacelli, 1994), 155.

22. Koolhaas, *Delirious New York*, 155.

23. Rem Koolhaas, "Kill the Skyscraper," in *Content*, ed. Rem Koolhaas, Brendan McGetrick, and Simon Brown (Cologne: Taschen, 2004), 473.

24. Margaret Rhodes, "NYC's $1.3B Supertall Skyscraper Was Inspired by a Trash Can," *Wired*, June 2, 2015, https://www.wired.com/2015/06/nycs-1-3b-supertall-skyscraper-inspired-trash-can.

25. Reinhold Martin, "In the Bank," *Thresholds* 41 (Spring 2013): 105.

26. Reinhold Martin, "Financial Imaginaries: Toward a Philosophy of the City," *Grey Room* 42 (Winter 2011): 71.

27. Frederic Jameson compares Wells Fargo Court in Los Angeles, designed by Skidmore, Owings & Merrill, to the monolith in Stanley Kubrick's *2001*. See Fredric Jameson, *Postmodernism, or,*

The Cultural Logic of Late Capitalism (Durham, NC: Duke University Press, 1992), 13.

28. Fredric Jameson, "The Brick and the Balloon: Architecture, Idealism and Land Speculation," *New Left Review* 228 (March–April 1998): 44.

29. Jameson, "Brick and Balloon," 44.

30. Peggy Deamer, *Architecture and Capitalism: 1845 to the Present* (New York: Routledge, 2014), 131.

31. Pier Vittorio Aureli, *The Project of Autonomy: Politics and Architecture within and against Capitalism* (New York: Temple Hoyne Buell Center for the Study of American Architecture and Princeton Architectural Press, 2008), 14, 53.

32. Pier Vittorio Aureli, "Rossi: The Concept of the Locus as a Political Category of the City," in *The Project of Autonomy*, 69.

33. Kim Moody, "Neoliberalism: The Shadow of Class," *Dialectical Anthropology* 32, nos. 1–2 (2008): 53.

34. Rafael Moneo, *Theoretical Anxiety and Design Strategies* (Cambridge, MA: MIT Press, 2004), 103.

35. Eugene T. Johnson, "What Remains of Man—Aldo Rossi's Modena Cemetery," *Journal of the Society of Architectural Historians* 41, no. 1 (March 1982): 39.

36. Johnson, "What Remains of Man," 44, 54. Also Rossi, as quoted in Johnson, "What Remains of Man," 45.

37. Moneo, *Theoretical Anxiety*, 119.

38. Moneo, *Theoretical Anxiety*, 109.

39. Adolf Loos, "Architecture," in *The Architecture of Adolf Loos: An Arts Council Exhibition*, 2nd ed., ed. Yehuda Safran and Wilfried Wang (London: Arts Council of Great Britain, 1987), 108.

40. Loos, "Architecture," 108.

41. "'Heaven': Will the Future Be Better Than We Can Imagine?," *CNN International*, June 19, 2006, http://edition.cnn.com/2006/TECH/science/06/19/heaven/.

42. Aldo Rossi, *The Architecture of the City*, trans. Diane Ghirardo and Joan Ockman (Cambridge, MA: MIT Press, 1982), 116.

Chapter 8: From Sci-Fi to Fi-Fi

Early ideas for this chapter were published in "From Sci-Fi to Fi-Fi: Fiction and the Socio-Technologies of Architectural Production," *Journal of Architectural Education* 69, no. 2 (October 2015): 220–27.

1. "What Is a Sears Modern Home?," Sears Archives, accessed June 3, 2019, http://www.searsarchives.com/homes/index.htm.

2. Gwendolyn Wright, *Building the Dream: A Social History of Housing in America* (Cambridge, MA: MIT Press, 1983), 252.

3. "Homeownership Rates," US Census Bureau, accessed June 3, 2019, https://www2.census.gov/programs-surveys/decennial/tables/time-series/coh-owner/owner-tab.txt. See also

"Homeownership Rate for the United States," Economic Research, Federal Reserve Bank of St. Louis, accessed August 17, 2020, https://fred.stlouisfed.org/series/RHORUSQ156N.

4. "Home Ownership Down and Renting Up for First Time in a Century," UK Office for National Statistics, June 19, 2015, https://www.ons.gov.uk/peoplepopulationandcommunity/housing/articles/.

5. Alicia Hall, "Trends in Home Ownership in Australia: A Quick Guide," Statistics and Mapping Section, Parliament of Australia, June 28, 2017, https://www.aph.gov.au/About_Parliament/Parliamentary_Departments/Parliamentary_Library/pubs/rp/rp1617/Quick_Guides/TrendsHomeOwnership.

6. Rose Neng Lai, Ko Wang, and Yuqing Zhou, "Sale before Completion of Development: Pricing and Strategy," *Real Estate Economics* 32, no. 2 (Summer 2004): 330.

7. Su Han Chan, Fang Fang, and Jing Yang, "Presales, Financing Constraints, and Developers' Production Decisions," *Journal of Real Estate Research* 30, no. 3 (July 2008): 374.

8. Lai et al., "Sale before Completion," 330.

9. Robert Edelstein, Peng Liu, and Fang Wu, "The Market for Real Estate Presales: A Theoretical Approach," *Journal of Real Estate Finance and Economics* 45, no. 1 (June 2012): 31.

10. "Understanding the Development Process: Part 2," Urbaneer, January 7, 2015, http://www.urbaneer.com/homewatch/understanding_the_development_process_part_2.

11. Kathy Tomlinson, "Flipping of Condo Units by Insiders Fuels Hot Vancouver Market," *Globe and Mail* (Toronto), April 29, 2018, https://www.theglobeandmail.com/canada/article-flipping-of-condo-units-by-insiders-fuels-hot-vancouver-market/.

12. Tomlinson, "Flipping of Condo Units."

13. Fredric Jameson, "The Brick and the Balloon: Architecture, Idealism and Land Speculation," *New Left Review* 228 (March–April 1998): 43.

14. Nancy Lin, "Architecture Shenzen," in *Great Leap Forward*, ed. Chuihua Judy Chung et al. (Cologne: Taschen, 2002), 167.

15. Lin, "Architecture Shenzen," 167.

16. Mark C. Taylor, *Abiding Grace: Time, Modernity, Death* (Chicago: University of Chicago Press, 2018), 52.

17. Mark C. Taylor, *About Religion* (Chicago: University of Chicago Press, 1999), 147.

18. Oliver Chiang, "Meet the Man Who Paid a Record $335,000 for Virtual Property," *Forbes*, November 17, 2010, https://www.forbes.com/sites/oliverchiang/2010/11/17/meet-the-man-who-paid-a-record-335000-for-virtual-property/.

19. "Decentraland," BitcoinWiki, accessed June 3, 2019, https://en.bitcoinwiki.org/wiki/Decentraland.

20. Camila Russo, "Making a Killing in Virtual Real Estate," *Bloomberg Businessweek*, June 12, 2018, https://www.bloomberg.com/news/articles/2018-06-12/making-a-killing-in-virtual-real-estate.

21. Architectural Institute of British Columbia, *Bulletin 55: Tariff for Market Multiple-Residential Section*, December 2001, 15, http://aibc.ca/wp-content/uploads/files/2016/01/Bulletin_55_Dec01.pdf.

22. Altus Group, *Canadian Cost Guide 2017*, January 2017, https://www.altusgroup.com/services/reports/2017-construction-cost-guide/. According to the Altus Group (a real estate services and consultancy company), condominiums between thirteen and thirty-nine stories cost between C$250 and C$315 (US$186 and US$234) per square foot to construct in Vancouver. For the sake of estimation, I have considered a 150-unit condo building at 112,500 square feet. This results in a construction cost of US$23,598,000 and architectural fees of 2.5 percent, for a total fee of US$589,950 (US$3,933 per unit).

23. The 2 percent fee is for marketing only and excludes sales commissions. It is a conservative estimate that is based on the author's conversations with developers in Vancouver.

24. Jack Self, "Default Grey: Autonomy and Anonymity," 2015, video, 5:00, https://vimeo.com/124924903.

25. "Product," Lumion, accessed February 22, 2019, https://lumion.com/product.html.

26. William Davies, "Elites without Hierarchies: Intermediaries, 'Agency' and the Super-Rich," in *Cities and the Super-Rich: Real Estate, Elite Practices and Urban Politics*, ed. Ray Forrest, Sin Yee Koh, and Bart Wissink (New York: Palgrave Macmillan, 2017), 23.

27. Reinhold Martin, "Financial Imaginaries: Toward a Philosophy of the City," *Grey Room* 42 (Winter 2011): 73.

28. Antoine Picon and Alessandra Ponte, eds., *Architecture and the Sciences: Exchanging Metaphors* (New York: Princeton Architectural Press, 2003), 10.

29. Rolf Torstendahl, "Technology in the Development of Society 1850–1980: Four Phases of Industrial Capitalism in Western Europe," *History and Technology: An International Journal* 1 (1984): 157–74.

30. Taylor, *Abiding Grace*, 44.

31. OMA, Rem Koolhaas, and Bruce Mau, *S,M,L,XL* (New York: Monacelli, 1995), xix, 88, 133.

32. OMA, *S,M,L,XL*, 1013, 1250.

33. Fredric Jameson, "Future City," *New Left Review* 21 (May–June 2003): 76.

34. Prashant Gandhi, Somesh Khanna, and Sree Ramaswamy, "Which Industries Are the Most Digital (and Why)?," *Harvard Business Review*, April 1, 2016, https://hbr.org/2016/04/a-chart-that-shows-which-industries-are-the-most-digital-and-why.

35. See Walter Mattli, *Darkness by Design: The Hidden Power in Global Capital Markets* (Princeton, NJ: Princeton University Press, 2019).

36. Matthew Blake, Peter Vanham, and Dustin Hughes, "5 Things You Need to Know about Fintech," World Economic Forum, April 20, 2016, https://www.weforum.org/agenda/2016/04/5-things-you-need-to-know-about-fintech/.

37. Deloitte Center for Financial Services, *Fintech by the Numbers: Incumbents, Startups, Investors Adapt to Maturing Ecosystem* (London: Deloitte, 2017), 7.

38. Andrew Baum, *PropTech 3.0: The Future of Real Estate* (Oxford: Saïd Business School, University of Oxford, 2017), 66, https://www.sbs.ox.ac.uk/sites/default/files/2018-07/PropTech3.0.pdf.

39. Dallas Rogers, "Becoming a Super-Rich Foreign Real Estate Investor: Globalising Real Estate Data, Publications and Events," in *Cities and the Super-Rich*, 92–94.

40. Jameson, "Brick and Balloon," 44.

41. Leigh Claire La Berge, "Introduction," *Scandals and Abstraction: Financial Fiction of the Long 1980s* (New York: Oxford University Press, 2014), 4, Oxford Scholarship Online, 2014, doi: 10.1093/acprof:oso/9780199372874.003.0001.

42. La Berge, *Scandals and Abstraction*, 4.

43. Leigh Clair La Berge, "Rules on Abstraction: Methods and Discourses of Finance," *Radical History Review* 118 (Winter 2014): 94.

44. La Berge, "Rules on Abstraction," 100.

Epilogue

Epigraph: Fredric Jameson, *Postmodernism, or, The Cultural Logic of Late Capitalism* (Durham, NC: Duke University Press, 1992), 47.

1. Tracey Tully and Stacey Stowe, "The Wealthy Flee Coronavirus. Vacation Towns Respond: Stay Away," *New York Times*, March 25, 2020, https://www.nytimes.com/2020/03/25/nyregion/coronavirus-leaving-nyc-vacation-homes.html; Kevin Baker, "Affluence Killed New York, Not the Pandemic," *The Atlantic*, August 27, 2020, https://www.theatlantic.com/ideas/archive/2020/08/who-new-york/615715/.

2. *Geographies of Racial Capitalism with Ruth Wilson Gilmore*, directed by Kenton Card (Antipode Foundation, 2020), https://www.youtube.com/watch?v=2CS627aKrJI.

Image Credits

Front cover
Photograph by Halkin Mason.
Courtesy of Rafael Viñoly
Architects

p 6
Courtesy of Imaginechina
Limited / Alamy

p 12
Photograph by Hufton+Crow.
Courtesy of the photographer
and Zaha Hadid Architects

p 14
Photograph by the author

p 17
Photograph by the author

pp 38–39
Photograph by the author

p 40
Photograph by the author

p 43
Photograph by Jim Bartsch

p 44
LEFT AND TOP RIGHT: Courtesy
of Pandiscio Green. BOTTOM
RIGHT: Photograph by Iwan
Baan

p 48
TOP AND BOTTOM:
Courtesy of James KM Cheng
Architects

p 52
Photograph by Graham Turner.
Courtesy of Redux Pictures

pp 58–59
Photograph by Josimar
Dominguez

p 61
Photograph by the author

pp 62–63
Photograph by the author

p 64
Photograph by Lőrinc Vass

pp 66–67
Photograph by the author

p 69
Photograph by the author

p 70
Photograph by Lőrinc Vass

p 71
Photograph by Josimar
Dominguez

p 74
Photograph by Tim Franco

pp 76–77
Photograph by Paulo Moreira

p 80
TOP: Photograph by Josimar
Dominguez. BOTTOM LEFT:
Photograph by the author.
BOTTOM RIGHT: Photograph
by Lőrinc Vass

p 83
Drawing by Lőrinc Vass,
redrawn from the original
drawing created by the architects

p 84
LEFT AND RIGHT: Courtesy of
Wolff Architects

p 85
LEFT: Courtesy of Basement
Design Studio.
RIGHT: Courtesy of Wolff
Architects

p 87
Photograph by the author

p 88
Photograph by the author

p 89
LEFT: *10,300 sq ft Homes. Los
Encinos, Ensenada, Mexico.
2000–present.* © Livia Corona
Benjamin. Courtesy of the
artist and Proxyco Gallery,
New York. RIGHT: *Backyards.
Durango, Mexico. 2000–present.*
© Livia Corona Benjamin.
Courtesy of the artist and
Proxyco Gallery, New York.

pp 90–91
*47,547 Homes, Ixtapaluca,
Mexico. 2000–present.* © Livia
Corona Benjamin. Courtesy of
the artist and Proxyco Gallery,
New York.

p 94
TOP: Photograph by
Robin Hill. Courtesy
of Arquitectonica.
BOTTOM: Courtesy of Emre
Arolat Architecture

p 95
Courtesy of ZinCo GmbH

p 97
Courtesy of SHoP Architects

p 98
Courtesy of SHoP Architects

pp 102–3
Photograph by the author

pp 110–11
Photograph by Paul Raftery

p 114
Courtesy of Rogers Stirk
Harbour + Partners

p 115
Courtesy of Rogers Stirk
Harbour + Partners

p 118
TOP: Courtesy of Zaha Hadid Architects. BOTTOM: Photograph by Hufton+Crow. Courtesy of the photographer and Zaha Hadid Architects

p 119
Photograph by Scott Francis. Courtesy of the photographer and Zaha Hadid Architects

p 122
Courtesy of Dogma

p 123
Courtesy of Dogma

p 125
Courtesy of Dogma

p 127
Copyright Charles Correa Associates. Courtesy of Charles Correa Foundation

p 143
Photograph by the author

p 145
TOP: Photograph by the author.
MIDDLE: Photograph by Josimar Dominguez.
RIGHT: Photograph by Lőrinc Vass

p 146
Photograph by the author

p 147
Photograph by the author

p 148
ALL: Photographs by the author

p 150
Photograph by Giovanni Nardi, © Boeri Studio

p 152
Rendering by Norm Li. Courtesy of UNStudio

p 155
Photograph by Koumin Lee. Courtesy of WOHA

p 158
Photograph by the author

p 160
TOP: Photograph by Arlen Redeko. Courtesy of Postmedia Network.
MIDDLE AND BOTTOM: Photographs by Vandy Muong

p 167
Photograph by the author

p 170
Photograph by Halkin Mason. Courtesy of Rafael Viñoly Architects

p 172
Drawing by Lőrinc Vass

p 174
TOP: Illustration from Henry O'Brien, *The Round Towers of Ireland: Or, The History of Tuath-de-danaans* (London: W. Thacker & Co., 1898), 72.
MIDDLE: Illustration from *Edward Ives, A Voyage from England to India* (London: Printed for Edward and Charles Dilly, 1773), facing 33.
BOTTOM: Etching by Toni Pecoraro

p 176
From *The American Architect*, March 26, 1913. Courtesy of the Skyscraper Museum

p 181
Photograph by Halkin Mason. Courtesy of Rafael Viñoly Architects

p 182
TOP: Courtesy of Rafael Viñoly Architects. BOTTOM: MAXXI Museo nazionale delle arti del XXI secolo, Roma. Collezione MAXXI Architettura Archivio Aldo Rossi, © Eredi Aldo Rossi

p 184
Photograph by Gabriele Basilico. Courtesy of Archivio Gabriele Basilico

p 186
Courtesy of the Albertina Museum, Vienna

p 188
Rendering by DBOX

p 190
Courtesy of www.sears.com

p 192
Photograph by Brent Holmes

p 197
Courtesy of Decentraland

p 198
Courtesy of Lumion

Back cover
10,300 sq ft Homes. Los Encinos, Ensenada, Mexico. 2000–present. © Livia Corona Benjamin. Courtesy of the artist and Proxyco Gallery, New York.

Index

iceberg homes and, 82
Manhattan, 18 (*see also*
  Manhattan)
MoMA, 128
Newmark Knight Frank
  and, 46
pencil towers and, 96, *97–98*,
  100, 163, 173
Rockefeller Center, 147
skyline of, *9*
superpodiums and, 93
superprime property and,
  115, *118*, 119-20, 128, 163
ultra-high net worth
  individuals (UHNWIs)
  and, 112
Woolworth Building, 173,
  176
zombie urbanism and, 53–54,
  56
New York City Housing and
  Vacancy Survey, 53
New York magazine, 153
New York Stock Exchange
  (NYSE), 92, 204
New York Times, 53–54, 79
New York University, 24
Nexus World Housing, 202
Nieuwenhuys, Constant, 153
Nixon, Richard, 30
Nouvel, Jean, 99

Oakridge Centre, 149
Occupy Wall Street, 50
Office for Metropolitan
  Architecture (OMA), 73,
  201–3
One57, 99–100, 128
One Hyde Park
  Aureli and, 18, 117, 124
  empty interior and, 124–25
  Schumacher and, 18, 117,
  120, 124
  superprime property and,
  18, 52, *110–11*, 112–17, 120,
  124–25
One Madison, 99
One Thousand Museum, *12*,
  104, 119
One World Trade Center, 188
Opus (Hillcrest II), *43*
Organisation for Economic
  Cooperation and
  Development (OECD),
  106–7
overbuilding, 56, 144, 168

Palisades condominiums, *148*
Panama City, 54, 100,
Panasjuk, Yan, 198

parametricism, 117, 120, 203
Paris, 17
  financial icons and, 101
  ultra-high net worth
  individuals (UHNWIs) and,
  110, 112
  zombie urbanism and, 20,
  53–55
Paris Urbanism Agency, 53
Pecoraro, Toni, *174*
pencil towers
  111 West 57th Street, *97–98*,
  100, 115
  220 Central Park South, 99
  432 Park Avenue, 18–19, 100,
  112, 169–71, *172*, 180–88,
  209
  accelerations and, 96
  access points and, 137-138
  Collins House, 100, 137
  condominiums and, 18, 96,
  99–100, 138, 169
  corner-to-floor area ratio
  and, 138–39
  design and, 99–100
  finance capitalism and, 17,
  20, 82, 99
  Highcliff, 99–100
  historical perspective on,
  171–74
  housing and, 171
  liquidity and, 96
  New York and, 16, 20,
  96–100, 163, 173
  One Madison, 99
  precrisis context and, 99
  real estate and, 99
  SHoP Architects and, *97–98*
  simplification and, 137–39
  slenderness ratio and, 96,
  99–100, 138, 169
  spirituality and, 169, 173,
  181, 188
  structural systems for, 105
  wealth storage and, 96, 99
penthouses, 42, 99–100, 112,
  114–15, 119, 128, 156
Pentominium, 42
Pérez Art Museum Miami
  (PAMM), 104
Phantom Urbanism, *9*
philanthropy
  Amazon and, 161
  avatars and, 166
  Buffet and, 159
  Carnegie and, 159
  Gates and, 159
  intermediaries and, 165–66
  one-for-one, 156, 159, 161–63
  Rockefeller and, 159

spatial, 161–63
substitution and, 163–65
taxes and, 104
TOMS and, 161–62
urbanism and, 166–68
Vancouver House and, 18,
  156, 159, 162, 167–68, 209
World Housing and, *160*,
  161–62, 164, 202
Žižek and, 157–58
Philosophy of Money, The
  (Simmel), 178–79
Phoenix, *14*
Picon, Antoine, 201
Piketty, Thomas, 42, 107, 128,
  163
Planet of Slums (Davis), 162–63
Pointe, *148*
Ponte, Alessandra, 201
Porta Nuova, 149
Portman, John, 10, 147
Portzamparc, Christian de, 99
posthousing, 173
posthumanism, 18, 175
postindustrialism, 33, 50, 56
postmodernism, 10, 12, 175, 201
*Postmodernism, or, the Cultural
  Logic of Late Capitalism*
  (Jameson), 10
postsocial space, 139, 141–44,
  146, 154, 165
poverty, 92, 164
predatory practices, 36, 209
presales
  accelerations and, 189, 206
  architectural futures and,
  194–95
  China and, 191, 195–96
  complexity and, 193
  condominiums and, 18, 119,
  191–93, 206
  design and, 199
  digital representation and, 19,
  189, 196, 200, 206
  finance capitalism and, 189–
  90, 194–95, 200, 206
  financialization and, 196, 200
  FinTech and, 19, 196, 200
  flips and, 194
  globalization and, 196
  housing and, 189–95
  increase of, 189, 191, 193–94
  markets and, 189–96, 200,
  206
  mutations and, 189
  occupation gap in, 193
  politics and, 200
  PropTech and, 19, 206
  real estate and, 19, 192–96
  sales centers and, 192–94

Matthew Soules is an associate professor of architecture at the University of British Columbia and a graduate of the Harvard University Graduate School of Design (GSD). Soules has been visiting faculty at the Southern California Institute of Architecture, a visiting associate professor at the GSD, and a guest critic at institutions throughout Canada and the United States. He is the founder and director of Matthew Soules Architecture.